# Religion and War

**Recent Titles in
Religion in Politics and Society Today**

Islam in America: Exploring the Issues
*Craig Considine*

Religion and Environmentalism: Exploring the Issues
*Lora Stone*

Antisemitism: Exploring the Issues
*Steven Leonard Jacobs*

Atheism and Agnosticism: Exploring the Issues
*Peter A. Huff*

Same-Sex Marriage: Exploring the Issues
*Scott A. Merriman*

# Religion and War

*Exploring the Issues*

Timothy J. Demy and Gina Granados Palmer

*Religion in Politics and Society Today*

An Imprint of ABC-CLIO, LLC
Santa Barbara, California • Denver, Colorado

Copyright © 2022 by ABC-CLIO, LLC

All rights reserved. No part of this publication may be reproduced, stored in a retrieval system, or transmitted, in any form or by any means, electronic, mechanical, photocopying, recording, or otherwise, except for the inclusion of brief quotations in a review, without prior permission in writing from the publisher.

Library of Congress Control Number: 2022026262

ISBN:  978-1-4408-7390-4 (print)
       978-1-4408-7391-1 (ebook)

26 25 24 23 22   1 2 3 4 5

This book is also available as an eBook.

ABC-CLIO
An Imprint of ABC-CLIO, LLC

ABC-CLIO, LLC
147 Castilian Drive
Santa Barbara, California 93117
www.abc-clio.com

This book is printed on acid-free paper ∞

Manufactured in the United States of America

# Contents

*Alphabetical List of Entries, vii*

*Topical List of Entries, ix*

*Series Foreword, xi*

*Preface, xiii*

*Overview, xv*

*Chronology, xxvii*

**A to Z**, 1

*Annotated Bibliography, 219*

*Index, 243*

# Alphabetical List of Entries

Afghanistan War
American Civil War
American Exceptionalism
American Peace Churches
American Revolution
Apocalypticism
Art
Buddhism and War
Christianity and War
Cold War
Conscientious Objection
Contemporary Non-U.S. Conflicts
Ecclesiastical Statements on War and Peace
Evangelicalism
Genocide
Graham, William Franklin, Jr. ("Billy")
Gulf War
Hinduism and War
Holocaust
Human Rights
Iraq War
Islam and War
Judaism and War
Just War Tradition
King, Martin Luther, Jr.
Korean War
Literature
Middle East Conflict
Military Chaplains
Music
Nongovernmental Organizations
Pacifism
Peace Movements
Peacemaking
Presidential Faith and War
Protestant Denominations
Religion, Conflict, and Geopolitics
Religious Freedom and Religious Persecution
Religious Identity in the Armed Forces
Religious Texts
Responsibility to Protect (R2P)
Rhetoric, Sermons, and Prayers
Rituals and Symbolism
Roman Catholicism
September 11, 2001, Terrorist Attacks
Terrorism
Torture
Ukraine War
United Nations
Vietnam War
Wars of Israel
Weapons of Mass Destruction (Nuclear, Biological, Chemical)
World War I
World War II

# Topical List of Entries

**Conflicts and Wars**
Afghanistan War
American Civil War
American Revolution
Cold War
Contemporary Non-U.S. Conflicts
Gulf War
Iraq War
Korean War
Middle East Conflict
Religion, Conflict, and Geopolitics
Ukraine War
Vietnam War
Wars of Israel
World War I
World War II

**Entities**
Military Chaplains
Nongovernmental Organizations
Presidential Faith and War
Religious Identity in the Armed Forces
United Nations
Weapons of Mass Destruction (Nuclear, Biological, Chemical)

**Events**
Holocaust
September 11, 2001, Terrorist Attacks

**Faith Traditions**
Buddhism and War
Christianity and War
Evangelicalism
Hinduism and War
Islam and War
Judaism and War
Protestant Denominations
Roman Catholicism

**Humanities**
Art
Literature
Music

**Concepts and Ideas**
American Exceptionalism
Apocalypticism
Conscientious Objection
Genocide
Human Rights
Just War Tradition
Pacifism
Peacemaking
Religious Freedom and Religious Persecution

Responsibility to Protect (R2P)
Terrorism
Torture

**Language and Texts**
Ecclesiastical Statements on War
  and Peace
Religious Texts
Rhetoric, Sermons, and
  Prayers

Rituals and Symbolism

**Movements**
American Peace Churches
Peace Movements

**People**
Graham, William Franklin, Jr.
  ("Billy")
King, Martin Luther, Jr.

# Series Foreword

Religion is a pervasive and powerful force in modern society, and its influence on political structures and social institutions is inescapable, whether in the United States or around the world. Wars have been fought in the name of faith; national boundaries have been shaped as a result; and social policies, legislation, and daily life have all been shaped by religious beliefs. Written with the reference needs of high school students and undergraduates in mind, the books in this series examine the role of religion in contemporary politics and society. While the focus of the series is on the United States, it also explores social and political issues of global significance.

Each book in the series is devoted to a particular issue, such as antisemitism, atheism and agnosticism, and women in Islam. An overview essay surveys the development of the religious dimensions of the subject and discusses how religion informs contemporary discourse related to that issue. A chronology then highlights the chief events related to the topic. This is followed by a section of alphabetically arranged reference entries providing objective information about people, legislation, ideas, movements, events, places, and other specific subjects. Each entry cites works for further reading and in many cases provides cross-references. At the end of each volume is an annotated bibliography of the most important print and electronic resources suitable for student research.

Authoritative and objective, the books in this series give readers a concise introduction to the dynamic interplay of religion and politics in modern society and provide a starting point for further research on social issues.

# Preface

This book is designed to provide students and general readers with a reference book and overview of about fifty topics in American history and contemporary society that explore how the convergence of religion, politics, and war have shaped present American culture. The intersecting of these three realms has shaped how Americans view themselves as well as how they understand the political relationship of the United States and the rest of the global community. No idea or event arises in a vacuum. There are always causes and influences that serve as catalysts. Values have consequences, and the political, religious, and other values in the history of a nation and its citizens have long-standing effects—for good and for ill. Each topic has contemporary significance and relevance for 21st-century American social and political life.

The entries presented in this volume are organized alphabetically. At the end of each entry, there is a list of related entries in the book that are significant to the content of the entry the reader has just completed. This cross-referencing of entries is designed to provide readers a broader perspective on the topic and to encourage readers to look for the connections between and among ideas, events, personalities, and subjects that have shaped the present. After these entries, there is a brief further reading section to point readers toward contemporary and significant articles, books, and websites that are pertinent to the entry.

Three additional items in the book are provided for reader reference. The overview orients readers to the interwoven strands of politics, religion, and war that provide much of the background of the colorful tapestry of 21st-century United States. Rather than compartmentalizing the American experience and separating the strands, the essay shows the influence of each upon the other.

The second item presented is a chronology. The sequence in it is not designed to be an exhaustive timeline of American religious, political, and military experiences. Rather, it is presented to give readers some signposts to help orient the reading audience to entries with respect to American history.

The third and final item presented is an annotated bibliography. The bibliography does not contain every item cited in the further reading sections. However, it does offer additional information on many of the books and articles cited. Present in it are the works the authors consider the most important from the further reading lists.

The events and ideas that shape a nation and its citizens are not static; they are fluid. Although one may pinpoint them on a timeline, their influence continues. Like a stone thrown into the water that creates circular ripples or waves upon the surface and underneath, so too do the events and ideas of the past and present shape the American experience—past, present, and future. To the extent that the words on these pages help illuminate the American past and provide thought for the American present and future, the authors will consider their time and effort in sharing their thoughts with others well spent.

# Overview

On the evening of June 6, 1944, D-Day, the Allied invasion of Europe during World War II—as American and Allied troops went ashore on the beaches of Normandy, France, after a surprise landing and bloody day of fighting—President Franklin D. Roosevelt announced the landings over national radio. His announcement of the critical military operations took the form of a prayer. It was not the first or last time that an American president, including Roosevelt, prayed during wartime. Presidential prayer, public and private, during American conflict has occurred frequently in the course of American history. However, on that particular June evening, technology in the form of the radio allowed millions of citizens to listen to and join with President Roosevelt as he prayed over the airwaves for the safety and victory of Allied forces.

For most Americans of the 20th century, that the president would lead the nation in prayer was not understood to be an aberration. Religion and politics have been two domains of American history and life that are prominent and ever present in the bold experiment known as the United States of America. They were prominent in the past and they remain so in the present.

### "I Am Bound for the Promised Land"

When Americans think and talk about war and the nation's history of warfare, there has often been an assumption or assertion that the war is just and that the United States is entering the conflict with divine favor. Such a belief is rooted deeply in the history of the United States that predates its existence as a nation. The arrival from Holland of English religious dissenters in 1620 and the subsequent establishment of the Plymouth Colony heralded the beginning of a colonial experiment that was infused with the belief that the colonists were mirroring the history of the biblical Israelites who journeyed from oppression to a wilderness wandering and finally arrived in a new "Promised Land" that would flow with "milk and honey" (cf. Exodus 3:8; Leviticus 20:24; Numbers 14:8; Joshua 5:6).

American Puritans saw many parallels between the Israelites of the Old Testament and themselves. In the New World, there was a sense of spiritual and historical recapitulation as the Puritans sojourned on their own "errand into the wilderness," an oft-used phrase alluding to the forty-year trek in the wilderness by the Israelites after their departure from Egypt as recorded in the Old Testament, as well as a prophetic journey into the wilderness detailed in Revelation 12:6–7 and understood by the Puritans as referring to themselves. American Puritan historian Perry Miller's *Errand into the Wilderness* (1956) attributes the phrase to a 1670 election sermon by Samuel Danforth (1626–1674) titled "A Brief Recognition of New England's Errand into the Wilderness," but the book's first essay with the same title fails to articulate the more significant biblical and prophetic Puritan identification with the phrase.

As a result of a long war with Great Britain, American independence served as a catalyst for how Americans would view religion, war, and politics in the future. The social and political reverberations from the American Revolution were long and loud. When, in 1836, American poet Ralph Waldo Emerson wrote in his poem "Concord Hymn" (commemorating the Battles of Lexington and Concord on April 19, 1775) the words "the shot heard round the world," his imagery was appropriate and realistic.

For many citizens of the newly founded United States, American independence confirmed religious and political sentiments and ideas regarding the uniqueness of the American people and the Puritan experiment in the New World. Puritan and first governor of Massachusetts John Winthrop's sermonic words, "We shall be as a City upon a hill. The eyes of all people are upon us," preached aboard a ship to newly arriving settlers in 1630, seemed as true in the days following the 1783 signing of the Treaty of Paris as they had a century and a half earlier. Winthrop was not alone in his thoughts and views. The biblical text for his sermon referenced the words of Jesus: "You are the light of the world. A city set on a hill cannot be hidden" (Matthew 5:14 ESV).

The United States' religiously grounded framework functioned well into the 20th century and was articulated in the 19th century by Herman Melville. The author of *Moby Dick* and one of America's greatest novelists declared, "We Americans are the peculiar, chosen people—the Israel of our time; we bear the ark of the liberties of the world. God has predestined, mankind expects, great things from our race; and great things we feel in our souls" (1979, 153).

George McKenna, professor emeritus of City College of the City University of New York, where he taught American government and American political thought for forty years, wrote of Americans' identification with their national forebears, the Puritans, "When the chips are down, when the stakes are high, American political leaders go back to the narrative and even the language of the Puritans; they do it then, especially, because that is when Americans especially want to hear it" (2007, xiii).

What was not in doubt among Puritans on American shores, and even to their children and grandchildren, was that they were part of a bold new religious and political experiment. This certainty was the seed of the political idea known in the 21st century as American exceptionalism. Rooted in the bold religious and political experiment of the Pilgrims and Puritans, extending through the 19th century with the concept of Manifest Destiny and into the 20th and 21st centuries with the idea of spreading democracy around the globe, Americans viewed their nation and its purpose as unique and even divinely ordained in human history.

## "Onward Christian Soldiers" (and Others)

Although war and conflict were not desired, it was understood by most Americans that they were sometimes necessary. And when Americans went (and go) to war, there often exists a religious component.

In his magisterial and oft-quoted book *On War* (*Vom Kriege*), Prussian general and military theorist Carl von Clausewitz states, "Military activity is never directed against material force alone; it is always aimed simultaneously at the moral forces which give it life, and the two cannot be separated" (1832). That was true when he wrote it in the 18th century, and it remains true in the 21st century. The weapons of war have changed, but the motivations for going to war have not.

Although historians and others often study warfare by viewing the weapons of war, the words of war—the ideas behind a war or in a war—are equally important. The ideas and words are the "moral forces" to which Clausewitz refers. Part of those "moral forces" are the religious values and ideas of the citizens, leaders, and warriors of every nation engaged in conflict. At times, the religious factor is significant, but at other times, it is not as prevalent. Yet, large or small, religion's presence is always a factor, just as politics is always a factor. If, as Clausewitz asserts, war is the continuation of politics by other means, then the assumptions, attitudes, and rhetoric that are found in war are also likely grounded in the assumptions, attitudes, and rhetoric that precede the war as prevalent in the politics and political environment. This is certainly true of American political history: American political thought is infused with religious engagement and religious perspectives, even with the long-standing interpretations and applications of the First Amendment of the U.S. Constitution.

Political scientist Eric D. Patterson writes in the concluding pages of his analysis of the ethics of the U.S. history of war: "During every U.S. conflict there has been robust public debate about whether or not to go to war in the first place, and after the decision has been made, debate continued on the ethics of how the war was fought" (2018, 178). Often, much of those debates was infused with religious values and the private and public support or nonsupport of a war that was voiced by American people of faith and the religious institutions to which they belonged. But unlike past grounding in religious values, the increasing secularization of American society in the 21st century has eradicated the spectrum of religious commitments held by many of the nation's citizens.

Religious values and political values are often intertwined and deeply held commitments by individuals. They can also be very contentious and divisive. For that reason, in many households in the 20th-century United States, a matter of etiquette was established in many families that religion and politics were two topics not discussed at the dinner table during family meals or in what was deemed polite society. Yet, there are also very public individual and collective expressions of religion and politics in American history and culture. Thus, religious values and political values have private and public manifestations—as previously stated, they also frequently overlap.

It is not surprising that when the storm clouds of war are on the horizon or erupting, many Americans seek the shelter and protection (in physical reality as well as ideologically) of religion. It is also logical that concerns and decisions about war would be infused with political perspectives and political rhetoric. Religion, politics, and war are frequently mixed together in American society.

### "Down by the Riverside"

Just as there has been strong political and religious support for American wars, so too has there been strong political and religious opposition to them. The diversity of American citizens in every area has ensured that a single perspective on any topic will not be achieved in private or in public. There is no single American viewpoint on anything—especially religion, politics, war, and the convergence of the three. There have always been individual and collective voices of pacifism in the United States. For some Americans, such as Quakers, Mennonites, the Amish, and other strands arising from 16th-century Anabaptism, the quest for peace is rooted deeply in a history of being persecuted in Europe because of beliefs. The desire for peace is experiential as well as theological.

Americans in other religious traditions in which the group or denomination has a history and ecclesiastical stance of pacifism also ground their beliefs in the religious texts of their faith. That some groups have an articulated pacifist position and others do not, but have strong segments or individual voices of pacifism within them, speaks to a core attribute of American religion and politics—individualism. Grounded ideologically and experientially in the history of the United States, many Americans are deeply imbued with religious and political mindsets that find strength in the collective expression of values, but they also do not hesitate to voice dissent.

Blending African rhythm and Christian themes, the 19th-century spiritual "Down by the Riverside" drew upon the biblical words of the prophet Isaiah 2:4: "They shall beat their swords into plowshares, and their spears into pruning hooks; nation shall not lift up sword against nation, neither shall they learn war anymore" (ESV). In part, the result was the lyrics "gonna lay down my sword and shield, down by the riverside . . . ain't gonna study war no more." First known during the American Civil War, the song had a renaissance during the 1960s, gaining wide popularity during the anti-war movement against the Vietnam War. To be sure, not all pacifists ground their pacifism in religion. There are religious and secular strands of pacifism. But in the American experience, it has been the religious variety that has been most prominent, although from the 1960s onward, secularization has eroded some of the religious pacifism and replaced it with pacifist thought not grounded in religious commitments.

## "Blest Be the Tie That Binds"

Like politics, religion has individual as well as group dynamics and facets. The term *religion* is derived from Anglo-Norman *religiun* and Latin *religare*—"to tie fast or bind together." (Indeed, many American Protestants know well the 19th-century gospel hymn "Blest Be the Tie

That Binds.") From a sociological perspective, that is what religion does in the lives of people and societies (so too does politics). Religion projects human order into the totality of being and provides order out of chaos. It provides a spiritual and philosophical framework for understanding ourselves and others. It can also provide insights into the personal, collective, and national experiences of war. If politics is the means by which perspectives and policies are made known in a nation, to and by its leaders, and within its assemblies, religion and religious values can be a forces that sustain, inform, and guide them. Such is not always the case, but it is frequently so.

Theologically, religions may be and often are very different. Sociologically, most religions are very similar. By this, it is understood that most religions

- include belief in the supernatural that is beyond but connected to human experience.
- distinguish between the sacred and the profane in terms of space, objects, and people.
- strongly encourage or require prescribed ritual activities for individuals and communities of faith.
- promote a moral code or ethical principles to guide individuals and communities.
- engage with and incorporate common emotional and intuitive feelings.
- encourage communication and provide ways to communicate or connect with the divine.
- provide a worldview through sacred stories and sacred scriptures.
- organize life for individuals in the context of their respective worldviews.
- promise inner peace and harmony despite the vicissitudes of life.
- require and promote social organization and institutional forms to carry out necessary functions of worship and leadership, preserving orthodox teachings and practices.
- offer a future hope through the coming of a new age or better existence in the afterlife.
- propagate themselves through the recruitment of new members and procreation.

Many of these characteristics can have political overtones or similar political functions. Legally and institutionally in the United States, the law separates religion and politics, but with respect to worldviews and making meaning of life, religion and politics often are interconnected.

Religion is a powerful force in the lives of the faithful. It gives meaning to individuals, communities, and groups. So too does politics; when the two are combined, the result can foster peace or war. With respect to the latter, the sociological characteristics of religions are the same, but the theological content is very different. The sociology is similar, but the theology is dissimilar. Therefore, in the realm of war, that which Geoffrey Chaucer, in *The Canterbury Tales* (1387–1400), called the "Temple of Mars" (the Greek god of war), it must always be asked by warriors, politicians, citizens, and the religious faithful, "What is the same?" and "What is different?" Doctrines matter; theology counts. The sociology of a religion may be confusing, but the theology of a religion can be lethal. Mission failure or defeat of one belligerent may be interpreted as the answer to prayer or even divine victory by another.

## "We Gather Together"

Within Christianity in the 20th-century United States, it was common to speak of *denominations* that functioned on the basis of shared historical and theological commitments and practices, sometimes using geographical or national descriptors that identified major ethnic constituents (e.g., Greek Orthodox Archdiocese of North America, Ukrainian Orthodox Church of the USA), including regions of the United States in which the denomination originated or was prevalent (e.g., Southern Baptist Convention, Cumberland Presbyterian Church, Lutheran Church–Missouri Synod). Indeed, American denominationalism was significantly shaped by the American Civil War, during which several Christian denominations fractured and separated along the boundaries of the famous Mason-Dixon Line (e.g., Southern Baptist Convention and Northern Baptist Convention; also Presbyterians and Methodists, though they reunited in the 20th century). Thus, in the same way that it was common in 19th- and 20th-century politics to speak of "Southern Democrats" or "Northern Republicans," religious groups, primarily Christian, identified in part with the diversity of the American experience.

Considering the interplay of religion, politics, and social change in the United States, in the *Handbook of Denominations in the United States*, religious scholars Craig D. Atwood and Roger E. Olson identify six factors that functioned and continue to function as catalysts in American religious life (2018, 1–11).

The first factor is the First Amendment of the Constitution of the United States and its Bill of Rights. This unique document broke away from earlier European assumptions that civic harmony depended in large part on religious conformity. Contending for the rights of individuals to practice any religion or no religion without state interference, this landmark document fostered growth of religion and new groups in the young nation. Coupled with the second factor, immigration, it was only a matter of time before the majority religious perspective, Protestant Christianity, experienced the growth of other perspectives. Though not without difficulties and even violence, many immigrants to the United States brought, and continue to bring with them, their religious values, practices, and identification. Historically, with respect to war, one sees the religious dimension in things such as the famed Irish Brigade at the Battle of Gettysburg and its well-known Roman Catholic chaplain, Father William Corby (1833–1897).

Theology is the third factor in the diversity of the American religious landscape. The various faith traditions not only have distinct populations and practices but also distinct doctrines and theological nuances. To be sure, many doctrines within a tradition overlap among the many groups of that tradition, but there also distinctions; some of those arise out of the American experience. Some religious groups find their origin in American history. For example, the Church of Jesus Christ of Latter-day Saints (Mormons) and its splinter groups are uniquely American in their origin (and not without political importance and some history of conflict, such as the 1838 Mormon War and the 1857–1858 Mormon Rebellion). Similarly, Pentecostalism began in the first decade of the 20th century.

Native American religion, at times blending Native beliefs and practices with aspects of Christianity, has also resulted in unique American religious groups and practices. With respect to conflict, one of the most tragic was the Ghost Dance movement among some Western Native American tribes. Warriors that performed the Ghost Dance believed that doing so would make them impervious to harm from enemy weapons. The movement began in the 1870s, matured in the 1880s, and culminated in 1889 in the defeat of the Lakota warriors at Wounded Knee Creek on the Lakota Pine Ridge Indian Reservation in South Dakota. Known as the Wounded Knee Massacre or Battle of Wounded Knee and fought on December 29, 1890, between Lakota warriors and members of the U.S. 7th Cavalry Regiment, the event became a symbol of Native American resistance to the U.S. government. From the 1970s to the present, it is looked to as a tragedy that requires continued political activism by Native Americans to ensure their rights. The movement had strong religious overtones and was understood by adherents to be a peaceful religious response to subjugation of Native Americans by the U.S. government. Adherents believed it was a means of enduring increasing hunger, hardship, poverty, disease, and reservation life in the aftermath of the Indian Wars of the 1860s and 1870s. At its height, the Ghost Dance movement found acceptance by tribes as far to the east and south as Colorado, the Dakotas, Nebraska, Kansas, Oklahoma, and Texas.

Cooperation in spite of religious competition and diversity has been a fourth factor of the American religious experience. Theologically, and not without strong opposition, this has resulted in the ecumenical movement. Politically, faith tradition and denomination often have become cobelligerents or partners in social action programs and in shared political perspectives. This has certainly been evident at times in opposition to specific wars (e.g., Vietnam War) and in opposition to weapons of mass destruction (WMDs). Such alliances have also fostered human rights, opposition to genocide, opposition to torture, opposition to religious persecution, and the promotion of religious freedom.

Closely aligned with and overlapping with the cooperation factor has been the fifth factor: the interconnectedness of the public practice of religious values and beliefs in support of political programs, popular culture, public morality, freedom of assembly, freedom of speech, and freedom of religion in very open and public environments. The sixth and final factor is the media. Secular and religious media have ensured that local concerns become national concerns and that national concerns become local concerns. Whether through print media, radio, television, or the Internet, communications technology aids the promulgation and amalgamation of religious and political perspectives. It was over the radio airwaves that most Americans learned of the Japanese attack on U.S. forces at Pearl Harbor on December 7, 1941. It was through television that Americans watched the Vietnam War on the evening news at dinnertime. It was also largely through television that Americans learned of the beginning of hostilities during the Gulf War; the four tragic flights of September 11, 2001, the operation of the Iraqi War and Afghanistan War; the collapse of Syria; and a score of other conflicts in the final years of the 20th century and the first decades of the 21st century.

In the 21st century, the term *denomination* is still used but alongside other terms such as *fellowship* or *network*, even if stressing autonomy and polity by using *independent* in the name. Additionally, denominational loyalism is eroding in the 21st-century United States—perhaps so too are political loyalties, with both being replaced by a more fluid individualism that seeks individual spirituality rather than corporate religion and social progress based on identity politics rather than party platforms. (With respect to the military, even the U.S. military has been transformed from a 20th-century draft to a 21st-century all-volunteer force.)

Even in an increasingly diverse and secular culture such as the 21st-century United States, religion remains a vibrant force that shapes many aspects of the lives of American citizens and all who live and work within the borders of the nation. There is not only a multiplicity of Christian faith traditions in the United States but also a history and spectrum of other traditions, among them, Buddhism, Judaism, Hinduism, Islam, and many others that have a smaller (but growing) representation. For each of these, interactions with American politics and political issues are active and diverse.

### "Mine Eyes Have Seen the Glory"

The joining of religion and politics in times of war has been commonplace in American history—even when Americans fought each other. During the American Civil War (1861–1865), Americans on both sides of the Mason-Dixon Line sought divine favor for victory, appealed to religious texts to bolster political views, and mixed religious and political themes of death, sacrifice, and rebirth to such an extent that they became commonplace in American civil religion and would be drawn upon by political and religious leaders throughout the 20th century and in the 21st century.

Julia Ward Howe's (1819–1910) "Battle Hymn of the Republic," written during the war in November 1861, continues to be one of the most popular patriotic and religious songs of Americans. Its ongoing popularity illustrates the ease with which many Americans blend religion, politics, and war. Yet, words from the song, spoken by minister and civil rights leader Martin Luther King, Jr. (1929–1968) in his last speech on April 3, 1968, on the eve of his assassination, remind singers and listeners of the hope and strength many Americans find in religion as they carry out political convictions—whether in war or peace.

That night, Americans were embroiled in a divisive war in Vietnam that King opposed. But closer to home, they were engaged in the struggle for civil rights, and on that too the nation was divided. King drew upon biblical imagery known so well to Americans—the Promised Land. To his audience in Memphis, Tennessee, at the end of his speech, he proclaimed, "I want you to know tonight, that we, as a people, will get to the Promised

Land. And I'm happy, tonight. I'm not worried about anything. I'm not fearing any man." He then closed with words of hope and affirmation for religion and politics: "Mine eyes have seen the glory of the coming of the Lord" ("I've Been to the Mountaintop").

## "Abide with Me"

The nation's founders hoped that war would not be as prevalent in the colonies and new nation as it had been in Europe. June 11, 1823, Thomas Jefferson wrote the following to James Monroe:

> I have ever deemed it fundamental for the US never to take active part in the quarrels of Europe. Their political interests are entirely distinct from ours. Their mutual jealousies, their balance of power, their complicated alliances, their forms and principles of government, are all foreign to us. They are nations of eternal war. All their energies are expended in the destruction of the labor, property and lives of their people. On our part, never had a people so favorable a chance of trying the opposite system of peace and fraternity with mankind, and the direction of all our means and faculties to the purposes of improvement instead of destruction. (National Archives, https://founders.archives.gov/documents/Jefferson/98-01-02-3559)

Regrettably, Jefferson's dream has yet to be realized in American history. The desire for peace has been strong, but so too have been the urges for war—often realized in the loss of America's greatest treasure, its sons and daughters. Even so, in the darkness of such days, most Americans, regardless of their political preferences, believed that there would be divine assistance or consolation in victory or defeat.

## "In God Is Our Trust"

No nation is immune from war. When the storm clouds of war appear on the horizon, Americans instinctively look to two of their most cherished values and institutions for guidance—the political and the religious. Both are dynamic, and both are complex—and they should be. Values have consequences.

The kaleidoscope of American history is remarkable. To be sure, it is imperfect, but every day brings a new turn and new opportunities to enact the principles and values of American citizens. Every day Americans can, if they so choose, draw upon their religious and political values to strive for a world of peace rather than war.

"The Star-Spangled Banner," the American national anthem (since 1931), arose out of the experience of Francis Scott Key (1799–1843) observing the bombardment of American forces at Ft. McHenry (Baltimore, Maryland) by the British during the War of 1812. Most Americans know the first stanza. Less well known are the others penned by Scott. With respect to religion, politics, and war, perhaps it is the fourth stanza that best captures and summarizes the perspective of many Americans throughout the 400-year experience of the birth and growth of the United States of America:

> O! thus be it ever when free men shall stand Between their loved homes and the foe's desolation; Bless'd with victory and peace, may our Heaven-rescued land Praise the Power that hath made and preserved us a nation Then conquer we must, for our cause it is just—And this be our motto—"In God is our trust!"

# Chronology

**1775–1783**—American Revolutionary War: The Americans in thirteen colonies gain independence from the British Crown and establish the United States of America under the U.S. Constitution.

**1861–1865**—American Civil War: Southern states secede from the Union over slavery and states' rights, and a civil war is then fought between Northern (Union) states and Southern (Confederate) states.

**1914–1918**—World War I originates in Europe in 1914 and is one of the deadliest and largest wars in history, with the United States participating from 1917 to 1918.

**1941**—December 7: The Imperial Japanese Navy launches a surprise attack against the United States at Pearl Harbor, Hawaii, leading President Franklin D. Roosevelt to join the Allies against the Axis powers in World War II.

**1944**—June 6: President Franklin D. Roosevelt addresses the United States on national radio, praying for the safety and victory of Allied forces on D-Day.

**1945**—April 25: Fifty national governments begin drafting the United Nations Charter with the aim of preventing future world wars and preserving world peace. The United Nations eventually grows to include 193 member states; the most recent to join was South Sudan in 2011.

August 6: The United States and Allies drop the atomic bomb on Hiroshima, Japan; the Soviet Union joins the war against Japan and invades Manchuria two days later on August 8.

August 9: The United States and Allies drop the atomic bomb on Nagasaki, Japan; Japanese emperor Hirohito announces the surrender of Imperial Japan to the Allies, ending the Pacific War on August 15.

**1946**—The Nuremberg trials are held after World War II by the Allied nations, prosecuting members of the leadership of Nazi Germany who participated in the Holocaust and other war crimes, including genocide.

**1947–1991**—Cold War era: Hostilities short of open warfare and the race for nuclear dominance between the Soviet bloc countries and the United States and allies begins with the Truman Doctrine and continues for more than forty years, until the collapse of the Soviet Union in 1991.

**1948**—December 9: The United Nations General Assembly unanimously accepts Resolution 217, the Universal Declaration of Human Rights (UDHR), affirming fundamental human and civil rights and freedoms as inalienable for all peoples and nations.

December 10: The United Nations General Assembly unanimously adopts the Genocide Convention, defining genocide in legal terms and committing to prevent and protect against the crime of genocide.

**1950–1953**—Korean War: The war between North and South Korea, fueled by China in the north and the United States and allies in the south, takes place.

**1955–1975**—Vietnam War or Second Indochina War: A war is fought between North Vietnam, supported by its communist allies, including China and the Soviet Union, and South Vietnam, supported by the United States and allies, with the bulk of U.S. participation from 1965 to 1973.

**1956**—July 30: President Dwight D. Eisenhower signs legislation passed by the Eighty-Fourth Congress making "In God We Trust" the official motto of the United States.

**1960**—November 8: John F. Kennedy is elected the first Roman Catholic U.S. president.

**1963**—November 22: Six-Day War or Third Arab-Israeli War: In the third of the Arab-Israeli wars, Israel defeats Egypt, Syria, and Jordan and captures territories that include the West Bank, Gaza Strip, and Golan Heights.

**1967**—April 4: Martin Luther King, Jr., the most prominent American civil rights movement leader, publicly denounces U.S. participation in the Vietnam War in his controversial speech "Beyond Vietnam: A Time to Break the Silence," delivered at Riverside Church in New York City.

**1968**—April 4: Martin Luther King, Jr., Baptist minister and civil rights leader, is assassinated, triggering nationwide race riots.

**1970**—The U.S. Supreme Court interprets exemption for conscientious objection in relation to the First Amendment in the court case *Welsh v. United States*, broadening exemption to include objection from nonreligious objection grounded in moral or ethical beliefs of right and wrong.

**1982**—June 7: President Ronald Reagan writes a letter to Pope John Paul II following their meeting in Vatican City, affirming their bond as recent survivors of attempted assassinations and their mutual desire for peacemaking and disarmament. In the following years, Reagan and Pope John Paul II actively work to undermine communism in Roman Catholic countries and eastern Europe, especially Poland, precipitating the end of the Cold War.

**1983**—May 3: The National Conference of Catholic Bishops publishes "The Challenge of Peace: God's Promise and Our Response," a pastoral letter addressing war, peace, and the use of force in a nuclear age, marking a shift toward nonviolence and pacifism in American Roman Catholicism and a move away from the just war tradition.

**1987–1993**—First Palestinian Intifada: Palestinian protests break out against Israeli occupation of the West Bank and Gaza Strip, resulting in the deaths of more than 1,900 Palestinians and 270 Israelis.

**1990–1994**—The Berlin Wall, the massive concrete barrier that physically and symbolically divided East and West Germany since 1961, is demolished, precipitating the reunification of Germany in 1990, the eventual collapse of the USSR, and end of the Cold War.

**1991**—January 15–February 28: The Gulf War takes place as United Nations Security Forces, including the United States, force Saddam Hussein's Iraqi army out of Kuwait.

**1993**—October 27: The U.S. Senate passes the Religious Freedom Restoration Act of 1993; it is signed into law by President William "Bill" J. Clinton on November 16.

November 17: The National Conference of Catholic Bishops publishes "The Harvest of Justice Is Sown in Peace" pastoral letter in commemoration of the tenth anniversary of "The Challenge of Peace" letter.

**1994**—April 7–July 15: The United Nations and international community fail to prevent genocide of the Tutsi minority group in the Rwandan Civil War, marking a major turning point in international concern regarding human rights, genocide, and the "Responsibility to Protect" (R2P).

**2001**—September 11: Nineteen people associated with the Islamist terrorist group al-Qaeda hijack four airplanes and carry out suicide attacks against targets in the United States, including the Twin Towers of World Trade Center in New York City and the Pentagon in Washington, DC, prompting the United States and its allies to embark on a "global war on terrorism."

**2003–2011**—Iraq War: A multinational coalition force led by the United States and the Bush administration invades and occupies Iraq, overthrowing the government of Iraqi president Saddam Hussein as part of the global war on terrorism and based on intelligence that Iraq possessed a program for weapons of mass destruction (WMDs).

**2003–Present**—Darfur conflict: After decades of civil war, non-Arab groups rebel in the Western Darfur region against the government of Sudan, resulting in major armed conflict and the ongoing oppression and killing of hundreds of thousands of civilians, eventually culminating in the secession of South Sudan from Sudan in 2011.

**2005**—The United Nations General Assembly unanimously adopts the "Responsibility to Protect" (R2P) principle at the 2005 World Summit, committing to protecting populations from genocide, war crimes, ethnic cleansing, and crimes against humanity.

**2005–2010**—The Second Palestinian Intifada against Israel gains international attention and divides nations and entities in their support or opposition to it.

**2006**—January: U.S. religious leaders at an international conference on theology, law, and torture sign an ecumenical statement, "Torture Is a Moral Issue," released by the National Religious Campaign Against Torture.

**2006–Present**—In 2006, U.S. forces kill Jordanian jihadist Abu Musab al-Zarqawi, the head of the Islamic State in Iraq and the Levant (ISIL; also known as ISIS, Daesh, and the Islamic State) that emerged from al-Qaeda in response to the U.S. invasion of Iraq. Zarqawi's vision of establishing a caliphate by stoking civil war between Sunnis and Shiites results in the Islamic State's takeover of parts of Iraq and Syria in 2014.

**2008–Present**—Post-Intifada Conflict: Although the Second Intifada generally ends in 2006, the Palestinian and Israeli conflict continues. Israelis kill or wound over 1,000 Palestinians in the Gaza Strip in 2008 and early 2009.

**2009–Present**—Boko Haram insurgency: The jihadist group Boko Haram launches an armed uprising against the Nigerian government in July 2009 with the aim of establishing a Muslim state.

**2011–Present**—Syrian Civil War and crisis: In March 2011, antigovernment marches spark conflict between the Ba'athist government of Bashar al-Assad and multiple opposition forces, resulting in a decade-long civil war and human rights violations, including the use of chemical weapons by the Assad government, and creating an ongoing refugee crisis.

**2014–Present**—Yemeni Civil War: A multifaction war breaks out in the Republic of Yemen between the Arab-led Yemeni government and Houthi forces and their allies.

**2015**—June 16: The U.S. Senate passes the McCain-Feinstein Anti-Torture Amendment, which rejects "enhanced interrogation," restricts interrogation techniques as authorized in the Army Field Manual, and requires Red Cross access to detainees.

**2020**—March–**Present**: The COVID-19 coronavirus pandemic begins; it results in millions of deaths and negative repercussions on national economies due to shutdowns worldwide.

**2022**—February: Russian invades Ukraine in a follow-up to 2014 incursions.

# Afghanistan War

The Afghanistan War (2001–2021) has deep roots and a long history. At the beginning of the 21st century, the United States was already involved in political efforts to suppress the terrorist organization al-Qaeda, headed by Saudi-born Osama bin Laden (1957–2011), and the Taliban government that harbored and supported it. U.S. interests in the region date to the Cold War and the Soviet invasion of Afghanistan and the subsequent war (1979–1989). In the decade following the 1989 Soviet withdrawal from Afghanistan and the war, the Taliban, an ultraconservative political and religious faction, emerged to gain political control of most of the nation, although there were significant areas of conflict and resistance. The Afghan Civil War (1996–2001) then occurred between the Taliban (officially, the Islamic Emirate of Afghanistan) and the Afghan Northern Alliance (officially, the United Islamic Front for the Salvation of Afghanistan).

In the aftermath of the September 11, 2001, terrorist attacks on the United States, which were planned and directed from Afghanistan, the United States demanded that the Taliban hand over Osama bin Laden and expel al-Qaeda from the country, ending the sanctuary that had been provided. When the Taliban refused, the United States led a military coalition and campaign against al-Qaeda and its protectors. Code-named Operation Enduring Freedom (2001–2014) and Operation Freedom's Sentinel (2015–2021) military operations commenced on October 7, 2001, to topple the Taliban government and deny safe haven and a base of operations to al-Qaeda. Over the course of the war, more than forty nations joined the U.S.-led coalition. Though initially successful in removing the Taliban government and supporting the new democratically elected Afghan government, the Taliban reemerged and gained control over most of the country, except for the major cities. The American endeavor resulted in the longest war in U.S. history.

Domestically, political support for the war rose and fell over the years. As the American presence grew and achieved military successes, there was hope that they would be long-lasting and that the newly established Afghan government and its military would soon require less U.S. and international support, development aid, and military assistance. This did not occur, and successive U.S. presidential administrations failed to end the war and ensure peace and stability in Afghanistan.

As military operations and strategies continued and shifted, domestic and political support for the war waxed and waned. Religious leaders and organizations in the United States also expressed concern regarding the goals and duration of the war. Many religious and political leaders rightly believed that the military operations in Afghanistan would lead to wider conflict, specifically against the regime of Iraqi president Saddam Hussein (1937–2006).

There was concern by the administration of President George W. Bush (and other nations such as the United Kingdom) that the global expansion of al-Qaeda might align with rogue regimes and acquire weapons of mass destruction to use in future terrorist attacks. Belief that Iraq was still in possession of such weapons, in violation of the cease-fire agreement reached after the Gulf War (1990–1991), and desire to oust Saddam Hussein from power led to expanded conflict and the Iraq War (2003–2011).

The war in Afghanistan—stemming from the religiously motivated terrorism of radical Islamic terrorists—brought to the forefront of the American experience the linking of militant Islamic thought with 21st-century domestic and global politics. Americans first became aware of power of political Islam during the Iran hostage crisis (1979–1981), when fifty-two American diplomats and citizens from the U.S. embassy in Tehran, Iran, were held captive by supporters of the Iranian Revolution. Other terrorist acts throughout the last two decades of the 20th century, primarily in the Middle East and Africa, were also strongly tied to militant Islam (Sunni and Shia). Yet, these acts did not generate the same level of awareness, information, misinformation, and antagonism against Islam as the 9/11 attacks and subsequent actions in Afghanistan. The ensuing U.S.-led international response and actions became known as the "global war on terrorism."

One aspect of the presence of the United States and its allies in Afghanistan is the enormous effort of religious and secular nongovernmental organizations (NGOs) to bring humanitarian and development aid to Afghanistan. Efforts to increase literacy, education, and opportunities for children, especially girls, have been especially prominent. Additionally, endeavors to enhance the rights and opportunities (social, economic, political) for women have garnered international attention and support. Regrettably, the war also resulted in the killing of many NGO workers as well as their being taken hostage.

In the first decade of the 20th century, the American population was generally supportive of the war effort, but the longer the war lasted, the more frustration increased domestically. Americans were torn between their desire for bringing American military forces home and bringing humanitarian development and political stability to Afghanistan. Americans wearied of the war, and critics called it a "quagmire," a term historically and politically identified with the Vietnam War.

The long history and complexity of the Afghanistan War generated qualified religious support for the war effort by many religious groups, religious leaders, and denominations that diminished through the years. Increasingly, U.S. religious leaders and groups called for the responsible transfer of power to the Afghan government as a precursor of U.S. withdrawal from the region. Withdrawal occurred in August 2021 under President Biden, but there were many critics of what was seen to be an uncoordinated and hasty withdrawal in the midst of the Taliban takeover of the elected government in Afghanistan. The ensuing humanitarian and refugee crisis reverberated strongly in the international area as well as in many faith traditions and religious organizations. In Afghanistan and Iraq, there were diverse religious opinions as to whether the conflicts could be supported within the moral and ethical framework of the just war tradition, and this too has made political and religious discourse challenging. Afghanistan has a centuries-long history of internecine warfare that has been compounded by regional hostilities and invasions by foreign powers. To date, no external power has successfully unified the region of deep tribal, ethnic, and religious factions. Although observers, prodemocracy nations, NGOs, and individuals have hoped, died, and worked for democracy in 21st-century Afghanistan, stability has thus far remained elusive.

*See also:* American Peace Churches; Christianity and War; Ecclesiastical Statements on War and Peace; Evangelicalism; Gulf War; Iraq War; Islam and War; Judaism and War; Just War Tradition; Middle East Conflict; Pacifism; Presidential Faith and War; Protestant Denominations; Religion, Conflict, and Geopolitics; Roman Catholicism; Terrorism; Torture; Weapons of Mass Destruction

## Further Reading

Congressional Research Service. "Afghanistan: Background and U.S. Policy in Brief." June 25, 2020. https://fas.org/sgp/crs/row/R45122.pdf

Council on Foreign Relations. "Timelines: The U.S. War in Afghanistan 1999–2020." August 2020. https://www.cfr.org/timeline/us-war-afghanistan

Jacobsen, Gary C. "A Tale of Two Wars: Public Opinion on the U.S. Military Interventions in Afghanistan and Iraq." *Presidential Studies Quarterly* 40, no. 4 (December 2010): 585–610.

Juergensmeyer, Mark. *Terror in the Mind of God*. 4th ed. Berkeley: University of California Press, 2017.

Kaplan, Robert D. *Soldiers of God: With Islamic Warriors in Afghanistan and Pakistan*. Rev. ed. New York: Vintage Books, 2001.

Maizland, Lindsay, and Zachary Laub. "The Taliban in Afghanistan." Council on Foreign Relations, March 11, 2020. https://www.cfr.org/backgrounder/taliban-afghanistan

National Association of Evangelicals. "Most Favor Continued U.S. Presence in Afghanistan." Evangelical Leaders Survey, August 2010. https://www.nae.net/most-favor-continued-u-s-presence-in-afghanistan/

Patterson, Eric. *Just American Wars: Ethical Dilemmas in U.S. Military History*. New York: Routledge, 2019.

Preston, Andrew. *Sword of the Spirit, Shield of Faith: Religion in American War and Diplomacy*. New York: Alfred A. Knopf, 2012.

Roy, Oindrila. "Religious Roots of War Attitudes in the United States: Insights from Iraq, Afghanistan, and the Persian Gulf." *Foreign Policy Analysis* 12, no. 3 (July 2016): 258–274. https://academic.oup.com/fpa/article/12/3/258/1751230

Tucker, Spencer C., and Paul G. Pierpaoli Jr., eds. *U.S. Conflicts in the 21st Century: Afghanistan War, Iraq War, and the War on Terror*. 3 vols. Santa Barbara, CA: ABC-CLIO, 2016.

United States Conference on Catholic Bishops. "Letter to Administration on U.S. Policy Towards Afghanistan." October 26, 2017. https://www.usccb.org/issues-and-action/human-life-and-dignity/global-issues/asia/afghanistan/letter-to-administration-on-afghanistan-2017-10-26

# American Civil War

Echoes of the American Civil War (1861–1865) are still heard in 21st-century American society, more than 150 years after its conclusion. Issues such as the removal of statues and images of Confederate leaders and the Confederate flag from buildings and public spaces, reparations for slavery, ensuring voting rights, and racial tensions are part of the legacy of the war and intersect with the personal, social, and religious values of many Americans. Just as the legacy of the war echoed in American society with such things as the rise of the civil rights movement in the 1950s and 1960s, the war and its lingering issues continue to reverberate in contemporary society.

Before, during, and after the war, religious communities and denominations were deeply and geographically divided, resulting in splits among many Protestant denominations. At the time of the war, the nation was one with deep religious commitments by the majority of its citizens. For example, in Virginia, where the bulk of major battles were fought, as many as two-thirds of the population attended Protestant churches at the time of the outbreak of the war. Census records from 1860 show that five out of six churchgoers in Virginia attended a Baptist, Methodist, Presbyterian, or Episcopal church. Of these Protestant denominations, all four would experience national division due to the war, geography, and politics. Some of the divisions, such as those in the Protestant Episcopal Church in the Confederate States of America, would quickly mend after the war's end in 1865. Other divisions, such as those in the Presbyterian Church, would resolve in the 20th century. Conversely, the Baptists still remain organizationally separate (i.e., Southern Baptist Convention). Whether one lived north or south of the dividing Mason-Dixon line, religion was an integral part of daily life for the majority of Americans.

The fervor of the reform movements of the 1830s and 1840s raised social and theological expectations and hopes. There were many areas of social concern, among them, better working conditions for sailors, the need for hospitals for the medically and mentally ill, and better public education, but the issue that had the most attention was slavery. Social, political, theological, and economic debates about slavery and the abolition of slavery were rampant in the North and the South.

For many people of faith in the North during the war, a major issue was the belief that the United States was a union and a Christian nation and that the rebellion of Southerners threatened to destroy a divinely ordained nation. Slavery was a concern, but for many, it was often subordinated to a larger theological-political vision of the nation. Christians in the North and the South had debated the biblical background regarding slavery and abolition for several decades prior to the war. Such debates were often not isolated but part of a broader theological and historical view of American exceptionalism. For many Protestants, part of this perspective was also a theological view of the future called *postmillennialism*. This was the view that the eradication of social and cultural problems in the world would be completed, and once accomplished, a millennial reign (1,000 years) of Jesus Christ upon the earth would be inaugurated. For those opposed to slavery on religious grounds, the defense was often a part of this theological perspective. As such, slavery was understood to be one of the widespread injustices to be remedied. Such a view imbued the war with enormous religious overtones (illustrated, for example, in the lyrics of Julia Ward Howe's song "Battle Hymn of the Republic").

Pious citizens in the South also believed in a divinely ordained nation but emphasized the rights of states and believed that they could create a godly republic that supported slavery as a key component of its economy. In many ways, the North and South were locked in confrontation, including dueling religious views of the covenantal nature and understanding of Christian America. It was an era of religious millennial hopes, political chaos, and competing claims of justice.

Once the war erupted, religious, political, and military leaders as well as soldiers and citizens on both sides prayed for victory and divine blessing. Both sides also portrayed their cause as a just war. Divine favor, guidance, and victory were sought and claimed by both sides throughout the war.

During the winters of 1862–1863 and 1863–1864, when the weather prohibited large battles and the armies settled into winter camps, there was a resurgence of religious enthusiasm in the camps. Religious revivals affected the armies on both sides, intensifying loyalty, improving morale, and deepening the sense of duty. The renewed commitment to personal religion may have also strengthened the resolve to fight and continue the war, especially among soldiers in the South. In this way, religion may have been a factor in prolonging the war.

Important during the war, in its aftermath, and to the present are the deeply rooted political and religious ideas that were expressed at the time. Themes of death, sacrifice, and rebirth entered American civil religion and have remained part of American religious imagery and discourse. Perhaps the clearest illustration of this is President Abraham Lincoln's Gettysburg Address, which he wrote and delivered in November 1863, after the Battle of Gettysburg in July 1863. Further, in subsequent wars, political and religious leaders have used the Civil War as a shared event of American heritage that could be looked to for the rallying of support for war efforts.

Many religious groups in the United States continue to support the need for reparations to the descendants of slaves. Most denominations have acknowledged the tragedy of slavery and the denominational and national guilt of historic participation in it. For example, in 1995, officials of the Southern Baptist Convention formally renounced the church's support of segregation and slavery. Subsequent to this renunciation, in 2009, the denomination issued an apology for its Civil War–era stance on slavery. Similarly, in 2017, the Jesuits and Georgetown University issued an apology for their participation in slavery. In 2019, in a first for an American Jewish organization, the Union for Reform Judaism issued a resolution for the creation of a federal commission to study and develop proposals for African American reparations. In recent state and national political elections, candidates looking to secure support, especially from African American voters, frequently face the issue of reparations. Such illustrations show the continued ramifications of the war on American politics and religion.

*See also:* American Exceptionalism; American Revolution; Human Rights; Just War Tradition; Military Chaplains; Music; Pacifism; Protestant Denominations; Rhetoric, Sermons, and Prayers; World War I; World War II

## Further Reading

Brodrecht, Grant. *Our Country: Northern Evangelicals and the Union during the Civil War Era*. New York: Fordham University Press, 2018.

Byrd, James P. *A Holy Baptism of Fire: The Bible and the American Civil War*. New York: Oxford University Press, 2021.

Faust, Drew Gilpin. *The Republic of Suffering: Death and the American Civil War*. New York: Random House, 2008.

Gamble, Richard M. A *Fiery Gospel: The Battle Hymn of the Republic and the Road to Righteous War*. Ithaca, NY: Cornell University Press, 2019.

Miller, Randall M., Harry S. Stout, and Charles Reagan Wilson, eds. *Religion and the American Civil War*. New York: Oxford University Press, 1998.

Miller, Robert J. *Both Prayed to the Same God: Religion and Faith in the American Civil War*. Lanham, MD: Lexington Books, 2007.

Noll, Mark A. *The Civil War as a Theological Crisis*. Chapel Hill: University of North Carolina Press, 2006.

Preston, Andrew. *Sword of the Spirit, Shield of Faith: Religion in American War and Diplomacy*. New York: Alfred A. Knopf, 2012.

Shattuck, Gardiner H., Jr. *A Shield and Hiding Place: The Religious Life of the Civil War Armies*. Macon, GA: Mercer University Press, 1987.
Stout, Harry S. *Upon the Altar of the Nation: A Moral History of the Civil War*. New York: Viking, 2005.
Woodworth, Steven E. *While God Is Marching On: The Religious World of Civil War Soldiers*. Lawrence: University of Kansas Press, 2001.

## American Exceptionalism

American exceptionalism is the belief that the United States is a unique nation in the history of the world with a special mission that makes it superior to other nations. For many, it means that the origin, existence, history, and future of the United States have divine blessing. American exceptionalism has often influenced and been a part of religious, political, and patriotic rhetoric. In times of war, it has been used to gain support for U.S. wars. American wars and victory in them have also enhanced the idea. The idea was widely used during the Cold War and in the post-9/11 efforts against global terrorism. In recent decades, even though it has been extensively debated by supporters and critics, it remains a central idea in many Americans' political views.

Words and phrases associated with the idea of American exceptionalism include viewing the American nation as an "empire of liberty" (Thomas Jefferson), the "last best hope of Earth" (Abraham Lincoln), and a "shining city on a hill" (John Winthrop). The latter phrase finds its source in the words of Jesus of Nazareth, as recorded in the Gospel of Matthew: "You are the light of the world. A city set on a hill cannot be hidden" (Matt. 5:14 NASB). The phrase has since been recited by many American presidents throughout the nation's history. In recent years, these include John F. Kennedy, Ronald Reagan, Bill Clinton, and Barack Obama. In American history, it was first used by Puritan leader John Winthrop (1587/8–1649) in a March 21, 1630, lecture and treatise titled "A Model of Christian Charity." This was given at Holyrood Church in Southampton, England, to a group of people who would be the first of the Massachusetts Bay colonists who embarked on the ship *Arabella* and sailed to Boston (Bremer 2005, 171).

American exceptionalism also shares the national optimism of the idea of *Manifest Destiny*, a term coined in 1845 by newspaper editor John

O'Sullivan, who used the term to promote the annexation of Texas and Oregon Country to the United States. Manifest Destiny contended that it was the destiny of the United States to be a nation from the Atlantic Ocean to the Pacific Ocean and to remake the West into an agrarian society based on the special virtues of Americans and their institutions.

Interestingly, the phrase *American exceptionalism* came to prominence through its use by Soviet leader Joseph Stalin (1878–1953) in 1929 as a critique of a faction of American communists who argued that aspects of the American political system exempted Americans from certain elements of Marxism. In 1840, French historian and political scientist Alexis de Tocqueville (1805–1859) wrote in his famous book *Democracy in America* that the United States was an "exceptional" country (*Democracy in America*, part 2, 36). "Exceptionalism" was also used by newspapers in the United States and England during the American Civil War. Additionally, the "Frontier Thesis" of historian Frederick Jackson Turner (1861–1932) and the writings of Alfred Thayer Mahan (1840–1914) coalesced to give Americans in the late 19th and early 20th centuries a sense of the rising importance of the United States on the global political stage.

Earlier, John Winthrop's use of the biblical phrase "city on a hill" expressed the Puritan idea that those individuals who immigrated to the New World and what would become the American colonies and, ultimately, the United States were in many ways replicating the history of the Israelites and their experiences as recorded in the Hebrew scriptures (Old Testament). In the New World, there was a sense of spiritual and historical recapitulation as the Puritans sojourned on their own "errand into the wilderness," an oft-used phrase alluding to the forty-year trek in the wilderness by the Israelites after their departure from Egypt, as recorded in the Old Testament, as well as a prophetic journey into the wilderness detailed in Revelation 12:6–7 and Jesus's words in Matthew 11:7. The phrase and idea were understood by the Puritans as referring to themselves. One example of this was the 1670 sermon by Massachusetts minister Samuel Danforth (1626–1674) titled "A Brief Recognition of New England's Errand into the Wilderness." This transference of and identification with Israel's history created an enduring belief in the uniqueness of the American experience. The fact that many came to the New World to have religious freedom further imbued in them a sense of religious destiny.

With the coming of the American Revolution and the victory obtained by it, the idea that the new nation had a special mission and purpose in the world became a firm part of American political ideology and American civil religion. Several decades later, it was during the War of 1812 with Great Britain that "The Star-Spangled Banner," what would become the American national anthem, was inspired and written by Francis Scott Key (1779–1843). The third stanza of the song clearly articulates the idea of the United States as a unique and divinely guided nation, especially in wartime. Key wrote, "Blest with victory and peace, may the heav'n rescued land, Praise the Power that hath made and preserved us a nation. Then conquer we must, when our cause it is just. And this be our motto: 'In God is our trust'" (Ferris 2014, 255–256). In the mid-19th century, famed American author Herman Melville (1819–1891) wrote in *White-Jacket*, "And we Americans are the peculiar, chosen people—the Israel of our time; we bear the ark of the liberties of the world" (Melville 1979, 153).

Belief in American exceptionalism continued in the 20th century, even after World War I, when the United States entered a time of international isolationism. After World War II, the phrase *Pax Americana* ("American Peace") became popular and signified an era of desired peace that was overseen by the United States (and to some extent the United Kingdom). As an extension of American exceptionalism, *Pax Americana* promoted the idea that American values and power should be spread across the globe. There was the Cold War in the latter half of the 20th century, but even that was understood by many to be an outgrowth of *Pax Americana* in the sense that it was not a third world war, even though conflicts in Korea and Vietnam occurred.

In the 21st century, the idea of American exceptionalism gained renewed visibility and popularity. Those sentiments continue despite years of conflict in Afghanistan and Iraq. For example, after the attacks of September 11, 2001, the idea grew such that it became and has continued to be a plank of the Republican Party platform since 2012. It defines American exceptionalism as "the notion that our ideas and principles as a nation give us a unique place of moral leadership in the world . . . requires the United States to retake its natural position as leader of the free world" (Republican National Committee n.d.).

Even in its secular representation, American exceptionalism traces its ideological roots to the religious values of the earliest European settlers in the New World. In times of war and peace, the idea has encouraged and sustained Americans who believed that their personal and national sacrifices had lasting—and at times eternal—significance.

*See also:* American Civil War; American Revolution; Cold War; Korean War; Presidential Faith and War; Religious Texts; Rhetoric, Sermons, and Prayers; World War I; World War II

## Further Reading

Bailyn, Bernard. *The Ideological Origins of the American Revolution.* Enl. ed. Cambridge, MA: Belknap Press, 1992.

Bremer, Francis J. *John Winthrop: America's Forgotten Founding Father.* New York: Oxford University Press, 2005.

Carlson, John D., and Jonathan H. Ebel, eds. *From Jeremiad to Jihad: Religion, Violence, & America.* Berkeley: University of California Press, 2012.

Cherry, Conrad, ed. *God's New Israel: Religious Interpretations of American Destiny.* Englewood Cliffs, NJ: Prentice-Hall, 1972.

Ferris, Marc. *Star-Spangled Banner: The Unlikely Story of America's National Anthem.* Baltimore, MD: Johns Hopkins University Press, 2014.

Guyatt, Nicholas. *Providence and the Invention of the United States, 1607–1876.* Cambridge, UK: Cambridge University Press, 2007.

Hall, David D. *The Puritans: A Transatlantic History.* Princeton, NJ: Princeton University Press, 2019.

Haselby, Sam. *The Origins of American Religious Nationalism.* New York: Oxford University Press, 2015.

Kupchan, Charles A. "The Clash of Exceptionalisms: A New Fight over an Old Idea." *Foreign Affairs* (March–April 2018). https://www.foreignaffairs.com/articles/united-states/2018-02-13/clash-exceptionalisms

McKenna, George. *The Puritan Origins of American Patriotism.* New Haven, CT: Yale University Press, 2007.

Melville, Herman. *White-Jacket: Or the World in a Man-of-War.* New York: New American Library, 1979.

Preston, Andrew. *Sword of the Spirit, Shield of Faith: Religion in American War and Diplomacy.* New York: Alfred A. Knopf, 2012.

Republican National Committee. "America Resurgent, Republican Platform." Accessed March 1, 2020. https://prod-cdn-static.gop.com/media/documents/DRAFT_12_FINAL%5B1%5D-ben_1468872234.pdf

Roberts, Timothy, and Lindsay DiCuirci, eds. *American Exceptionalism.* 4 vols. London: Pickering & Chatto Publishers, 2012.

Rogers, Daniel T. *As a City on a Hill: The Story of America's Most Famous Lay Sermon.* Princeton, NJ: Princeton University Press, 2018.

Rojecki, Andrew. "Rhetorical Alchemy: American Exceptionalism and the War on Terror." *Political Communication* 25, no. 1 (2008): 67–88.

Shalev, Eran. *American Zion: The Old Testament as a Political Text from Revolution to the Civil War.* New Haven, CT: Yale University Press, 2013.

Spragg, Dennis M. *America Ascendant: The Rise of American Exceptionalism.* Lincoln, NE: Potomac Books, 2019.
Tocqueville, Alexis de. *Democracy in America.* New York: G. Dearborn & Co., 1838.
Van Egan, Abram C. *City on a Hill: A History of American Exceptionalism.* New Haven, CT: Yale University Press, 2020.
Wilsey, John D. *American Exceptionalism and Civil Religion: Reassessing the History of an Idea.* Downers Grove, IL: InterVarsity Press, 2015.
Winship, Michael P. *Godly Republicanism: Puritans, Pilgrims, and a City on a Hill.* Cambridge, MA: Harvard University Press, 2017.

# American Peace Churches

Historically, *American peace churches* is a phrase that refers to three Protestant denominations that have prominently and consistently opposed war and participation in it since before the American Revolution (though they are not the only pacifist churches and religious organizations in the United States). These denominations are the Mennonites, the Society of Friends (or Quakers), and the Church of the Brethren. Their opposition to war is firmly grounded in the history and theology of each denomination. In general, peace churches are Christian denominations or groups that advocate Christian pacifism or biblical nonresistance. It is their belief that pacifism is the teaching of the New Testament and Jesus of Nazareth and that Christians are to actively pursue peace and resist war. As with other pacifist groups, American peace churches reject the just war tradition as a viable political and religious response to warfare.

While conscientious objection to war has always been a part of American history, until 1940, most conscientious objectors came from American peace churches. During the Vietnam War, there was a broadening of legal, political, and religious views on conscientious objection such that there was a significant increase in the number of men granted conscientious objector status with respect to military service who came from other churches. Many now came from Protestant mainstream denominations (e.g., Methodist, Lutheran, Episcopal, Presbyterian, and others) or from a secular nonreligious perspective.

When the draft ended in 1975, the peace churches lost a major visible source of objection. While there remained the ability for some to gain conscientious objector status with the Selective Service System, public protest to the draft was no longer necessary. Peace churches had always had a strong focus on humanitarian assistance, and these efforts continued and were reinvigorated with calls for just peace, peacemaking, and support for the concept of the "Responsibility to Protect" (R2P). The R2P doctrine asserts that the international community has a duty to protect against mass atrocities such as genocide, war crimes, and crimes against humanity. The peace churches also turned their focus on opposing various conflicts, such as the 1991 Gulf War, as well as armed conflicts in the Balkans and elsewhere throughout the 1990s. This continued as new conflicts emerged in the 21st century.

In the aftermath of the September 11, 2001, terrorist attacks and the American response, the Church of the Brethren passed resolutions in 2001 and 2011 against war in Afghanistan and called for a just peace. In 2003, the denomination passed a resolution titled "Call for a Living Peace Church." This resolution acknowledged the denomination's historic peace posture and encouraged its continuation. This resolution was followed in 2008 with one promoting the R2P doctrine that has arisen in the international realm in the last thirty years and, more specifically, was accepted by all member states of the United Nations in 2005.

Similarly, in 2005, the Mennonite Church USA issued a statement on the war in Iraq in which it encouraged the American nation to repent for the ways it had contributed to the war and to work for peace, justice, and reconciliation. Mennonites have often worked in war zones, primarily through the Mennonite Central Committee, which is a relief, service, and peace agency that represents Mennonite, Amish, and Brethren in Christ groups in North America. It has more than 19,000 field workers, and in its more than 100-year history, only two have been killed in a war zone—the most recent being the death of Glenn Lapp in Afghanistan in 2010.

As with the other two peace churches, the Quakers have a long history of pacifism that is centuries old and antedates their arrival in colonial America. In the aftermath of September 11, 2001, Friends organizations called for a peaceful response grounded in social justice and international law enforcement rather than war. The primary agency pursuing Quaker social and political ideals is the American Friends Service Committee (AFSC), which was founded in 1917 to assist civilian victims of World War I.

The historic voice and actions of American peace churches remain strong and vibrant in the 21st century. Beyond pacifism, they are active in supporting human rights, peaceful resolutions of conflict, and social justice nationally and internationally.

***See also:*** Ecclesiastical Statements on War and Peace; Genocide; Human Rights; Pacifism; Peace Movements; Peacemaking; Protestant Denominations; Religious Texts; Responsibility to Protect

**Further Reading**

Bogaski, George. *American Protestants and the Debate over the Vietnam War: Evil Was Loose in the World*. Lanham, MD: Lexington Books, 2014.

Brown, Dale. *Biblical Pacifism: A Peace Church Perspective*. Elgin, IL: Brethren Press, 1985.

Chiba, Shin, and Thomas J. Schoenbaum. *Peace Movements and Pacifism after September 11*. Cheltenham, UK: Edward Elgar Publishing, 2008.

Church of the Brethren Annual Conference 2011. "Resolution on the War in Afghanistan." http://www.brethren.org/ac/statements/2011resolutionafghanistan.html

Griggs, Walter S., Jr. "The Selective Conscientious Objector: A Vietnam Legacy." *Journal of Church and State* 21, no. 1 (Winter 1979): 91–107.

Horsch, John. *The Principle of Nonresistance as Held by the Mennonite Church*. Ephrata, PA: Eastern Mennonite Publications, 1999.

Koontz, Ted. "Thinking Theologically about War against Iraq." *Mennonite Quarterly Review* 77 (January 2003): 93–108.

Mennonite Church USA. "Statement on the War in Iraq." July 9, 2005. https://anabaptistwiki.org/mediawiki/index.php?title=Statement_on_the_War_in_Iraq_(Mennonite_Church_USA,_2005)

Miller, Grant. "A Peace Witness Transformed: The Mennonite Response to the Gulf Wars in 1990–1991 and 2002–2003." *Mennonite Quarterly Review* 87 (October 2013): 467–501.

Moskos, Charles C., and John Whiteclay Chambers II. *The New Conscientious Objection: From Sacred to Secular Resistance*. New York: Oxford University Press, 1993.

Quinley, Harold E. "The Protestant Clergy and the War in Vietnam." *Public Opinion Quarterly* 34 (Spring 1970): 43–54.

Settje, David E. *Faith and War: How Christians Debated the Cold and Vietnam Wars*. New York: New York University Press, 2011.

Smylie, James H. "American Religious Bodies, Just War, and Vietnam." *Journal of Church and Staten* 11, no. 3 (Autumn 1969): 383–408.

# American Revolution

The American Revolution (1775–1783) was a watershed event in Western political history. The intellectual roots of the revolution can be found in

17th- and 18th-century philosophical, political, and theological ideas regarding the purpose and function of the nation-state and the nature of the rights, responsibilities, and relationship of citizens to the state. Deeply embedded in the ideology and the events of the revolution was religion. Issues such as the relationship between religion and the state were first articulated in the context of the revolution and its immediate aftermath, including the writing of the U.S. Constitution and its amendments.

Religion was key in the outworking and worldview of the American Revolution and played a significant role in providing moral sanction for opposition to the British. Colonial resistance was transformed into a religious cause as well as a political cause, although the political aspects remained primary in the minds of the colonial clergy and their congregations.

For several hundred years in Europe, there was a religious and political belief in the divine right of monarchs to rule. Those who held the perspective contended that political legitimacy was grounded in the belief that monarchs were not subject to any earthly authority. Rather, the king or queen was only responsible to God. If true, then on what religious or political grounds could the subjects of a monarch revolt? Whether true or not, ideas and images such as General George Washington praying in the snow during the winter of 1777–1778 at Valley Forge made a strong impression in the minds of many of the citizens and have been a part of the American story ever since.

Warfare in the American colonies was not a new experience during the American Revolution. War was a central fact of life and thought for the colonial Puritans on the frontier. It was part of their history and daily life, and at times, they looked to the just war tradition for validation of their experience of war. Events such as the Pequot War (1636–1637), the English Civil Wars (1642–1651), King Philip's War (1675–1678; also known as Metacom's War), the French and Indian War (1754–1763), and other conflicts abroad and in the colonies tempered colonial acceptance of war. When coupled with the Pilgrim and Puritan heritage and ideology of the experience in the New World as a recapitulation of the exodus and conquest events of the Hebrew scriptures (Old Testament), warfare did much to shape the ideas of liberty and American exceptionalism.

Protestant Christianity was not the only faith tradition in the American colonies, but it was by far the most dominant religious perspective. Although there were Anglicans, Roman Catholics, and Jews in the colonies, the prevailing religious heritage was that of Protestant Calvinism. Since the 16th century, there had arisen in England, Scotland, and Europe a strong resistance ideology that inferior magistrates may actively resist tyrants. The colonists revolting against King George III used this political and religious perspective to ground and justify revolution. Drawing on thinkers such as John Calvin (1509–1564), John Ponet (ca. 1514–1556), Christopher Goodman (1520–1603), and George Buchannan (1506–1582), there was fertile soil for growing the idea of revolution against the Crown and Parliament. John Locke (1632–1704), especially in his 1689 work *Second Treatise on Civil Government*, secularized Calvinist political theory.

Political and religious rhetoric blended to create the language of liberty that resonated among many of the colonists and fueled the growing patriotic fervor and revolutionary spirit. For some, this included a history and mixture of political and religious millennial expectations in which the colonies, often termed by the New England Puritans as "the errand into the wilderness" (see, for example, the election sermon of Samuel Danforth delivered on May 11, 1670: *A Brief Recognition of New England's Errand into the Wilderness*), understood their presence in the New World as part of the outworking of God's plan of history and the end of time. Millennialism and providentialism were two persistent and complementary religious streams of thought flowing before the outbreak of the war.

In the years prior to the American Revolution, there was a growth in and linking of political and religious thought with respect to ideas of individual liberty and its relationship to authority. Much of this was nurtured by the religious revival in the colonies known as the Great Awakening during the 1730s and 1740s that fostered individualism in theological matters and was subsequently aligned with political orientation undermining political authoritarianism, establishments, and hierarchies. For example, in 1750, on the one hundredth anniversary of the execution of Charles I, Boston minister Jonathan Mayhew (1720–1766) preached a sermon declaring that civil liberty and religious liberty were ordained by God and that resistance to tyranny was a Christian duty. Titled *Discourse Concerning Unlimited Submission and Non-Resistance to Higher Powers*, the sermon was published and widely distributed in Boston and New England. Presbyterian minister John Witherspoon (1723–1794) of New Jersey was another staunch supporter of the revolution and a signatory of the Declaration of Independence on July 4, 1776.

Additional background considerations include the perception among many colonists that there was a struggle between emerging national morality in the colonies and moral corruption of the monarchy and Parliament in

England. There was also fear that the Church of England would appoint an Anglican bishop for America and entrench church and state matters in the colonies as it was in England. Further, after the Quebec Act of 1774, there was a concern among Protestants about the spread of Roman Catholicism in the colonies, especially given the strong Roman Catholic presence in Quebec, to the north of the New England colonies that were steeped in Puritanism. Additionally, the Southern Colonies faced Spanish Florida to their south, a territory controlled by staunchly Roman Catholic Spain.

For many advocates of the American Revolution, their religious orientation raised perceptions of the new American national cause to almost the level of a crusade. The patriotic response was strong.

It is often assumed that the religious sentiments in the colonies were such that nearly all religiously devout colonists supported the revolution. Such was not the case. Members and clergy of the Church of England (Anglicans) were especially prominent among the loyalists (although many Anglicans favored the patriots). Many loyalist Anglicans in New York and New England fled the colonies and went to Canada rather than support what they believed to be an illegitimate new government. Similarly, some Methodists and Roman Catholics remained loyal to the British. Some Presbyterians as well as Congregationalists and Baptists also supported the loyalist perspective. Jews in colonies (about 1,500) were also divided on support for the revolution. Interestingly, for those Jews who participated and fought in the war, it was the first time since the Jewish exile from Jerusalem in the 1st century that Jews fought alongside Christians as equals. There was no single religious group that was monolithic in its support for or against the revolutionary cause.

There were also religious groups that refused to become involved in the war and advocated pacifism on the basis of religious values. Pacifist groups included Quakers, Mennonites, Moravians, and Church of the Brethren.

With respect to religion and the course of the war, religious leaders were more concerned about justifying revolution than they were the subsequent warfare that ensued once independence was declared. Perhaps more than at any other time in American history, the clergy played a vital role in the war, not only as chaplains but also as political advocates and interpreters of the events of the war. The prestige of the clergy in communities was very high, and the sermons in support of them were instrumental in gaining and sustaining support for the war. Military victories and defeats were frequently interpreted as being the result of divine favor.

The coupling of religion, specifically Protestant Christianity, and patriotism during the American Revolution set a precedent that would be developed throughout the 19th and 20th centuries, with remnants evidenced in the 21st century. By the end of the Revolutionary War, politics had become sacralized, and religious ideas had become secularized, creating the beginnings of civil religion and American exceptionalism in the new United States.

*See also:* American Civil War; American Exceptionalism; Just War Tradition; Military Chaplains; Pacifism; Protestant Denominations; Rhetoric, Sermons, and Prayers; World War I; World War II

## Further Reading

Bailyn, Bernard. *The Ideological Origins of the American Revolution.* Enl. ed. Cambridge, MA: Belknap Press, 1992.

Baldwin, Alice M. *The New England Clergy and the American Revolution.* New York: Ungar, 1958.

Byrd, James P. *Sacred Scripture, Sacred War: The Bible and the American Revolution.* New York: Oxford University Press, 2013.

Dreisbach, Daniel L., and Mark David Hall, eds. *Faith and the Founders of the American Republic.* New York: Oxford University Press, 2014.

Endy, Melvin B., Jr. "Just War, Holy War, and Millennialism in Revolutionary America." *William and Mary Quarterly* 3rd set 42 (1985): 3–25.

Frazer, Gregg L. *God against the Revolution: The Loyalist Clergy's Case against the American Revolution.* Lawrence: University Press of Kansas, 2010.

Hatch, Nathan O. *The Sacred Cause of Liberty: Republican Thought and the Millennium in Revolutionary New England.* New Haven, CT: Yale University Press, 1977.

Kidd, Thomas S. *God of Liberty: A Religious History of the American Revolution.* New York: Basic Books, 2010.

Larson, Mark J. *Calvin's Doctrine of the State: A Reformed Doctrine and Its American Trajectory, the Revolutionary War, and the Founding of the Republic.* Eugene, OR: Wipf & Stock, 2009.

Mailer, Gideon. *John Witherspoon's American Revolution.* Chapel Hill: University of North Carolina Press, 2017.

Noll, Mark A. *Christians in the American Revolution.* 2nd ed. Vancouver: Regent College Publishing, 2006.

Preston, Andrew. *Sword of the Spirit, Shield of Faith: Religion in American War and Diplomacy.* New York: Alfred A. Knopf, 2012.

Sandoz, Ellis, ed. *Political Sermons of the American Founding Era, 1730–1805.* 2 vols. Indianapolis: Liberty Fund, 1991.

Stout, Harry S. "War." In *The New England Soul: Preaching and Religious Culture in Colonial New England*, 233–255. 2nd ed. New York: Oxford University Press.

# Apocalypticism

Apocalypticism is the religious belief in the cataclysmic ending of history and the end of the world. It is the belief that at some future divinely appointed time, the world as known to us will end through the cataclysmic confrontation between the forces of good and evil. For some interpreters, this is a spiritual confrontation only, but for others, it is understood to be a spiritual and physical confrontation. From this confrontation, the eternal, righteous Kingdom of God will emerge. Apocalypticism is not found in every religion, but it is a doctrine in Christianity, Islam, and Judaism, although with significant differences in interpretations. For example, Christians and Muslims have different interpretations between the religions and within each religion as to the reality and nature of a future conflict that is often known as the Battle of Armageddon.

In recent decades, some Christians and Muslims have sought to interpret international political events, among them the Six-Day War (1967), the Gulf War (1990–1991), the Iraq War (2003–2011), and the War in Afghanistan (2001–2021), in light of their respective religious interpretations and sacred texts. For Americans, this has usually taken the form of interpreting various verses and passages in the Bible that deal with prophecies.

In American culture, belief in Bible prophecy has a long and varied history. Within the study of theology, for any religious belief system, the doctrine of eschatology is the study of last things and is usually associated with the end of time and end of the world. Eschatology is a detailed field of theological inquiry with many terms and concepts, and it is part of every Christian theological framework (as well as Jewish and Islamic frameworks). Apocalyptic beliefs are not an aberration of theology; they are inherent in doctrinal systems. But pursuing violence as a consequence of apocalyptic belief *is* contrary to orthodox beliefs in Christianity, Judaism, and Islam.

There are hundreds of biblical verses that pertain to eschatology and apocalypticism, and there are scores of statements in Christian creeds throughout the centuries that affirm apocalyptic beliefs. For example, there is this Christian declaration: "He will come to judge the living and the dead." These words from the Apostles' Creed date to the 2nd and 3rd centuries CE, and similar words from other Christian affirmations of faith have been voiced for centuries as public declarations of belief in the yet future return of Jesus Christ to earth. Likewise, there are the words "Thy kingdom come. Thy will be done, on earth as it is in heaven" (Matthew 6:10; Luke 11:2). Countless times every day for almost 2,000 years, Christians around the globe have voiced this prayer that models one Jesus gave to his disciples (as recorded in the New Testament, Matthew 6:9–13 and Luke 11:2–4). Many Christians (usually Protestant) understand these statements to address the fulfillment of Bible prophecy and be part of contemporary and future world events. For the majority of Christians, it is anticipation; for a minority, it is violence.

All Christians believe that Jesus Christ will someday return to earth in an event known as the Second Coming or Second Advent. They also believe in something known as the millennium. According to the New Testament passage Revelation 20:1–7, there is a period of 1,000 years during which Jesus Christ will establish a kingdom and rule over the world. However, there is disagreement on the nature and timing of that kingdom in relation to the Second Advent. Some Christians view the millennium as a literal physical kingdom lasting 1,000, while others view it as a spiritual kingdom. In answer to the question, "What is the relationship of the millennium to the Second Coming?" there are three possibilities: amillennialism, postmillennialism, and premillennialism.

Christian amillennialism contends that there will not be a future 1,000-year physical reign of Jesus Christ upon the earth. Rather, from the 1st century until the return of Jesus Christ, there is a spiritual form of the Kingdom of God that is experienced by Christians. Jesus Christ will physically come again at some point in the future, after which the eternal state will ensue.

Christian postmillennialism contends that Christ's kingdom is presently being extended throughout the world through the proclamation of the Gospel—the Christian message of salvation brought to humans in the person and work of Jesus Christ in his first coming to earth as taught in the New Testament. There will be the gradual Christianization of the world, and at some point in the future, not a literal 1,000 years, Jesus Christ will return.

Christian premillennialism contends that at some point in the near or distant future, Jesus Christ will appear in the sky and gather all Christians, living and dead, to heaven in an event known as the Rapture. After this event, there will be a period of tribulation, natural catastrophes, and global war. The period of tribulation will end with the physical return of Jesus Christ to earth to establish a worldwide physical and political kingdom over which Jesus Christ will reign in fulfillment of Bible prophecy. At the end of the 1,000 years, there will be final judgment of Christians and non-Christians and the ensuing of eternity with God for Christians.

Each of these provides a detailed biblical and theological understanding of the doctrine of eschatology and, within it, apocalypticism. What is significant for many Christians, especially those who support the system of premillennialism, is the belief that current global political and military events *may have* (but not necessarily) apocalyptic significance.

As a result of the three Christian interpretive systems of eschatology noted above, things such as weapons of mass destruction, present and historic wars and politics in the Middle East, the Cold War, and the role of the United States in global affairs are often interpreted by some Christians through a lens of apocalypticism. This has been especially prevalent in American evangelicalism. Historically, an aberration of eschatological views has at times led to violence.

Apocalyptic violence is not new in Christian history. Two examples from the past are the populist millennial revolt led by Thomas Müntzer during the 1525 Peasant's War in Germany and the Anabaptist revolt in Münster during 1533–1535. In more recent U.S. history, the April 1993 tragedy in Waco, Texas, at the Branch Davidian compound under the religious leadership of Vernon Howell, more commonly known as David Koresh, is a vivid example of apocalyptic faith coupled with armed violence. Such incidents have occurred for centuries. Eschatology is part of every Christian theological framework. Apocalyptic beliefs are not an aberration of theology, but pursuing violence as a consequence of apocalyptic belief *is* contrary to orthodox Christianity.

Within Islam and Judaism, there are also varying apocalyptic interpretations. With respect to war, terrorism, and geopolitical events in the 21st century, apocalyptic ideology and apocalyptic violence have been foundational to and prevalent in the actions of groups such as the Islamic State (IS or ISIS). These groups have as part of their political ideology that is grounded in their theology a belief that their violent actions are sanctioned by God and that the actions are a catalyst to the realization of their religious beliefs about the future. For them, temporal violence, terrorism, and warfare have spiritual significance, divine favor, and the effect of helping bring forth the future as they understand it within their theological framework. Through their actions, they are, in essence, "jump-starting" or "hot-wiring" the apocalypse.

Within every religious tradition, there is a spectrum of belief and practice regarding war and peace. To fully understand and appreciate the religious perspectives, one must also consider the extent contemporary geopolitical events are being viewed within an apocalyptic framework of belief and interpretation by the adherents of a specific religion.

*See also:* Christianity and War; Evangelicalism; Gulf War; Iraq War; Islam and War; Judaism and War; Middle East Conflict; Religion, Conflict, and Geopolitics; Religious Texts; Terrorism; Wars of Israel; Weapons of Mass Destruction

## Further Reading

Boyer, Paul. *When Time Shall Be No More: Prophecy Belief in Modern American Culture.* Cambridge, MA: Harvard University Press, 1992.
Cook, David. *Contemporary Muslim Apocalyptic Literature.* Syracuse, NY: Syracuse University Press, 2008.
Demy, Timothy J. "Arming for Armageddon: Myths and Motivations of Violence in American Christian Apocalypticism." In *Armed Groups: Studies in National Security, Counterterrorism, and Counterinsurgency*, edited by Jeffrey Norwitz, 225–235. Newport, RI: Naval War College Press, 2008.
Ice, Thomas, and Timothy J. Demy. *Fast Facts on Bible Prophecy from A to Z.* Eugene, OR: Harvest House Publishers, 1997.
Newport, Kenneth G. C., and Crawford Gribben, eds. *Expecting the End: Millennialism in Social and Historical Context.* Waco, TX: Baylor University Press, 2006.
Oren, Michael B. *Power, Faith, and Fantasy: America in the Middle East, 1776 to the Present.* New York: W. W. Norton & Co., 2007.
Ostransky, Bronislav. *The Jihadist Preachers of the End Times: ISIS Apocalyptic Propaganda.* Edinburgh, UK: Edinburgh University Press, 2019.

# Art

Though not as prominent in the 21st-century United States, religion, politics, and war are three topics that are frequently portrayed in visual art. For example, depictions of religious leaders, saints, and events from sacred texts are well known in many religious traditions. Similarly political cartoons have been drawn for centuries. Artistic depictions of war are also millennia old—whether one thinks of Assyrian stone reliefs and panels, trench art of World War I, or paintings such as Emanuel Leutze's *Washington Crossing the Delaware* (1851). The United States Marine Corps War Memorial, designed by Felix de Weldon (1954), which portrays the raising of the American flag on Iwo Jima as depicted in the famous photograph taken by Associated Press photographer Joe Rosenthal on February 23, 1945, is recognized worldwide.

The combination of any two, or all three, of the topics of religion, politics, and war can generate strong reactions, both positive and negative. Such works of art evidence the long and profound cultural influence of religion, politics, and war on societies and nations. Art can be a strong catalyst for enhancing religious and political commitment and enthusiasm, whether viewed as propaganda or as visual statements of faith, ideology, or national history.

Examples from American history of combinations of the blending of religion, politics, and war in art include various depictions of late 19th-century and 20th-century paintings and engravings of the legend of General George Washington praying in the snow at Valley Forge during the winter of 1777–1778. Similarly, *The First Thanksgiving* (1914) painting by Jeannie Augusta Brownscombe (1850–1936) portrays Pilgrims praying before sharing a common meal with Native Americans. In recent decades, the best-known example is *The Prayer at Valley Forge* (1975) by illustrator and painter Arnold Friberg (1913–2010).

The deaths of George Washington and Abraham Lincoln were frequently portrayed in art as an apotheosis, the glorification of an individual to a divine level—portraying an individual as becoming divine or almost divine. Portrayals of deification in art were common in Greek and Roman art, and neoclassicism was prominent in American (and European) art and architecture from 1750 to 1900. Perhaps most prominent in the United States, there are many examples of it in government buildings such as the U.S. Capitol and White House. Much of the art within the U.S. Capitol follows this style, and *The Apotheosis of Washington* is the fresco in the eye of the U.S. Capitol Rotunda, painted in 1865 by Constantino Brumidi (1805–1880). It depicts George Washington upon his death being carried into heaven by female figures or angels of Liberty and Victory/Fame. It was completed in eleven months during the final year of the American Civil War. The idea of apotheosis was also used in illustrations and prints portraying Washington welcoming President Abraham Lincoln into glory upon Lincoln's assassination in 1865. The coupling of images of these two presidents in an 1865 photographic print on carte de visite mount titled *Washington & Lincoln* became part of American civil religion.

During World War II, the cover art and forty-four tear sheet illustrations for the *Saturday Evening Post* magazine by Norman Rockwell (1894–1978) portrayed life on the American home front. Among the most notable of these were the 1943 *Four Freedoms* series of oil paintings (*Freedom of Speech*, *Freedom of Worship*, *Freedom from Want*, and *Freedom from Fear*) and *Rosie the Riveter* (1943). The latter was the Memorial Day, May 29, 1943, cover of the *Saturday Evening Post*. *Four Freedoms* and *Rosie the Riveter* were used widely in war bond drives.

Although there has been much political art in the 21st century, as well as art that blends politics and war (mostly political cartoons), there has yet to arise an American body of art that combines art, religion, and war in expressions of support or nonsupport of 21st-century war and military operations. Internationally, the violent responses by Islamist terrorists and critical responses by other Muslims around the globe to the publication of cartoons portraying the Prophet Muhammad in the Dutch newspaper *Jyllands-Posten* in September 2005 brought international attention to the controversy. In Islam, visual depictions of Muhammad are considered blasphemous. Similarly, the French satirical weekly newspaper *Charlie Hebdo* was the target of terrorist attacks in which the offices were firebombed in 2011 and twelve people were killed and eleven wounded in a shooting attack in 2015. Acknowledging that many found the cartoons offensive but also wanting to support democracy and free speech rights, the Obama administration did not criticize the French magazine for publishing the cartoons. In 2020, a schoolteacher in Paris was killed and beheaded by a lone attacker after the teacher taught students about the cartoon incident and showed some of the cartoons in a class about democracy and free speech.

The events of September 11, 2001, have generated artistic responses. One aspect of the attacks that is often overlooked is the amount of artwork that was destroyed in the Twin Towers of the World Trade Center and the Pentagon. There were extensive public and private collections of art in the Twin Towers estimated at more than $100 million, as well as art studios on the ninety-first and ninety-second floors of Tower One. Art, icons, and relics at the Church of St. Nicholas were also destroyed (Heritage Preservation 2002, 3).

The terrorist attacks and the wars in Afghanistan and Iraq that resulted from the September 11 attacks have left deep cultural memories in the American public that have affected many citizens, families, veterans, and members of the military. No 21st-century conflict has been a rallying cause in American politics and religion. Instead, the nation has been deeply and equally divided politically, and religious groups and denominations have also lacked unanimity with respect to politics and war. With few exceptions, such as the post-9/11 art of Dario Robleto (1972–present), which focuses on war, individuals, memory, peace, and salvation, this fragmentation and division has resulted in a paucity of visual art with respect to the intersection of religion, politics, and war. Instead, the visual arts have focused on aspects of globalization, cultural pluralism, gender, consumer culture, politics, and spirituality.

*See also:* Gulf War; Literature; Military Chaplains; Music; Presidential Faith and War; Religious Texts; Rhetoric, Sermons, and Prayers; Rituals and Symbolism; September 11, 2001, Terrorist Attacks

## Further Reading

Architect of the Capitol. "*Apotheosis of Washington.*" Accessed March 2, 2020. https://www.aoc.gov/explore-capitol-campus/art/apotheosis-washington

Blake, Aaron. "How Do Americans about Muhmmad Cartoons?" *Washington Post*, January 5, 2015. https://www.washingtonpost.com/news/the-fix/wp/2015/01/07/how-do-americans-feel-about-muhammad-cartoons/

Bleiker, Roland. "Art after 9/11." *Alternatives: Global, Local, Political* 31, no. 1 (January–March 2006): 77–99.

Bourke, Joanna, ed. *War and Art: A Visual History of Modern Conflict*. London: Reaktion Books, 2017.

Heritage Preservation. *Cataclysm and Challenge: Impact of September 11, 2001, on Our Nation's Cultural Heritage*. Washington, DC: Heritage Preservation Inc., 2002. https://cool.culturalheritage.org/byorg/hp/PDFS/Cataclysm.pdf

Klapper, Bradley. "US Tempers Criticism of Muhammad Cartoons after Paris Attack." *Seattle Times*, January 14, 2015. https://www.seattletimes.com/nation-world/us-tempers-criticism-of-muhammad-cartoons-after-paris-attack/

Knaff, Donna B. *Beyond Rosie the Riveter: Women of World War II in American Popular Graphic Art*. Lawrence: University Press of Kansas, 2012.

U.S. Army Center of Military History. *Army Artists Look at the War on Terrorism 2001 to Present: Afghanistan, Iraq, Kuwait, and the United States*. Washington, DC: U.S. Army Center of Military History, 2009. https://history.army.mil/books/wot_artwork/wot_artbook.html

# B

## Buddhism and War

Buddhism is practiced individually and corporately and is increasing in prominence in the 21st-century United States. According to a 2017 study on global religion by Pew Research Center, approximately 500 million adherents practice Buddhism worldwide, with one to four million in the United States. With respect to warfare, Buddhism has not played a prominent role in U.S. wars, although it is a significant factor in 21st-century international conflict.

Buddhism originated from the teachings known as *dharma*. The Buddha, born Prince Siddhartha in Lumbini, Nepal, in the 5th or 6th century BCE, was the son of King Suddhodana and Queen Mahamaya, heads of the Shakya clan in India. Raised as royalty, Siddhartha studied humanities, sciences, and the arts of war and politics. At the age of twenty-nine, leaving his wife and child, he began a spiritual pilgrimage hoping to find the end of *samsara*, or perpetual suffering. Eventually attaining *nirvana* (enlightenment) and departing from Hinduism, he became known as the Buddha ("one who is awake") and found what he believed to be the path to ending the cycle of reincarnation and endless suffering.

Practitioners who follow the way of the Buddha toward enlightenment adhere to what are known as the Four Truths for the Noble (or the Four Noble Truths), which roughly emulate the journey of Prince Siddhartha. These truths are (1) the truth of suffering, (2) the truth of the origin of suffering, (3) the truth of the cessation of suffering, and (4) the truth of the path that leads to the end of suffering. They are called "noble" because it is believed to be the knowledge of these truths that liberates humans from persistent suffering in this world.

Over a period of 2,500 years, Buddhism spread through various countries, beginning in East Asia, and split into three major sects: Theravada,

Mahayana, and Vajrayana. These three sects, in turn, divided further into various branches, including Tibetan and Zen Buddhism.

Buddhists have immigrated to the United States from China and Japan since the 19th century. In the 20th and 21st centuries, additional countries from which Buddhists have migrated include (but are not limited to) Bangladesh, Burma (Myanmar), Bhutan, Cambodia, Korea, Laos, Mongolia, Nepal, Sri Lanka, Taiwan, Thailand, Tibet, and Vietnam. Each Buddhist group or faction established from these various influxes is independently structured, with many different practices and teachings. Although these groups may be loosely affiliated as Buddhist, there is generally no universal or national unifying organization.

Although there is a significant number of Americans who convert to Buddhism, much of the remainder of its adherents are offspring of Buddhist immigrant parents. A 2010 religious census by the Association of Statisticians of American Religious Bodies (ASARB) estimated that there are more than 990,000 Buddhists in nearly 3,000 congregations in the United States, primarily in metropolitan areas on the West and East Coasts.

In addition to the many forms of Buddhism passed down from migrant families, three branches of Buddhism are prevalent in the contemporary United States; most converts to Buddhism choose one of these branches: Vajrayana, Vipassana (a branch of the Theravada tradition), and Zen (an offshoot from the Mahayana school). Of these three, Zen is the one to which most individuals convert or adopt due to its popularity in American culture for philosophical thought and meditative practices. Because Buddhism is often understood as being compatible with other religions, many people identify with it in combination with another religion. This compatibility and blending also make it difficult to ascertain who is Buddhist and to get an accurate census of the U.S. population of Buddhists.

Buddhism is well known in many U.S. branches as forwarding paths to enlightenment, compassion, and peace, and a significant number of Americans drawn to the different forms of Buddhism seek mindfulness practices such as meditation. However, similar to Christianity, Islam, and other traditions, Buddhism also bears historical roots supporting violence throughout the ages to protect its followers. For example, medieval and feudal Japan's Sōhei warrior monks protected land and challenged competing Buddhist schools in the 10th through 17th centuries, somewhat similar to the various orders of Christian knights during the era of the Crusades. Buddhist priests helped to liberate China from Mongol rule in the 14th century.

In Tibet, where Tibetan Buddhists follow the nonviolent teaching of the Dalai Lama, who they worship as the embodiment of compassion, Buddhist monks and nuns took up arms in uprisings to protect the fourteenth Dalai Lama (1935–) and to rebel against the 1950 Chinese military invasion, occupation, and political rule of Tibet. The Tibetan Buddhist rebels were supported and trained by the U.S. government. This support continued during the Cold War until the 1970s. In recent years, the Dalai Lama has acknowledged that although peace is desirable, just war is at times necessary. In so doing, he cites World War II and the Korean War as examples of just wars. For many Americans, the photographic image of the self-immolation of Buddhist monk Thich Quang Duc (1897–1963) in the streets of Saigon, South Vietnam, in protest of the government of President Ngo Dinh Diem (1901–1963) was one of the earliest photographs of the Vietnam War that was to politically divide Americans in the 1960s and 1970s.

Internationally, recent events in Sri Lanka evidence continued Buddhist participation in violence, as monks protect their community from what they purport is a Muslim threat to their religion and community from Hindu Tamils. Some religious scholars and historians have argued that 19th-century U.S. Buddhist thinkers had an integral role in espousing anti-Tamil sentiment in the name of preserving Buddhist culture.

Anti-Tamil nationalism and ethnic and political violence continue in the 21st century. Buddhist Sinhalese nationalists use violence in Sri Lanka to continue the perceived purification of their religious ranks against Tamil Muslims and in competition with other Buddhist sects. The roots of the conflict bear some similarity to past religious wars and tensions. In Sri Lanka and elsewhere, the combinations of religious, political, economic, and ethnic tensions perpetuate civil war and unrest. In Buddhist religious history, this protective stance has resulted in militant monks participating in killings, fighting, attacks, and rape of minorities.

This same dynamic is at work in contemporary Myanmar, where a Buddhist majority led by extremist monk Ashin Wirathu (1968–) and his militant organization, Ma Ba Tha, currently seek to purge their country of the Rohingya Muslim minority. Supported by the Myanmar government and military, the Buddhist movement continues to attack and exile Rohingya Muslims despite their lower economic standing and inability to wage a significant and sustained kinetic threat. Myanmar political leader Aung San Suu Kyi (1945–) has been criticized by human rights advocates for her failure to provide a solution to the conflict or to protect the Rohingya in the Rakhine State against attack by the militant majority. These two examples of Buddhist violence in Sri Lanka and Myanmar continue to receive international and U.S. attention.

Buddhists are not monolithic on the issue of resorting to violence in the name of religion and culture. Thich Nhat Hanh (1926–2022), the Dalai Lama, and other contemporary Buddhist leaders have called for adherence to nonviolence and compassion toward the Rohingya Muslims and all peoples irrespective of religion and ethnicity. In the United States, the Buddhist teachings of compassion and nonviolence have a strong appeal among U.S. Buddhists, and numerous U.S. charities and nonprofit organizations promote those values in their work. There are also Buddhists serving in the U.S. Congress and U.S. military. Although Buddhism is not a major religion numerically in the United States, its popularity and influence at all levels of American life, politically and culturally, is increasing.

*See also:* Cold War; Hinduism and War; Just War Tradition; Korean War; Vietnam War; World War II

## Further Reading

Barylski, Szymon, Michael Grunwald, Timothy Noah, and John F. Harris. "The Genocide the U.S. Didn't See Coming." *POLITICO Magazine*, March/April 2018. https://www.politico.com/magazine/story/2018/03/04/obama-rohingya-genocide-myanmar-burma-muslim-syu-kii-217214

Dalai Lama. "The Reality of War." Accessed June 17, 2022. https://www.dalailama.com/messages/world-peace/the-reality-of-war

Dunham, Michael. *Buddha's Warriors; The Story of the CIA-Backed Tibetan Freedom Fighters, the Chinese Communist Invasion, and the Ultimate Fall of Tibet*. New York: Penguin Group.

Jerryson, Michael K. "Buddhist Traditions and Violence." In *The Oxford Handbook of Religion and Violence*, edited by Mark Juergensmeyer, Margo Kitts, and Michael K. Jerryson, 41–66. New York: Oxford University Press, 2016.

Jerryson, Michael K., and Mark Juergensmeyer. *Buddhist Warfare*. New York: Oxford University Press, 2010.

Pew Research Center. "The Changing Global Religious Landscape." Religion & Public Life Project, April 5, 2017. https://www.pewforum.org/2017/04/05/the-changing-global-religious-landscape/

*Religion & Ethics NewsWeekly*. "Comments on Tensions in American Buddhism." PBS, July 6, 2001. https://www.pbs.org/wnet/religionandethics/2001/07/06/july-6-2001-comments-on-tensions-in-american-buddhism/15941/

US Religion Census. "U.S. Religion Census 1952 to 2020." Accessed March 10, 2020. http://usreligioncensus.org/

Wilson, Jeff. "Buddhism in America." *Oxford Research Encyclopedia of American History*, August 5, 2016. https://doi.org/10.1093/acrefore/9780199329175.013.320

Wuthnow, Robert, and Wendy Cadge. "Buddhists and Buddhism in the United States: The Scope of Influence." *Journal for the Scientific Study of Religion* 43, no. 3 (2004): 363–380.

# C

## Christianity and War

The 21st-century landscape of American religion is changing rapidly and is more diverse than previously, but, by far, Christianity remains the dominant religion. As such, the variety of views regarding war and peace within Christianity continue to affect public opinion and foreign policy. This does not mean that the United States is a "Christian nation," as has been argued by some individuals. Rather, Christianity has informed and, at times, guided American citizens and political leaders (including some presidents) as they engaged in warfare. Religion has been a major or minor factor in every American conflict. Although U.S. wars have not been crusades or holy wars, religion (primarily Christianity) has informed and guided support for and against the wars of the United States. This influence continues in the 21st century, though many observers believe the role of religion is diminishing due to the growing secularization of the nation. Even so, according to the 2014 Pew Forum survey of 21st-century U.S. religious demographics, just over 70 percent of Americans identify as Christian.

There is no single Christian doctrine or perspective on war. The responses of Christians through the centuries, and American Christians since the colonial era, are on a spectrum that ranges from absolute rejection of engaging in or participating in any war (pacifism) to full participation and support for war in the belief that the war has divine support or blessing. At the furthest extreme in Christianity (and in other religions), there is the belief that a war is divinely mandated. In Christianity, this is the crusade perspective. The predominant perspective throughout the centuries and in American history has been what is known as the *just war tradition*.

Regardless of where Christians are on the spectrum of belief regarding war, a core component of the Christian viewpoint is a belief in the brokenness of humanity from a moral and ethical perspective. This belief is grounded in the story of Adam and Eve as recorded in Genesis (chapters 1–3), the first book of the Bible. Christians interpret this story, known as the fall of Adam and Eve, to mean that every person and every aspect of one's personal life and corporate life has been affected by the original sin of Adam and Eve, and the ramifications of that sin result in other sins (missing the mark of what God desires for all of humanity). Ultimately, war exists in the world because of original sin and subsequent sins.

Some Christians believe that every individual has the nature of a sinner, and this mars or corrupts not only interpersonal relations but also international relations. Just as individuals have conflicts at times, so too do groups of people and nations have conflicts. War may be fought on battlefields, but for Christians, they are first waged in the hearts of individuals; war then becomes the physical result. For Christians, war is ultimately the result of sin—and yet, the prevailing Christian view through the centuries has been that war may sometimes be necessary to bring about a just peace in defense of those who have been unjustly attacked (just war tradition). The Christian just war position shares Christian pacifism's desire for peace but argues that there must be a just peace, noting that a dictator or tyrant can ensure peace but that it will not be a just peace. Rather, it may be a regime of severe oppression and abuse of human rights.

Apart from the strong tradition of Christian pacifism, Christians do not believe that war is avoidable or should be avoided in all cases. The Christian pacifist believes that all wars are immoral and to be avoided. The Christian just war proponent believes that war is tragic, but in some instances, participation is necessary. All Christians believe that the death, destruction, trauma, tragedy, and horrors of war are real. There has not been unanimity of perspective on war and participation in war by Christians, but the tragedy of all warfare has been normative in Christian thought. Christians believe that to wrestle with the issue of war is to think about the theological and philosophical issue of the problem of evil in the world.

Throughout the Bible (Hebrew and Christian scriptures), there are many verses that are cited as support for whichever Christian position one advocates. Central to these passages are prohibition against murder in Deuteronomy 5:15 and 20:13 and deciding how this prohibition relates to war (i.e., is murder the same as killing) and the words of Jesus in Matthew 5:12 and St. Paul in Romans 12 and 13. Interpretation of every passage in the Bible must be considered in view of the intended audience and reader.

That is, to whom is the passage applicable? Is it applicable only to individuals or the Christian church at large or also (or only) to other institutions, such as the nation-state? Most Christians would argue that not all passages are applicable to all people, groups, and entities. Spirituality and statecraft are two vastly different realms.

There have been numerous Christian thinkers and groups through the centuries whose writings and thought have been incorporated into the various Christian positions on war and peace. In part, this occurred because they believed that Christian ethics and Christian theology were greater and more important than any individual, group, political position, nation, or era of history. For example, in early Christianity, Tertullian (ca. 160–225 CE) argued against military service on the basis of idolatry, and Origen (185–254 CE) argued against it because killing is not the way of Jesus Christ. Both rejected Christian participation in the military. Other early Christian voices include Cyprian (d. 258 CE), Clement of Alexandria (150–215 CE), and Hippolytus of Rome (170–235). However, there also are more than two dozen records and accounts of early Christians in military service who became martyrs because of their Christian faith.

Among the many proponents of what became the just war tradition, major Christian thinkers include Ambrose (340–397 CE), Augustine of Hippo (354–430), and Thomas Aquinas (1225–1274). In the early modern era, the writings of Christian thinkers on war and peace, such as Francisco de Vitoria (ca. 1483–1546), Francisco Suárez (1548–1617), and Hugo Grotius (1583–1645), enormously affected the development of law and international relations. Christian voices across the political spectrum and the representation of Christian pacifism and Christian just war thought have been central to the development of Western ideas about ethics, war, peace, and justice.

Major Christian thinkers in the 20th and 21st centuries who addressed the subject of war include proponents of the pacifist and just war traditions: John Courtney Murray (1904–1967), Paul Ramsey (1913–1988), William V. O'Brien (1923–2003), Jean Bethke Elshtain (1941–2013), James Turner Johnson (1938–), Glen H. Stassen (1936–2014), John Howard Yoder (1927–1997), and Oliver O'Donovan (1945–).

The history of American warfare, including the 21st century, is filled with Christian participation and objection. Protestants, Roman Catholics, and Orthodox Christians and denominations in the United States have supported and opposed U.S. wars and issues surrounding war, such as nuclear proliferation, torture, terrorism, and conscientious objection. Individual citizens (as members of the military and otherwise) and national leaders have drawn upon personal Christian faith and aspects of American civil religion for guidance, inspiration, and support for their efforts in times of war and for national victory in those wars. They have upheld and departed from normative interpretations of the Bible. For many Americans, Christianity has been a resource for personal strength and comfort amid the depravations of war.

Christian images of events in early American history, such as accounts of General George Washington praying in the snow at Valley Forge in the winter of 1777–1778 during the American Revolution and Julia Ward Howe's "Battle Hymn of the Republic," which was written and popularized during the Civil War (1861–1865), set a pattern of imbuing the wars of the United States with Christian rhetoric and national identification. Similarly, in the 20th century, during World War II, events such as President Franklin D. Roosevelt's nationally broadcast prayer on D-Day (June 6, 1944), General George Patton's request for a prayer for victory from his chaplain during the December 1944 Battle of the Bulge (subsequently distributed to every member of the Third Army), and popular music such as "Praise the Lord and Pass the Ammunition" (1942) and "Coming in on a Wing and a Prayer" (1943) continued the coupling of Christianity and American warfare. During the Vietnam War, as the war continued and especially after the 1968 Tet Offensive, many Christian leaders and denominations opposed the United States' continued involvement in the war. Late in the 20th century, during the 1990–1991 Gulf War, there was again a strong identification of Christianity and war popularly evidenced in things such as composer-singer Lee Greenwood's "God Bless the USA" and the proliferation of bumper stickers bearing an American flag and the words "Psalm 91."

The same examples that were used during the Gulf War carried into the 21st century, especially after the September 11, 2001, terrorist attacks on the United States and subsequent American operations against international terrorism and the conflicts in Afghanistan and Iraq. At the same time, however, there has been a persistent perspective of Christian pacifism wherein many have called for a complete abstinence and avoidance of war, while others have participated in the military or alongside the military as noncombatants providing medical support and other services.

Christian leaders, theologians, and laity have grounded their beliefs about war and peace in their Christian faith. As with all religious traditions, there is a spectrum of belief and commitment to matters of war and peace and how one's faith is to inform personal and national endeavors.

*See also:* American Peace Churches; Ecclesiastical Statements on War and Peace; Gulf War; Iraq War; Islam and War; Judaism and War; Just War Tradition; Pacifism; Presidential Faith and War; Protestant Denominations; Religious Texts; Rhetoric, Sermons, and Prayers; Roman Catholicism

**Further Reading**

Charles, J. Daryl, and Timothy J. Demy. *War, Peace, and Christianity: Questions and Answers from a Just-War Perspective.* Wheaton, IL: Crossway Publications, 2010.

Clouse, Robert G., ed. *War: Four Christian Views.* Downers Grove, IL: InterVarsity Press, 1981.

Cole, Darrell. *When God Says War Is Right: The Christian Perspective on When and How to Fight.* Colorado Springs, CO: Waterbrook, 2002.

Demy, Timothy J. "War." In *The Oxford Encyclopedia of the Bible and Ethics*, edited by Robert L. Brawley, vol. 2, 395–403. New York: Oxford University Press, 2014.

Holmes, Arthur F., ed. *War and Christian Ethics: Classic and Contemporary Readings on the Morality of War.* 2nd ed. Grand Rapids, MI: Baker Books, 2005.

Pew Research Center. "Religious Landscape Study." Pew Forum, 2014. https://www.pewforum.org/religious-landscape-study/

# Cold War

The Cold War was a decades-long era (1945–1990) of geopolitical tension in the aftermath of World War II. The rivals in it were the United States and its allies in western Europe and the former Soviet Union and its satellites states in eastern Europe, known as the Eastern Bloc. Formal political-military alliances opposing each other during the Cold War were the North Atlantic Treaty Organization (NATO) and the Warsaw Pact, the former supporting the United States and the West and the latter supporting the Soviet Union and its client states. The political, geographical, and physical boundaries that separated the rivals was termed the "Iron Curtain." The phrase in this context is attributed to its use in a speech given by Winston Churchill on March 5, 1946, at Westminster College in Fulton, Missouri, that was titled "The Sinews of Peace." In that speech, he declared, "An iron curtain has descended across the Continent [Europe]" (Churchill 1946).

The word "cold" is used because there was no large-scale military fighting between the two entities. There were, however, numerous proxy wars, including regional conflicts around the globe. Some of these, including the Korean War (1950–1953), Vietnam War (1955–1975), and Cuban Missile Crisis (1962), directly involved U.S. military forces. The two superpowers in the conflict were the United States and the Union of Soviet Socialist Republics (USSR or Soviet Union), each having significant political and economic differences that fueled major military buildups and enormous militaries with global reach.

In the United States, religion was a significant component of support for the United States, NATO, and their allies, in part to stand in opposition to the atheistic stances of Marxism and communism. For many, the war was understood to be a spiritual battle for global influence as well as economic and political influence. During the early decades of the Cold War, religious ideas and personalities, especially Protestant ones, were prevalent and important in creating what one historian calls a "diplomatic theology of containment" (Inboden 2010, 102). Interestingly, many of the religious ideas and foundations for fighting communism came not from religious groups but from religiously minded individuals holding significant positions of political power and influence in Washington, DC (including Presidents Harry Truman and Dwight Eisenhower). Unlike the strong base of conservative evangelicals that created the mid-1970s Moral Majority and strongly supported the political agenda of President Ronald Reagan, early Protestant cold warriors were from what are known as mainline Protestant denominations (e.g., Presbyterians, Methodists, Episcopalians, Lutherans).

This era drew upon the ideas of American exceptionalism and American civil religion. These concepts were deeply embedded in American history and culture. Devoid of most doctrinal specifics that would identify them with a particular denomination or religion, the concepts promote a view of American history and purpose that accepts and promotes a national spirituality that is acceptable regardless of a citizen's particular religious tradition and commitments. Although there were dissenting voices throughout the Cold War regarding the use of religion as an ideological or propaganda tool, few people denied its presence and political power. It was during the Cold War that the motto "In God We Trust" became the official motto of the United States by means of legislation passed by the Eighty-Fourth

Congress (P.L. 84–851) and signed by President Eisenhower on July 30, 1956. Two years earlier, out of a desire to differentiate the values of the United States from the official atheism of the Soviet Union, the two words "under God" were added to the Pledge of Allegiance and signed into law by President Eisenhower.

By the 1960s, some of this religious influence began to subside as many major Protestant denominations shifted to a more liberal political and theological stance and also experienced a steep decline in membership. This fragmentation prevented a united Protestant perspective on the Cold War. This fragmentation is also seen in the religious divisions that occurred regarding American participation in the Vietnam War and all subsequent military conflicts, including those in the 21st century.

In the 1970s and 1980s, the public and private efforts of Pope John Paul II (previously, Cardinal Wojtyla of Poland) were significant in being a spiritual inspiration and catalyst for the collapse of communism in Poland and central and eastern Europe. In this regard, he worked closely with President Ronald Reagan to strengthen U.S.-Vatican relations, force the Soviet Union out of Poland, and hasten the collapse of communism. Earlier, President Truman sought to gain support and ally with Pius XII, another staunch anticommunist.

In the same way that religion was used as an instrument in fighting communism during the Cold War, religion was also an instrument in keeping the Cold War from becoming a "hot war." The triumph of democratic civil society over totalitarianism was aided by churches and religious organizations that promoted peaceful opposition by workers' unions, associations, guilds, educational institutions, and the masses. While the world of the 1990s was one that heralded the rise of secularism and a post-Christian Europe, this was made possible in part by religion that helped the West to prevail over Soviet-led or Soviet-supported totalitarian regimes.

As a result of the collapse of European communism, the fall of the Soviet Union, and the democratization of many former Eastern Bloc nations, there was a renewal of religious fervor in many countries where state-supported atheism, religious persecution, and communism had previously existed. This religious resurgence crossed religious boundaries (Protestant, Roman Catholic, Orthodox, Islam, etc.) and generated new social, religious, and political dynamics that remain prevalent in the present. Some of these included militant religious ideologies that fomented religiously motivated terrorism and attempts to propagate religious extremism through social and political means. The end of the Cold War, inspired in part by religion, resulted in a new era of national and international politics in which religion continues to be a prevalent factor seeking to shape personal, national, and international affairs.

*See also:* American Exceptionalism; Apocalypticism; Evangelicalism; Graham, William Franklin, Jr. ("Billy"); Korean War; Protestant Denominations; Roman Catholicism; Vietnam War

## Further Reading

Churchill, Winston. "The Sinews of Peace." Speech at Westminster College, Fulton, Missouri, March 5, 1946. https://winstonchurchill.org/resources/speeches/1946-1963-elder-statesman/the-sinews-of-peace/

Gaddis, John Lewis. *The Cold War: A New History*. New York: Penguin Books, 2006.

Inboden, William C. *Religion and American Foreign Policy, 1945–1960*. Cambridge, UK: Cambridge University Press, 2010.

Kengor, Paul, and Robert Orlando. *The Divine Plan: John Paul II, Ronald Reagan, and the Dramatic End of the Cold War*. Wilmington, DE: Intercollegiate Studies Institute, 2019.

Kirby, Diane, ed. *Religion and the Cold War*. New York: Palgrave Macmillan, 2013.

Mojzes, Paul. *North American Churches and the Cold War*. Grand Rapids, MI: Eerdmans, 2018.

Muehlenbeck, Philip. *Religion and the Cold War: A Global Perspective*. Nashville, TN: Vanderbilt University Press, 2012.

Padgett, Timothy D. *Swords & Plowshares: American Evangelicals on War, 1937–1973*. Bellingham, WA: Lexham Press, 2018.

Preston, Andrew. *Sword of the Spirit, Shield of Faith: Religion in American War and Diplomacy*. New York: Alfred A. Knopf, 2012.

Settje, David E. *Faith and War: How Christians Debated the Cold and Vietnam Wars*. New York: New York University Press, 2011.

# Conscientious Objection

Conscientious objection is the belief that there is a moral and human right to refuse to perform military service. It has a centuries-long history, and every nation has its own unique history of the idea—some favorably and some unfavorably. Historically, it was primarily tied to religious beliefs and religious traditions. However, there is also a secular strand, and in the United States, both the religious and secular strands are accepted as valid by the Department of Defense; individuals may apply for conscientious objector status on the grounds of either.

The Department of Defense defines conscientious objection as a "firm, fixed, and sincere objection to participation in war in any form or the bearing of arms, by reason of religious training and/or belief" (CFR 32, Sec.75.3). In the United States, there are two kinds of conscientious objection status that an individual may be given by the Selective Service System: those who object to all military service and those whose beliefs permit them to serve in the military but not to carry weapons. Conscientious objectors must be opposed to all war, not specific ones. Under the Selective Service System a person who is classified as 1-A is considered available for military service. Conscientious objectors available for noncombatant military service are classified as 1-A-O. Conscientious objectors who oppose all military service are classified as 1-O and remain available for civilian work supporting the national cause.

In the broader international realm, the idea of conscientious objection is considered a part of Article 18 of the 1948 United Nations' Universal Declaration of Human Rights (UDHR): "Everyone has the right to freedom of thought, conscience and religion; this right includes freedom to change his religion or belief, and freedom, either alone or in community with others and in public or private, to manifest his religion or belief in teaching, practice, worship and observance" (United Nations 1948).

Historically, the United States has always recognized the role of conscience in participating or not participating in military service and war. Early in the nation's history, the granting of conscientious objector status was the function of individual states. Conscription began during the Civil War (1861–1865), though not without opposition, such as during the New York City draft riots of July 1863. During World War I, conscientious objectors were allowed to serve in noncombatant military roles. Those who refused all service were imprisoned (about 2,000). During World War II, individuals who received conscientious objector status were offered the alternative of Civilian Public Service. During the Vietnam War, there was a broadening of legal, political, and religious views on conscientious objection such that there was a large increase in the number of men granted conscientious objector status who came from Protestant mainstream denominations (e.g., Methodist, Lutheran, Episcopal, Presbyterian) or a secular background. In part, this was made possible by two U.S. Supreme

Court cases that broadened the qualifications for conscientious objector status: *United States v. Seeger* in 1965 and *Welsh v. United States* in 1970.

In the *Seeger* case, which arose from the Vietnam War, there was an expansion of the court's understanding of religious belief such that an applicant for conscientious objection status could be morally and ethically opposed to war based on religious study yet without believing in a Supreme Being or having religious training in their background. Similarly, in the *Welsh* case, also arising out of the Vietnam War, there was agreement by the court that one could be a conscientious objector based on philosophical objections rather than religious objections. Both of these decisions broadened the understanding of who could be classified by the government as a conscientious objector with respect to required military service.

In the aftermath of the American experience in the Vietnam War, the military draft ended in the United States in 1973, and the military became an all-volunteer force. While there is no draft in effect, American males between the ages of eighteen and twenty-five are still required to register with the Selective Service System. Women are not subject to registration. Before the 1991 Gulf War, there were about 2,500 service members who refused to continue service. During the 21st century, in the wars in Afghanistan and Iraq, the number of service members seeking status as conscientious objectors was very small.

American religious groups and denominations that actively support and promote conscientious objection include historic American peace churches (i.e., Mennonites, Society of Friends or Quakers, and Church of the Brethren). A person need not be affiliated with one of these groups to claim religious conscientious objection. Within many denominations and religious organizations, there are leaders and individuals who affirm pacifism based on religious values, and a consequence of this may be either promotion of or application for conscientious objector status. Conscientious objection is not a matter of political persuasion or political ideology.

*See also:* American Peace Churches; Ecclesiastical Statements on War and Peace; Human Rights; Pacifism; Peace Movements; Peacemaking; Protestant Denominations; Roman Catholicism

## Further Reading

Code of Federal Regulations (CFR), Title 32—National Defense, Section 75.3. https://www.govinfo.gov/content/pkg/CFR-2000-title32-vol1/xml/CFR-2000-title32-vol1-sec75-3.xml

Griggs, Walter S., Jr. "The Selective Conscientious Objector: A Vietnam Legacy." *Journal of Church and State* 21, no. 1 (Winter 1979): 91–107.

Hall, Mitchell K. *Because of Their Faith: CALCAV and Religious Opposition to the Vietnam War*. New York: Columbia University Press, 1990.

Moskos, Charles C., and John Whiteclay Chambers II. *The New Conscientious Objection: From Sacred to Secular Resistance*. New York: Oxford University Press, 1993.

Office of the Under Secretary of Defense for Personnel and Readiness. "DoD Instruction 1300.06: Conscientious Objectors." July 12, 2017. https://www.esd.whs.mil/Portals/54/Documents/DD/issuances/dodi/130006_dodi_2017.pdf

Schlissel, Lillian, ed. *Conscience in America: A Documentary History of Conscientious Objection in America, 1757–1967*. New York: Dutton, 1968.

Selective Service System. "Conscientious Objectors." Accessed March 1, 2020. https://www.sss.gov/conscientious-objectors/

United Nations. "Universal Declaration of Human Rights." 1948. https://www.un.org/en/universal-declaration-human-rights/index.html

# Contemporary Non-U.S. Conflicts

The 21st century has been a violent and bloody century with more than one hundred armed conflicts occurring around the globe. Several of these conflicts have involved U.S. military forces, the largest being the Iraq War, beginning in 2003 and ending in 2011, and the ongoing presence of U.S. military forces in Afghanistan, beginning in 2001 and ending in 2021 with the complete withdrawal of U.S. troops. However, U.S. forces and internal problems in Iraq continue. Other conflicts have had a smaller U.S. military presence (usually special operations forces), and many conflicts have had no U.S. military presence but included U.S. humanitarian assistance. Finally, there have been and continue to be conflicts in which the United States is not presently a direct participant with a military, humanitarian aid, or other presence.

The deadliest conflicts in which there has been either minor U.S. military participation or no participation include the Second Congo War (1998–2003), the Syrian Civil War (2011–present), the Darfur conflict (2003–present), the war against Boko Haram (2009–present), the Yemeni Civil War (2004–present), and the Ukraine conflict (2014–present). Other conflicts, such as the Gaza War (2008–2009), the Somali Civil War (2009–present), the South Sudanese Civil War (2013–2020), and many others, are tied historically and politically to earlier wars and conflicts. War is rarely, if ever, an isolated event.

Even in instances of conflict in which the United States is not a belligerent, religious and political entities within the United States are often working to bring about resolution. The political dimensions are the responsibility of the U.S. Department of State, and the religious efforts are often through ecclesiastical statements and resolutions, international networks of religious bodies, and humanitarian assistance provided by religious nongovernmental organizations (NGOs), such as American Friends Service Committee, American Jewish World Service, American Muslim Council, Catholic Relief Services, Lutheran World Relief, World Vision, and many others, that are working in the nations and regions where the conflicts are occurring. In these instances, the organizations and agencies frequently work alongside or in coordination with other international and secular NGOs, such as the International Committee for the Red Cross (ICRC).

Probably the most prevalent conflict in the international arena is the Syrian Civil War, with its many dimensions, factions, and shifting allegiances. The Syrian Civil War has destroyed much of the country, created more than five million refugees and six million internally displaced persons, resulted in hundreds of thousands of deaths, and fomented continued Middle East instability and the presence of powers such as Iran, Russia, and the United States. Additionally, groups such as the Islamic State (IS), Hezbollah, and others have participated in the civil war. Many religious groups, including the Vatican, the United States Conference of Catholic Bishops, the National Council of Churches, and the National Association of Evangelicals, have called for resolution of the conflict and the refugee crisis. American religious leaders and organizations have also issued statements calling for restraint in the use of military force by the United States in response to repeated chemical attacks by the regime of Syrian president Bashar al-Assad.

All conflicts exacerbate current conditions on the ground and give ample opportunity for the exploitation, subjugation, and persecution of civilians and citizens ensnared in the conflict and caught in the war zone. The violation of human rights, including genocide, is also a frequent religious and humanitarian issue. For religious observers in the United States as well as the U.S. Department of State, issues of religious freedom and religious persecution around the globe, especially in nations where there is conflict or a very strong regime, are closely monitored concerns. The international principle termed a "Responsibility to Protect" (R2P) may also become a factor that potentially draws in outside nations and forces.

The combination of religion and politics, whether on a national level or an international level, can be a force for war or for peace. Because religious values are deeply held, those who neglect the religious dimension of politics or conflict do so at the peril of misunderstanding some conflicts and missing opportunities to engage religious communities in conflict resolution and peacebuilding.

*See also:* Ecclesiastical Statements on War and Peace; Human Rights; Middle East Conflict; Peacemaking; Religious Freedom and Religious Persecution; Responsibility to Protect; United Nations; Weapons of Mass Destruction

## Further Reading

Ahram, Ariel I. *War and Conflict in the Middle East and North Africa*. Cambridge, UK: Polity Press, 2020.

Council on Foreign Relations. "Global Conflict Tracker." August 2020. https://www.cfr.org/global-conflict-tracker/

Ferris, Elizabeth. "Faith-Based and Secular Humanitarian Organizations." *International Review of the Red Cross* 87, no. 858 (June 2005): 311–325. https://www.icrc.org/en/doc/assets/files/other/irrc_858_ferris.pdf

Kerr, Robert. *Syrian Civil War: The Essential Reference Guide*. Santa Barbara, CA: ABC-CLIO, 2020.

Omer, Atalia, R. Scott Appleby, and David Little, eds. *The Oxford Handbook of Religion, Conflict, and Peacebuilding*. New York: Oxford University Press, 2019.

Pinaud, Clémence. *War and Genocide in South Sudan*. Ithaca, NY: Cornell University Press, 2021.

Ray, Michael. "8 Deadliest Wars of the 21st Century." *Encyclopedia Britannica*. Accessed June 13, 2022. https://www.britannica.com/list/8-deadliest-wars-of-the-21st-century

United States Institute of Peace. "Special Report: Faith-Based NGOs and International Peacebuilding." October 22, 2001. https://www.usip.org/sites/default/files/sr76.pdf

Ware, Anthony, and Costas Laqutides. *Myanmar's "Rohingya" Conflict*. New York: Oxford University Press, 2018.

# E

## Ecclesiastical Statements on War and Peace

Religious pronouncements regarding war and peace are common in history. In Christianity, one finds them in creeds, catechisms, the works of the historic councils of Christianity's early centuries, and denominational declarations of later centuries and the present day. Sometimes they address war and peace generally; at other times, they address specific conflicts, wars, or even weapons, as in the case of weapons of mass destruction.

Though most prominent in Christianity, such statements are not unique to it. One finds them in both Judaism and Islam, especially in the 20th and 21st centuries. Though religious leaders can make statements, such as papal decrees in Roman Catholicism or fatwas in Islam, in American history, it has been denominations and organizations such as the North American Imam's Federation, the National Council of Churches, the National Association of Evangelicals, the Southern Baptist Convention, the United Synagogue of Conservative Judaism, the United States Conference of Catholic Bishops—and scores of other groups and organizations—that have influenced the greatest number of people and American politics. To be sure, individual leaders such as Martin Luther King, Jr. (1929–1968), William "Billy" Franklin Graham, Jr. (1918–2018), Harry Emerson Fosdick (1878–1969), Fulton J. Sheen (1895–1979), William Sloane Coffin, Jr. (1924–2006), Reinhold Niebuhr (1892–1971), and others have had a significant impact on public discourse about American wars and the quest for peace, but it has been the group and denominational statements that have continuing influence for the masses.

Deeply rooted in faith traditions and derived from sacred texts—and interpretations of them—religious and ecclesiastical statements articulate and disseminate the beliefs and policies of religious groups. With the rise of the printing press in the 15th century and mass media communications in the

20th and 21st centuries, the dissemination of religious statements expanded beyond the printed word and afforded wider distribution of the content.

Probably the most influential ecclesiastical statement in the 20th and 21st centuries with respect to war and peace is "The Challenge of Peace: God's Promise and Our Response," a pastoral letter issued by the National Conference of Catholic Bishops in 1983. Issued in the midst of the Cold War and nuclear arms race, the document was applauded and criticized for its "presumption against war" rather than support of the historic just war tradition position of Christianity in general. Specifically, the Roman Catholic Church had previously held to a presumption against injustice, arguing that war is sometimes necessary, even though it is tragic and must be avoided when possible (National Conference of Catholic Bishops 1983, 2). In 1993, "The Challenge of Peace" was followed by another statement from the bishops: "The Harvest of Justice Is Sown in Peace."

Since September 11, 2001, there been have been many religious statements on specific things, such as the war in Afghanistan, the Iraq War, conflict in Syria, refugees, terrorism, and torture. Statements from across the religious spectrum, including from the historic American peace churches, have set forth theological and political positions on matters of war and peace in the 21st century.

Although individual members may support or not support the declarations, the issuing of such statements can have political influence in American politics. Even with the separation of religion and politics as presented in the First Amendment of the U.S. Constitution, public pronouncements of political and religious values are guaranteed in the Constitution through freedom of assembly and freedom of the press. Each and all of these guarantees afford citizens the opportunity to articulate and promulgate religious and political values with respect to war and peace. In so doing, religious and ecclesiastical statements continue a long tradition of support and nonsupport of U.S. wars and conflicts.

*See also:* American Peace Churches; Christianity and War; Cold War; Genocide; Human Rights; Islam and War; Judaism and War; Just War Tradition; Peacemaking; Protestant Denominations; Religious Texts; Responsibility to Protect; Roman Catholicism; Terrorism; Torture; Weapons of Mass Destruction

## Further Reading

Braun, Christian Nikolaus. "James Turner Johnson and the Roman Catholic Just War Tradition." In *Responsibility and Restraint: James Turner Johnson and the Just War Tradition*, edited by Eric D. Patterson and Marc LiVecche, 125–158. Middletown, RI: Stone Tower Press, 2020.

Central Conference of American Rabbis. "The Use of Torture or Lesser Forms of Coercion to Obtain Information from Prisoners." March 2005. https://www.ccarnet.org/ccar-resolutions/the-use-of-torture-or-lesser-forms-of-coercion-to-obtain-information-from-prisoners/

Evangelicals for Human Rights. "An Evangelical Declaration against Torture: Protecting Human Rights in an Age of Terror." *Review of Faith & International Affairs* 5, no. 2 (2007): 41–58.

National Association of Evangelicals. "Peace, Freedom and Security Studies: Resolution." January 1, 1986. https://www.nae.org/530/

National Conference of Catholic Bishops. "The Challenge of Peace: God's Promise and Our Response." May 3, 1983. https://www.usccb.org/upload/challenge-peace-gods-promise-our-response-1983.pdf

National Conference of Catholic Bishops. "The Harvest of Justice Is Sown in Peace." 1993. http://www.usccb.org/beliefs-and-teachings/what-we-believe/catholic-social-teaching/the-harvest-of-justice-is-sown-in-peace.cfm

National Council of Churches. "Nuclear Disarmament: The Time Is Now." November 12, 2009. http://nationalcouncilofchurches.us/common-witness/2009/nuclear-disarm.php

Pew Research Center. "Religious Groups Issue Statement on War with Iraq." Compiled by Religious News Service, March 19, 2003. https://www.pewforum.org/2003/03/19/publicationpage-aspxid616/

Reichberg, Gregory M., Henrik Syse, and Endre Begby, eds. *The Ethics of War: Classic and Contemporary Readings*. Oxford: Blackwell Publishing, 2006.

Reichberg, Gregory M., Henrik Syse, and Nicole M. Hartwell, eds. *Religion, War, and Ethics: A Sourcebook of Textual Traditions*. New York: Cambridge University Press, 2014.

Weigel, George. *Tranquillitas Ordinis: Present Failure and Future Promise of American Catholic Thought on War and Peace*. New York: Oxford University Press, 1987.

# Evangelicalism

Evangelicals, and their ideological and religious precursors, have participated in all of the American wars and continue to be strong supporters of the U.S. military and its 21st-century operations. Evangelicals are a vibrant, visible, and vocal part of 21st-century religious life in the United States. Increasingly, they span the educational, socioeconomic, and ethnic spectra. American evangelicalism's history has roots that precede the

American colonial experience and date to the era of the European Reformation of the 1500s. According to a 2015 survey and report by the Pew Research Center, 25.4 percent of Americans identify as evangelicals and not as members of mainline Protestant denominations (Lutheran Church in America, Presbyterian Church in the United States, United Methodists, Episcopal Church in America, United Congregational Church, etc.).

Although most evangelicals are Protestant and are not members of mainline denominations, there are individuals and groups of evangelicals in the denominations., Some American evangelicals also self-identify as being either Orthodox Christians or Roman Catholics. Ethnically, in addition to what has historically been a religious movement that was largely Caucasian, there are presently large and growing expressions of evangelicalism in the religious experiences of Hispanic, Asian, and African Americans.

Self-identification as an evangelical is one of the key components of American evangelicalism, and it draws on the democratic spirit of individualism that is seen and experienced in many aspects of life in the United States as well as the theological perspective of a religious conversion, or "born again," experience that is grounded in the words of Jesus as recorded in the Gospel of John (3:1–21).

To understand the relationship between evangelicals and war, one must first understand what is meant by the term *evangelical*. Evangelicalism is not a uniquely American phenomenon; it has a global presence. Although evangelicalism in the United States began as a transatlantic movement in the 1700s with religious roots in the Reformation era of the 1500s, by the late 1800s, it had become an international movement, and its 21st-century presence is growing exponentially.

In 1989, British historian David Bebbington published a seminal volume on British evangelicalism titled *Evangelicalism in Modern Britain: A History from the 1730s to the 1980s*. In addition to noting the deep and wide transatlantic ties between evangelicalism in the British Isles and evangelicalism in the United States, Bebbington articulated what has come to be known by religious studies scholars as the "Evangelical Quadrilateral." What is meant by this is that Bebbington identified four central elements or characteristics of the evangelical experience: (1) *biblicism*, a particular regard for the Bible (e.g., all essential spiritual truth is to be found in the Bible); (2) *crucicentrism*, a focus on the sacrificial death and atoning work of Jesus Christ on the cross; (3) *conversionism*, the belief that all human beings need to be converted to Christianity; and (4) *activism*, the belief that the Gospel message of Christianity needs to be expressed in efforts such that it is proclaimed and applied to one's personal daily life and the issues of society.

Evangelicals are a slice of American society, and like most segments and aspects of American life, politics, and culture, American evangelicalism is not monolithic. American evangelicals are part of a multifaceted, multigenerational, and multiethnic religious culture. Politically, evangelicals are also diverse. While the majority of American evangelicals self-identify as moderate or conservative, broader and left-wing politics have also influenced evangelicalism since the mid-1960s. This is also true for the social issues that are frequently a part of political discourse and posturing in the United States—especially with respect to matters of war and peace.

The topic of evangelicals and war is a subset of the broader subject of the relationship between evangelicals and the state. Evangelicals understand issues of war and peace as part of the understanding and application of the words of Jesus in the synoptic Gospels, in which Jesus states, "Render unto Caesar the things that are Caesar's, and to God the things that are God's" (Matthew 22:21; Mark 12:17; Luke 20:25). This statement by Jesus has been understood by evangelicals and other Christians as part of a larger issue of a spiritual-temporal reality in which Christians' loyalties to the state and loyalties to God may conflict at times. The nature of this relationship is a centuries-old concern that has been addressed by Christian thinkers such as Augustine of Hippo (354–430), Martin Luther (1483–1546), and John Calvin (1510–1564).

With respect to evangelicals and war, the subject entails such issues as military service, military chaplains, pacifism, the just war tradition, foreign policy advocacy, and support for and against specific conflicts in which the United States is a belligerent or has an interest. There is no single evangelical perspective with respect to American evangelicals and the state, nor are evangelicals monolithic in their responses to the multifaceted issues and dimensions of war and peace.

The rise of evangelicals as a distinct and identifiable population with respect to politics and issues of war and peace arose in the post–World War II era and became most visible in the mid-1970s and 1980s. This visible and influential presence continued in the 1990s, though it became less vocal. In the aftermath of the September 11, 2001, terrorist attacks, evangelicals once again became a noticeable part of American religious and political discussions and debate with respect to American military operations in Afghanistan and Iraq, the civil war in Syria, and in combating terrorism around the world.

During the American experience in Vietnam in the 1960s and 1970s, evangelicals, like the rest of the nation, were divided on support of the war effort. However, while many religious leaders in the mainline Protestant denominations were pacifistic, evangelical leaders such as Carl F. H. Henry (1913–2003), Harold Lindsell (1913–1998), Billy Graham (1918–2018), and others argued for a responsible use of military force. Yet, not all evangelicals supported the war. One prominent and outspoken evangelical against the Vietnam War effort was a Republican U.S. senator from Oregon, Mark O. Hatfield (1922–2011). Based on his experiences as a naval officer in the Pacific theater during World War II and in its aftermath, Hatfield believed that American participation in the war in Vietnam was not justified under the tenets of the just war tradition—an ethical framework that is often used by policymakers, political decision-makers, and military leaders in bounding military operations at all levels (tactical, operational, and strategic). Evangelicals and other Christians in the United States have frequently looked to the just war tradition for a framework for religious and ethical considerations of war.

On the whole, evangelicals supported American conflicts in the Middle East, beginning with Operations Desert Shield and Desert Storm (1990 and 1991, respectively) as well as smaller conflicts such as military operations in Grenada (1983) and Panama (1989–1990). They also supported the United Nations' endeavors in Operation Allied Force in Kosovo (1999).

One major organizational voice for matters of war and peace and a wide range of other social and political issues in the United States has been the National Association of Evangelicals (NAE), which was founded in 1942 during World War II. The NAE has been proactive in participation of the endorsement process of evangelicals for service as military chaplains as well as in providing policy support for matters of war, peace, and security during the Cold War. One example of this was its 1986 "Guidelines: Peace, Freedom, and Security Studies," which articulated an evangelical perspective on issues of war and peace in the era of weapons of mass destruction. Similarly, in 2007, the NAE issued an extensive resolution titled "An Evangelical Declaration against Torture."

Notable contemporary evangelical scholars writing and working within the just war framework include Eric D. Patterson, J. Daryl Charles, and Daniel R. Heimbach. Each of these individuals addresses issues of war prevention and postconflict resolution as well as matters of actions during war. However, there have been dissenting voices within evangelicalism of American military efforts and policy, among them Ronald J. Sider (1939–), Jim Wallis (1948–), and Glen Stassen (1936–2014).

After the September 11, 2001, terrorist attacks on the United States, evangelicals gave broad, though not unanimous, support to military operations in Iraq and Afghanistan. Among the most prominent of the dissenting voices with respect to the war in Iraq was former president Jimmy Carter, a Southern Baptist. In 2003, Carter wrote an editorial in the *New York Times* arguing that U.S. intervention in Iraq was not justified.

One interesting aspect of evangelicals and war as well as evangelicals and U.S. foreign policy is that there is frequently a linkage that is understood to be present between current events and Bible prophecy and doctrine, notably the doctrine of eschatology, which deals with what is perceived to be the catastrophic end of the world and end of time. In some views of Bible prophecy and eschatology within evangelicalism, there is the belief that some of the prophetic passages in the Bible are being fulfilled in recent, current, or near-future events that will culminate in the return of Jesus Christ to earth. Military conflicts and all that surrounds them are frequently seen as harbingers of the future and as precursors to the realization of apocalyptic beliefs. This is especially true of instances of war and potential warfare in the Middle East, though the rise of military strength in China and Russia is also viewed as potentially prophetically significant. Such interpretations were common in the aftermath of the June 1967 Six-Day War in the Middle East, during Operation Desert Storm in 1991, and, to a lesser extent, in 21st-century military actions in Afghanistan and Iraq. Aspects were also present throughout the Cold War.

Since the mid-20th century, American evangelicals have supported most U.S. foreign policies pertaining to war and peace. They have provided chaplains for the military and been strong supporters of U.S. military forces. This support has been based on religious and political considerations of evangelicals as individuals, groups, and denominations. Although there is more ethnic, social, cultural, and political diversity within evangelicalism in the 21st century than previously, there remains broad support for the U.S. government with respect to matters of war and peace.

***See also:*** Apocalypticism; Christianity and War; Cold War; Graham, William Franklin, Jr. ("Billy"); Gulf War; Just War Tradition; Middle East Conflict; Military Chaplains; Peacemaking; September 11, 2001, Terrorist Attacks; Terrorism; Torture; Vietnam War; Wars of Israel

## Further Reading

Bebbington, David. *Evangelicalism in Modern Britain: A History from the 1730s to the 1980s*. Grand Rapids, MI: Baker Books, 1989.

Borg, David. "The End of Evangelical Support for Israel? The Jewish State's International Standing." *Middle East Quarterly* 21, no. 2 (Spring 2014). http://www.meforum.org/3769/israel-evangelical-support

Carter, Jimmy. "Just War—or a Just War?" *New York Times*, March 9, 2003. https://www.nytimes.com/2003/03/09/opinion/just-war-or-a-just-war.html

Laing, John D. *In Jesus' Name: Evangelicals and Military Chaplaincy*. Eugene, OR: Wipf and Stock Publishers, 2010.

Mojzes, Paul, ed. *North American Churches and the Cold War*. Grand Rapids, MI: William B. Eerdmans, 2018.

Olson, Jason M. *America's Road to Jerusalem: The Impact of the Six-Day War on Protestant Politics*. Lanham, MD: Lexington Books, 2018.

Padgett, Timothy D. *Swords & Plowshares: American Evangelicals on War, 1937–1973*. Bellingham, WA: Lexham Press, 2018.

Patterson, Eric. "Just War Theory & Terrorism." *Providence: A Journal of Christianity & American Foreign Policy*, no. 4 (Summer 2016): 38–44.

Pew Research Center. "America's Changing Religious Landscape." May 12, 2015. https://www.pewforum.org/2015/05/12/americas-changing-religious-landscape/

# G

## Genocide

Genocide is understood to be the "intent to destroy, in whole or in part, a national, ethnic, racial, or religious group" (United Nations 1948). However, diplomatic and legal nuances in the use of the term often make international response to genocide difficult. Religious organizations have focused on preventing genocide as part of their missions and ministries to assist civilians in need, prevent harm, and protect the human rights of victims of oppression, persecution, violence, and conflict. In 2014, Pope Francis wrote, "The most basic understanding of human dignity compels the international community . . . to do all that it can do to stop and prevent further systematic violence against ethnic and religious minorities and to protect innocent peoples" (Pope Francis 2014).

This 2014 statement addressing genocide in a letter to the United Nations illustrates the ongoing concern of religious communities to address issues of genocide in the 21st century. It urges the United Nations and international community to employ international laws and norms to protect Christians and other ethnic, national, and religious minorities against violence in the Middle East. In so doing, Pope Francis employed a basic understanding of human dignity to protect innocent people against religious and ethnically motivated systematic violence without explicitly naming such acts "genocide." There is good reason to avoid the word if action is required: in the seventy-five years since the word's creation, *genocide* has been subject to much political, social, legal, and human rights debate concerning its definition.

Despite overwhelming evidence of systematic violence perpetrated against minority groups, the definition of the word *genocide* is not universally accepted as legally binding. The term is considered modern in origin, coming into mainstream international discourse after World War II and the

Nuremberg trials in 1946 in which Nazi leaders were prosecuted for "crimes against humanity" and the Holocaust. The Nuremberg indictments included text explicitly defining genocide as a war crime to exterminate racial and national groups or to destroy particular races and classes of people. This closely matches the legal origin of the word, coined by Raphaël Lemkin, combining the Greek word *genos* (referring to kin, race, or lineage) with the Latin suffix *-cide* (referring to the act of killing). Lemkin coined the term around 1944 while writing the first draft of the Convention on the Prevention and Punishment of the Crime of Genocide (commonly known as the Genocide Convention), which the United Nations adopted in December 1948. In addition to the Article 2 definition of genocide as the intent to destroy a group, it specifies the mechanism as acts that include killing, causing serious mental or bodily harm, inflicting conditions intended to destroy the group in whole or in part, preventing births, and forcibly transferring a group's children to an external group.

Although religious and faith-based organizations arise from specific faith commitments, recipients of their work are not limited to specific religious values or commitments. These organizations provide aid and protect vulnerable populations from violence and persecution regardless of one's religious or secular values and faith. Critics evaluating religion and genocide in the post–World War I era argue that religion has played a key role in state-based outbreaks of genocide, including cases in Armenia, Rwanda, and Bosnia (Bartov and Mack 2001). However, religious and faith-based organizations working to defend religious freedom and human rights among populations serve a critical role in protecting *against* genocide, regardless of the state-based motivation for violence. Well-known religious nongovernmental organizations (NGOs) aiding victims of war and serving as watchdogs to protect individuals from violence include American Friends Service Committee (Quaker), Catholic Relief Services (Roman Catholic), World Vision International (Christian), Samaritan's Purse (Christian), the Islamic Relief (Muslim), the Adventist Relief and Development Agency (Christian), and Lutheran World Relief (Christian).

As faith-based organizations often provide aid to local populations on an ongoing basis, they provide a useful monitoring function to protect refugees, the marginalized, and the persecuted from human rights abuses. Reporting from local church councils can provide early warnings of violence and genocide. In the 21st century, examples of early warnings of genocide and potential genocide include (but are not limited to) watchdog monitoring of the Pygmy population in Eastern Congo (2002–2003), the

Tamil Eelam in Sri Lanka (1956–2009), killings in Darfur in Sudan (2003–present), the Muslim Rohingya refugee crisis and crackdown in Myanmar (2015–present), and the persecution of the Muslim Uyghur population in the Xinjian Uyghur Autonomous Region of China by the Chinese government under the direction of the Chinese Communist Party (2014–present).

In part, it is because of instances of genocide in the last thirty to forty years, such as the genocide in Rwanda in 1994, that the concept of the "Responsibility to Protect" (R2P) has become part of the international commitment by members of the United Nations to protect individuals and groups against genocide. Though, as noted earlier, garnering international will to act in specific instances is difficult.

In the United States, religious groups, denominations, and individuals actively monitor conflict, war, and civil war, often with a specific interest in preventing genocide. Because genocide is such an egregious crime against human rights, one often finds it to be something closely connected to other violations of human rights, such as religious persecution.

*See also:* American Peace Churches; Human Rights; Pacifism; Responsibility to Protect; United Nations

## Further Reading

Abrams, Elliott. *The Influence of Faith: Religious Groups and U.S. Foreign Policy*. New York: Rowman & Littlefield, 2002.

Barnett, Michael, and Janice Gross Stein. *Sacred Aid: Faith and Humanitarianism*. Oxford, UK: Oxford University Press, 2012.

Barnett, Victoria. "I. Teaching and Theologizing about Religion and Genocide: Some Reflections." *Horizons* 47, no. 1 (2020): 69–76. https://doi.org/10.1017/hor.2020.50

Bartov, Omer, and Phyllis Mack. *In God's Name: Genocide and Religion in the Twentieth Century*. New York: Berghahn Books, 2001.

Dallaire, Roméo. *Shake Hands with the Devil: The Failure of Humanity in Rwanda*. Toronto: Random House Canada, 2003.

Ferris, Elizabeth. "Faith-Based and Secular Humanitarian Organizations." *International Review of the Red Cross* 87, no. 858 (2005): 311–325.

Irvin-Erickson, Douglas. *Raphaël Lemkin and the Concept of Genocide*. Philadelphia: University of Pennsylvania Press, 2017.

Menendian, Stephen. "A 21st Century Problem: Lessons from the Armenian Genocide." Othering & Belonging Institute, March 1, 1970. https://belonging.berkeley.edu/21st-century-problem-lessons-armenian-genocide

Pope Francis. "Letter of the Holy Father to the Secretary General of the United Nations Organization concerning the Dramatic Situation in Northern Iraq." August 9, 2014. http://www.vatican.va/content/francesco/en/letters/2014/documents/papa-francesco_20140809_lettera-ban-ki-moon-iraq.html

Power, Samantha. *A Problem from Hell: America and the Age of Genocide*. New York: Basic Books, 2002.

United Nations. "No. 1021: Convention on the Prevention and Punishment of the Crime of Genocide. Adopted by the General Assembly of the United Nations on 9 December 1948." United Nations Treaty Series—Genocide Convention, December 9, 1948. https://treaties.un.org/doc/publication/unts/volume 78/volume-78-i-1021-english.pdf

United States Conference of Catholic Bishops. "Letter to House on Genocide Prevention Resolution, May 31, 2018." May 31, 2018. www.usccb.org/committees/religious-liberty/letter-house-genocide-prevention-resolution-2018-05-31

## Graham, William Franklin, Jr. ("Billy") (1918–2018)

A Baptist evangelist with international name recognition, evangelist William "Billy" Franklin Graham, Jr. (1918–2018) was the most well-known evangelist of the 20th century. His prominence in American Christianity afforded him opportunities of being heard by millions of people through his evangelistic meetings, through radio, and on television. His monthly periodical *Decision* and his many books had a national and international readership. Beginning in 1949 and throughout the next half century, he was the face and voice of American evangelicalism in the post–World War II United States. The era of Graham's ministry paralleled the rise and duration of the Cold War, the conflicts in Korea and Vietnam, and the Gulf War.

Billy Graham was born of Scottish Presbyterian heritage in Charlotte, North Carolina, on November 17, 1918. As a youth, he was skeptical of Christianity and religion. However, in 1934, Graham attended a revival meeting and experienced conversion to Christianity upon hearing a sermon preached by Baptist fundamentalist evangelist Mordecai Ham (1877–1961).

Graham began his higher education at Bob Jones College (now Bob Jones University) in 1936; transferred to Florida Bible Institute (now Trinity College of Florida) in 1937, from which he graduated; and was subsequently ordained as a minister in the Southern Baptist Convention.

He later attended Wheaton College (Illinois), earning a bachelor of arts in 1943.

In 1949, Graham scheduled a series of evangelistic meetings in Los Angeles and attracted national media coverage through the influence of the conservative newspaper magnate William Randolph Hearst (1863–1951). These meetings set him on a trajectory that would lead to global recognition and influence. Over the next half century, he conducted more than 400 evangelistic crusades in 185 countries and territories and was extremely influential in the rise of American evangelicalism. His ministry touched millions of people, including U.S. presidents and many international leaders. Three days after the September 11, 2001, terrorist attacks on the United States, Graham was invited to lead a worship and prayer service at the Washington National Cathedral.

Graham retired from active ministry at the age of ninety-five and died on February 21, 2018, at the age of ninety-nine. Shortly after his death, for two days, on February 28 and March 1, 2018, Graham became the fourth private U.S. citizen in the nation's history to lie in honor at the U.S. Capitol Rotunda.

Throughout his ministry, Graham was an outspoken critic of communism and a staunch supporter of U.S. foreign policy, including U.S. involvement in the Vietnam War. Yet, from the 1970s, there was a gradual shift in Graham's rhetoric and writings to focus on peace more than conflict with respect to matters of war and peace. This was not a solitary shift but a change of course that paralleled thought in U.S. politics and society. As the Cold War progressed through the decades and the former Soviet Union and Eastern Bloc nations collapsed and dispersed in the late 1980s and early 1990s, Graham changed emphases in his message. In his ministry, Graham framed the threat of communism as a threat to Christianity and never backed away from that perspective. He believed that communism threatened democracy, the American way of life, and the individual and collective faith of Christians around the globe. He was not a solitary voice against communism but, rather, one of numerous public figures, which included names such as Dean Acheson (1893–1971) and John Foster Dulles (1888–1959), who commanded respect for their views regardless of their political party affiliation.

Graham visited with and preached to troops in Korea and Vietnam during both wars in those nations. His Christmas 1953 visit to troops in South Korea was recorded in his diary of the trip and published as a small book titled *I Saw Your Sons at War*. He was also a guest, friend, and confidant of many political leaders, including U.S. presidents—though not without controversy. During the administrations of Presidents Kennedy, Johnson, and Nixon, Graham was a vocal supporter of the war in Vietnam. However, as the war continued, he became more ambivalent, and his support for the war wavered in his private communications. He had private conversations and correspondence with each of the three presidents. As the war continued, Graham, like many religious leaders and citizens, wanted to see it come to a quick conclusion. However, Graham also did not want the United States to experience defeat. Although some religious leaders spoke publicly against the war, Graham did not do so. He believed that to make such pronouncements would limit his unique access to the White House and other national leaders.

On April 15, 1969, Graham wrote a thirteen-page personal letter to President Richard Nixon, with whom he had been friends for many years. In the letter, Graham, claiming to speak for a group of missionaries in Vietnam, expressed grave concern regarding the administration's execution of the war in Vietnam. He also offered several scenarios that he believed might bring the war to a conclusion. His letter has been a controversial document for those studying his life and work in that he is seen as speaking naively and beyond his expertise regarding the military and political realities of the war and U.S. foreign policy. On several occasions over the years, Graham acknowledged that some of his political statements were at times not fully informed or were excessive.

The decades of Graham's public life concerning matters of war and peace can be categorized as the following: the 1950s were decisively anticommunist, the 1960s were supportive of the Vietnam War, the 1970s were focused on the threat of nuclear weapons and support for their limitation, and the 1980s and 1990s emphasized the need for Christians to focus on being peacemakers. In the late 1960s and 1970s, Graham's sermons and writings frequently linked prophetic passages of the Bible with current events as a foreshadowing of the fulfillment of biblical prophecy. In 1968, Graham visited the Nazi death camp Auschwitz, and it made a lasting impression on his views. With the rise of nuclear weapons proliferation, he feared a "nuclear holocaust" if there was not a peaceful solution to the stockpiling of them by the United States and Soviet Union. Graham also repeatedly spoke of the tragedy of war and the effects from it on civilians and those who want nothing to do with any given conflict. He was passionate but also compassionate.

Although he was fervent in his views and preaching, Graham did not propound a holy war perspective. He held the mediating position of the just war tradition. Graham's thoughts regarding war changed with the times and also became more nuanced and reflective. Publicly, Graham and his ministry, the Billy Graham Evangelistic Association (BGEA), supported American war efforts because of his concern regarding the atheistic nature of the global communist threat. He believed communism was a national threat as well as a threat to global Christianity.

*See also:* Christianity and War; Cold War; Evangelicalism; Gulf War; Just War Tradition; Korean War; Presidential Faith and War; Rhetoric, Sermons, and Prayers; Vietnam War; Weapons of Mass Destruction

**Further Reading**

Gibbs, Nancy, and Michael Duffy. *The Preacher and the Presidents: Billy Graham in the White House*. New York: Center Street, 2007.

Graham, Billy. "Billy Graham's 9/11 Message from the Washington National Cathedral." Billy Graham Evangelistic Association, September 9, 2018. https://billygraham.org/story/a-day-to-remember-a-day-of-victory/

Graham, Billy. *I Saw Your Sons at War: The Korean Diary of Billy Graham*. Minneapolis, MN: Billy Graham Evangelistic Association, 1953.

Graham, Billy. *Just as I Am*. New York: HarperOne Publishers, 1997.

Hatfield, Jeremy. "The Great Undecided Group: Billy Graham, Jerry Falwell, and the Evangelical Debate over Nuclear Weapons." In *North American Churches and the Cold War*, edited by Paul Mojzes, 418–432. Grand Rapids, MI: William B. Eerdmans, 2018.

Jenkins, Philip. "Billy Graham and the Hell Bombs." *Patheos*, February 23, 2018. https://www.patheos.com/blogs/anxiousbench/2018/02/billy-graham-hell-bombs/

Learned, Jay Douglas. "Billy Graham, American Evangelicalism, and the Cold War Clash of Messianic Visions, 1945–1962." Unpublished PhD diss., University of Rochester, Rochester, NY, 2012.

Martin, William. *A Prophet with Honor: The Billy Graham Story*. Grand Rapids, MI: Zondervan, 2007.

Pierard, Richard V. "Billy Graham and Vietnam: From Cold Warrior to Peacemaker." *Christian Scholar's Review* 10, no. 1 (1980): 37–51.

Settje, David E. *Faith and War: How Christians Debated the Cold and Vietnam War*. New York: New York University Press, 2011.

Wacker, Grant. *America's Pastor: Billy Graham and the Shaping of a Nation*. Cambridge, MA: Harvard University Press, 2014.

Wallace, Marissa Lowe. "Billy Graham's Cold War Rhetoric: Evangelical and Civil Religious Revival." In *The Rhetoric of American Civil Religion: Symbols, Sinners, and Saints*, edited by Jason Edwards and Joseph M. Valenzano III, 77–94. London: Lexington Books, 2016.

# Gulf War

The Gulf War (August 1990–February 1991) occurred as a response by a coalition of thirty-five nations led by the United States against Iraq. The war is linked to much of the recent military and political history of the United States in the 21st-century Middle East as well as military operations in Afghanistan.

On August 2, 1990, Iraq invaded and annexed Kuwait in a quick two-day operation. The response to the Iraqi invasion was the largest international military coalition since World War II. Much of the equipment and personnel were staged in Saudi Arabia, and the country also funded a significant portion of the international effort. The presence of Western and non-Muslim troops on Saudi soil was one of the grievances Saudi national and terrorist leader Osama bin Laden voiced before and after the September 11, 2001, attacks on the United States.

The Gulf War was the first large-scale conflict of the post-Vietnam and all-volunteer military era. It was also the first major conflict of the post–Cold War era. The war occurred in two phases, Operation Desert Shield (August 2, 1990–January 17, 1991) and Operation Desert Storm (January 17, 1991–February 28, 1991). The military and political goals of both operations against Iraq included expelling Iraqi forces from Kuwait, destroying Iraqi capabilities to wage war, and encouraging future regime change. From the perspective of the allied coalition, the conflict was one with limited objectives and was viewed as a response to Iraqi aggression.

President George H. W. Bush understood the actions taken by the coalition to be affirmed by and grounded in the just war tradition and vocalized principles of the tradition to give ethical and moral support for the political and military endeavor. Many religious leaders, especially among conservative Protestants and Roman Catholic laity, also appealed to the just war tradition. However, the just war framework for supporting the war was not accepted by all U.S. religious leaders, political leaders, commentators, and citizens. Within Protestant Christianity, the more liberally minded mainline denominational leaders did not support the war effort or provide strong leadership in national moral discourse regarding the war. Nor was the leadership of American Roman Catholicism strongly supportive. The National Council of Churches was highly critical of U.S. policy and actions. For Jews and Arabs, whether secular or religious, the conflict created unique concerns and many mixed emotions.

After weeks of air assaults, the ground assault by coalition forces began on February 24, 1991, and following an overwhelming victory, a cease-fire was called one hundred hours later. There were many dimensions to the conflict, including the launching of Scud missiles by Iraq into Saudi Arabia and Israel. Attacks on Israel occurred in hopes of imperiling the U.S.-led coalition, which had several Arab and Muslim member states. If successful, such a fragmentation may have led to a broader Middle East conflict, with Israel as a major belligerent. The United States encouraged Israel not to retaliate, and those desires were followed.

The war was not a religious war, but there were strong religious overtones, with the conflict at times being portrayed as a Christian versus Muslim conflict or a West versus Islam conflict in propaganda coming from Iraq. Some Christians in the United States believed the events in the Middle East should be understood through the interpretive framework of Bible prophecy, thus giving the events apocalyptic importance. Religious rhetoric of crusade and jihad was frequently used, often blurring political and strategic issues.

Because Iraq was an overwhelmingly Muslim nation in its demographics (although the government was Ba'athist and not officially Muslim), this created false impressions that the war was religious. There were also extensive efforts made by Western members of the allied coalition not to offend the religious sensitivities of Saudi Arabia, the host nation. To that end, one action taken by the coalition was to have Christian military chaplains remove the collar device of the cross from their uniforms. From a Muslim perspective, the powerful blending by Saddam Hussein of Arab nationalism and Islam generated strong support by some Arabs and Muslims in the Middle East. Even though Iraq was defeated, Arab nationalism and Islamic fervor remained strong in Iraq and the region and became part of the ideological backdrop of the attacks of September 11, 2001.

In the immediate aftermath of the war, there were several unsuccessful uprisings in Iraq in an effort to overthrow Saddam Hussein. Among these was the ongoing conflict with Kurds in northern Iraq and subsequent humanitarian assistance by the U.S. and coalition forces that lasted from 1991 to 1996 in what was called Operation Provide Comfort. This endeavor prefigured humanitarian assistance operations supported by military forces in Africa, the Middle East, and elsewhere throughout the 1990s. However, if understood as a secondary result of the Gulf War, they were very influential in similar activities in the opening years of the 21st century, giving great impetus to religious and political statements and actions regarding genocide, human rights, and the "Responsibility to Protect" (R2P).

Without the Gulf War, events in Iraq post-9/11, including the Iraq War (2003–2011), would have been very different and perhaps would not have occurred. The Gulf War did not bring about stability and peace in the Middle East. To the contrary, it likely hardened attitudes and actions as the region entered the 21st century.

The Gulf War brought to the forefront of public religious and political discourse the moral questions regarding war and peace and a reevaluation of the just war tradition. Technological advances in weapons systems generated some of the discussion of whether to validate or invalidate the tradition in the present age. Those concerns have continued in the decades since the conflict, especially with unmanned weapons, helping to mark the war as a significant turning point and event in post–Cold War American life with respect to the intersection of politics and religion.

*See also:* American Peace Churches; Apocalypticism; Christianity and War; Ecclesiastical Statements on War and Peace; Evangelicalism; Genocide; Human Rights; Iraq War; Islam and War; Judaism and War; Just War Tradition; Middle East Conflict; Military Chaplains; Music; Pacifism; Presidential Faith and War; Protestant Denominations; Religion, Conflict, and Geopolitics; Responsibility to Protect; Roman Catholicism

## Further Reading

Cole, Darrell. "The First and Second Gulf Wars." In *America and the Just War Tradition*, edited by Mark David Hall and J. Daryl Charles, 251–270. Notre Dame, IN: University of Notre Dame Press, 2019.

Elshtain, Jean Bethke, et al. *But Was It Just? Reflections on the Morality of the Persian Gulf War*. New York: Doubleday, 1992.

Goldman, Ari L. "War in the Gulf: For American Jews and Arabs, the Tug of Divided Emotions; Words of Support for U.S. Goals and Support for Israel." *New York Times*, January 19, 1991: S1, 13. https://www.nytimes.com/1991/01/19

/us/war-gulf-for-american-jews-arabs-tug-divided-emotions-words-support-for-us-goals.html

Gordon, Michael R., and Bernard E. Trainor. *The General's War: The Inside Story of the Conflict in the Gulf.* New York: Little, Brown and Co., 1994.

Heimbach, Daniel R. "The Bush Just War Doctrine: Genesis and Application of the President's Moral Leadership in the Persian Gulf War." In *From Cold War to New World Order: The Foreign Policy of George H. W. Bush*, edited by Meena Bose and Rosanna Perotti, 441–464. Westport, CT: Greenwood Press, 2002.

Johnson, James Turner, and George Weigel. *Just War and the Gulf War.* Washington, DC: Ethics and Public Policy Center, 1991.

Long, Jerry M. *Saddam's War of Words: Politics, Religion, and the Iraqi Invasion of Kuwait.* Austin: University of Texas Press, 2004.

Patterson, Eric. *Just American Wars: Ethical Dilemmas in U.S. Military History.* New York: Routledge, 2019.

Preston, Andrew. *Sword of the Spirit, Shield of Faith: Religion in American War and Diplomacy.* New York: Alfred A. Knopf, 2012.

Weigel, George. "The Churches & War in the Gulf." *First Things*, March 1991. https://www.firstthings.com/article/1991/03/the-churches-war-in-the-gulf

## Hinduism and War

Although Hinduism is a significant religious tradition globally, it does not have a dominant presence in the United States. There is a long history of Hindu conflict and warfare in Hindu literature and history. Still, the ramifications of that history and contemporary American society have been and continue to be minimal. According to a 2017 study on global religion by the Pew Research Center, over 1.1 billion adherents practice Hinduism worldwide, with over one million in the United States.

The concept of Hinduism originated as a way to describe Eastern religion and practice originating in India—generally agreed by scholars as proximal to the Indus valley. A precursor to Buddhism, Hinduism is compatible with many religions and may be practiced in many forms, including polytheistic (belief in many gods), monotheistic (belief in one god), and atheistic (disbelief in a god or gods). Expanding through East Asia, Hinduism split into four major denominations: Saivism, Shaktism, Vaishnavism, and Smartism.

Hinduism has no singular leader or founder. Historians commonly trace a lineage of *dharma*, or way of life, rooted in religious oral history and texts, including the *Bhagavad Gita*, *Ramayana*, and Vedas scriptures and the Manusmriti manuscripts. Addressing duty, law, conduct, and other dharma concerns, the Manusmriti proscribes the well-known, archaic, and controversial caste system still widely imposed in many contemporary Hindu communities. The caste system, established before 1000 BCE, designates four social classes: (1) Brahmins (priests, teachers); (2) Kshatriyas (rulers, warriors); (3) Vaishyas (farmers, merchants); and (4) Shudras (manual workers). Human rights advocates criticize the caste system as outdated, especially concerning the treatment of those born into families of Dalits, or outcasts. Proponents of the caste system have historically discouraged intermarriage between castes, reinforcing hierarchies to elite and colonial economic and political advantage. This formality is eschewed by Hindu society at the time of this writing; discrimination against lower castes has been outlawed since 1947. Nonetheless, the formal structure is a source of still-existing tensions, including caste-based violence against Dalits.

Americans were interested in Hindu teachings and philosophy long before the transference of Hinduism through immigrant practitioners. Prior to the Immigration and Naturalization Act of 1965—when migration restrictions were loosened, allowing a more significant number of Hindus to move from India to the United States—Hinduism was taught through emissaries brought to address American interests. This initial influx focused more on studying Hinduism through gurus and yogis. South Asian diaspora scholars note a shift in emphasis, from a public fascination with Hinduism and practice to South Asian immigrant preservation of Hindu cultural and religious tradition. It is with this 1960s immigration that temples and organizations began to establish themselves as part of a Hindu American (and in conjunction, a majority of Indian American) infrastructure.

Unlike Buddhism, conversion is not a significant form of Hindu population growth in the United States. Major Hindu umbrella organizations include Vishwa Hindu Parishad of America (VHPA) and Hindu Swayamsevak Sangh (HSS). These organizations are a unifying mechanism that advocates for American Hindus in conjunction with their overseas counterpart organizations in India. Various movements within American Hinduism are political in nature, including conservative and militant factions that support Hindu nationalist causes. Nationalist groups aim to unite Hindus across sectarian lines, often including the controversial and questionable interest of solidifying the creation of a Muslim or Islamic "other."

Before addressing Hindu nationalism, it is worth recognizing the ancient historical background relationship between Hinduism and violence. As Henry O. Thompson notes in his seminal work *World Religions in War and Peace*, "The record of Hindu history is close to unmitigated war" (1988). Hindu ancient history is a story of warriors and conquest throughout the ages. Nomadic Aryans created vast kingdoms as early as the 7th century BCE; the *Ramayana* epic details conquests and violent destruction. Hindu warriors have fought wars against invasion, including against the Greeks, Muslims, and the British. Fighting between Hindus and Muslims in Pakistan and India, ignited by a history of conflict culminating in colonial division, continues in contemporary Asia today.

Participation in violence and war notwithstanding, there are essential components of Hinduism that support peace and nonviolence. Primary in this balance is the concept of *ahimsa*, or nonviolence, in the Padma Purana as one's "highest duty." This respect and reverence for all life is prevalent in Hinduism today. This duty, however, does not preclude the necessity of killing in cases of self-defense or mercy killing.

Is Hindu nationalism relevant in contemporary American geopolitics, and if so, how? Some scholars place the emergence of Hindu nationalism in late 19th-century upper-caste Hindu mobilization as an ideological reaction to European domination. Others focus on the influence of cultural nationalism that started in the 1980s. Hindu nationalist scholar Chetan Bhatt contends that even the newer forms of Hindu nationalism evolved through synthesizing 19th-century archaic concepts with politicized spirituality, religious nationalism, and regional nationalism. To complicate things further, multiple trajectories result in distinct Hindu nationalist movements. Most applicable to contemporary Hindu nationalism in the United States is Bhatt's focus on ideological Hindu nationalism: "that Hindus did or should constitute 'a nation,' and that Indian nationalism was solely or largely coextensive with, and to be based on, Hindu religious or ideological precepts" (Bhatt 2001, 4). More specific to the period following the 1960s, two main political groups dominate the nationalist space: the Bharatiya Janata Party (BJP) and the Vishwa Hindu Parishad (VHP). Both political groups are proponents of Hindu nationalism commonly characterized by human rights groups as authoritarian, populist, xenophobic, and focused on Muslims as "other" and a perceived threat to Hinduism.

In 2014, Narendra Modi of the BJP was elected prime minister of India. A Hindu nationalist, Modi was recently reelected in April and May 2019. The majority of Indian American diaspora identify as Democrats, and only half of Indian Americans are Hindu. Yet, populist support of Modi and Hindu nationalism is significant, as evidenced by the crowd of more than 50,000 people in attendance at a September 2019 "Howdy, Modi" rally held in conjunction with President Donald J. Trump in Houston, Texas. Hindu nationalism enjoys support from this portion of the Indian American diaspora, despite protests from the majority supporting a secular, inclusive concept of Indian democracy and Modi's recent anti-Muslim actions in India. These include the blocking of nearly two million mostly Muslim Indians from Indian citizenship, planned detention camps for people who cannot prove legal Indian residence, and violence against mass arrests of Muslims in Kashmir.

U.S. groups opposed to Modi and Hindu nationalism include the Alliance for Justice and Accountability; groups associated with Indian Christian, Muslim, Sikh, Buddhist, and Dalit minorities; and the U.S. Commission on International Religious Freedom (USCIRF). USCIRF controversially denied Modi a U.S. visa during President George W. Bush's administration, citing violations against religious minorities. Hundreds of Hindu nationalist groups support Modi and the BJP, including the Texas India Forum (a group associated with a far-right precursor to BJP, Rashtriya Swayamsevak Sangh (RSS)), the Hindu Swayamsevak Sangh (HSS), and the Hindu American Foundation.

A strong partnership between the United States and India is generally conducive to world democracy and the world economy. Partnering with Modi and the BJP is a complex geopolitical bargain with both short- and long-term implications for human rights and the support of minorities both in the United States and abroad. To be sure, India is a critical piece of contemporary geopolitical populist and nationalism puzzles.

*See also:* Buddhism and War; Christianity and War; Islam and War; Judaism and War

## Further Reading

Bhatt, Chetan. *Hindu Nationalism: Origins, Ideologies and Modern Myths*. Oxford, UK: Berg, 2001.
Chapple, Christopher Key. "Peace, War, and Violence in Hinduism." *Oxford Bibliographies Online*, January 27, 2011. https://doi.org/10.1093/obo/97801953-99318-0038
Ferguson, John. *War and Peace in the World's Religions*. New York: Oxford University Press, 1978.
Frost, J. William. *A History of Christian, Jewish, Hindu, Buddhist, and Muslim Perspectives on War and Peace*. Lewiston, NY: Edwin Mellen Press, 2004.
Gupta, Vidya Bhushan. *Hinduism in America*. Demarest, NJ: Vid Publications, 2004.
Hemeyer, Julia Corbett. *Religion in America*. London: Routledge, 2016.
Jaffrelot, Christophe. *Hindu Nationalism: A Reader*. Princeton, NJ: Princeton University Press, 2009.
Kumar, Rashmee. "The Network of Hindu Nationalists behind Modi's 'Diaspora Diplomacy' in the U.S." The Intercept, September 25, 2019. https://theintercept.com/2019/09/25/howdy-modi-trump-hindu-nationalism/

Lucia, Amanda. "Hinduism in America." *Oxford Research Encyclopedia of Religion*, January 25, 2017. https://doi.org/10.1093/acrefore/9780199340378.013.436

Mohammad-Arif, Aminah. "The Paradox of Religion: The (Re)Construction of Hindu and Muslim Identities amongst South Asian Diasporas in the United States." *South Asia Multidisciplinary Academic Journal*, no. 1 (2007). https://doi.org/10.4000/samaj.55

Neusner, Jacob, Bruce Chilton, and Robert E. Tully. *Just War in Religion and Politics*. Lanham, MD: University Press of America, 2013.

Reichberg, Gregory M. *Religion, War, and Ethics: A Sourcebook of Textual Traditions*. New York: Cambridge University Press, 2014.

Ross, Jeffrey Ian. *Religion and Violence: An Encyclopedia of Faith and Conflict from Antiquity to the Present*. Armonk, NY: M. E. Sharpe, 2011.

Sharma, Jyotirmaya. *Hindutva: Exploring the Idea of Hindu Nationalism*. New York: HarperCollins, 2016.

Sorabji, Richard, and David Rodin. *The Ethics of War: Shared Problems in Different Traditions*. Aldershot, Hants, UK: Ashgate, 2006.

Subramanian, Courtney. "India Election 2019: Echoes of Trump in Modi's Border Politics." BBC News, May 21, 2019. https://www.bbc.com/news/world-asia-india-48334689

Thompson, Henry O. *World Religions on War and Peace*. Jefferson, NC: McFarland, 1988.

# Holocaust

More than seventy-five years after the end of World War II in 1945, the Holocaust continues to influence American religious, cultural, and political life—especially for American Jews. References to it abound in American political discourse, and its legacy affects many U.S. foreign policy issues, such as human rights, genocide, Palestinian statehood, and U.S.-Arab relations. The memory of the Holocaust is also a concern regarding rising neo-Nazism and anti-Semitism in Europe and elsewhere in the 21st century. Religiously, in the United States and elsewhere, the legacy of the Holocaust affects Jewish-Christian and Jewish-Muslim interfaith dialogue as well as reflection and dialogue within contemporary Judaism and Christianity.

The Holocaust refers to the intentional systematic and state-sponsored persecution and murder of six million European Jews (about two-thirds of the European Jewish population) by the Nazi regime and its allies during World War II. The Nazi regime believed that Jews were racially inferior to Germans and a threat to Germans, the future of Germany, and the Nazi regime. The regime referred to the annihilation of European Jewry as "the Final Solution," a shortening of the German phrase "the Final Solution of the Jewish Question."

The term *holocaust* is derived from Greek, meaning "sacrifice by fire." Presently, and in large part due to the Holocaust, there are only about 1.4 million Jews living in Europe. While Jews were not the only group singled out for destruction by the Nazis, they were by far the largest persecuted group.

Anti-Semitism predates the Holocaust by centuries, but the scale and effects of it during World War II were unparalleled in history. In the United States, before and during the war, there was institutional and individual anti-Semitism that curtailed Jewish immigration policy and also affected the complex political and military response to Jewish persecution and the Holocaust. There were Christian and Jewish leaders in the United States who pleaded for a greater U.S. response, but they were a minority. Ambivalence was a common response, but it was not the only response. There was some anti-Semitism among Protestants and Catholics. For religious leaders who spoke out against the Nazi regime, the alarm often took one of two forms: the persecution was viewed as racial or the persecution was viewed as religious. When it was the latter, it was frequently presented as a forerunner of greater religious persecution, specifically of Christians. Before the war, some religious leaders and denominations did explicitly condemn Nazi anti-Semitism.

Immediately upon release from concentration camps, there were pledges by survivors of "never again" and "never forget." These two commitments have become not only a part of the Holocaust legacy of remembrance and memorialization but also a part of the strong national commitment by Israel as a nation that an event such as the Holocaust will not be repeated and that the nation of Israel will not be destroyed or defeated. These fervent commitments affect U.S.-Israeli relations in that although the two countries are staunch allies, Israeli concerns regarding the proliferation of nuclear weapons in the region, or other political or military threats from other nations, though also a U.S. concern, might strain U.S.-Israeli relations if Israel acted unilaterally. Though such actions are always a difficulty in any international coalition or alliance, the unique history of the Holocaust and Israeli nationhood accentuates the challenges of contemporary international relations.

Despite the revelations of the Holocaust after World War II, anti-Semitism remained part of the last half of the 20th century and continues in the present, as does Holocaust denial. The growing indications and incidents of 21st-century anti-Semitism, especially in the United States and Europe, are a reality, and incidents of contemporary violent anti-Semitism are alarming. Incidents of anti-Semitism on U.S. university campuses are also increasing.

In the United States, education regarding the Holocaust and its memory is found in the common practice of high school students having Holocaust survivor and Nobel Peace Prize recipient Elie Wiesel's book *Night* assigned as part of the educational curriculum. Many students also read Holocaust victim Anne Frank's posthumously published book, *Anne Frank: The Diary of a Young Girl*. The establishment of the United States Holocaust Memorial Museum in Washington, DC, and similar but smaller other museums throughout the country afford the opportunity for further education and awareness. Further, in 2005, the United Nations General Assembly adopted a general resolution (A/RES/60/7, November 1, 2005) declaring January 27 to be an international day of Holocaust remembrance. Along with many nations, the United States annually observes this day of remembrance.

In 2015, almost three-fourths (73%) of responding American Jews in a Pew Research Center survey stated that remembering the Holocaust is an essential aspect of their personal Jewish identity. In part, this also explains why there is strong support for Israel among American Jews. Forty-three percent of respondents stated that caring for Israel was essential to their Jewish identity. Similarly, in the United States, awareness of the Holocaust and religious and political support for Israel is very strong among American evangelicals.

Probably more than any other single event in the last one hundred years, the Holocaust has shaped international law with respect to war crimes, genocide, and human rights. The Holocaust remains a human tragedy that will be a perpetual scar on nations that did little or nothing to prevent it.

***See also:*** Evangelicalism; Genocide; Human Rights; Middle East Conflict; Responsibility to Protect; Wars of Israel; World War II

## Further Reading

Alper, Becka A. "70 years after WWII, the Holocaust Is Still Very Important to American Jews." Pew Research Center, August 13, 2015. https://www.pewresearch.org/fact-tank/2015/08/13/70-years-after-wwii-the-holocaust-is-still-very-important-to-american-jews/

Bergen, Doris L. *The Holocaust: A Concise History*. Rev. ed. New York: Rowman & Littlefield, 2009.

Frank, Anne. *Anne Frank: The Diary of a Young Girl*. New York: Bantam, 1993.

Gordis, Daniel. *We Stand Divided: The Rift between American Jews and Israel*. New York: HarperCollins, 2019.

Greene, Daniel, and Frank Newport. "American Public Opinion and the Holocaust." Gallup Polling Matters, April 23, 2018. https://news.gallup.com/opinion/polling-matters/232949/american-public-opinion-holocaust.aspx

Lipka, Michael. "A Closer Look at Jewish Identity in Israel and the U.S." Pew Research Center, March 16, 2016. https://www.pewresearch.org/fact-tank/2016/03/16/a-closer-look-at-jewish-identity-in-israel-and-the-u-s/

Lipstadt, Deborah E. *Antisemitism: Here and Now*. New York: Schocken Books, 2019.

Mazzenga, Maria, ed. *American Religious Responses to Kristallnacht*. New York: Palgrave Macmillan, 2009.

Pew Research Center. "A Portrait of Jewish Americans." October 1, 2013. https://www.pewforum.org/2013/10/01/jewish-american-beliefs-attitudes-culture-survey/

Pew Research Center. "What Americans Know about the Holocaust." January 22, 2020. https://www.pewforum.org/2020/01/22/what-americans-know-about-the-holocaust/

Popescu, Diana I., and Tanja Schult. "Performative Holocaust Commemoration in the 21st Century." *Holocaust Studies: A Journal of Culture and History* 26, no. 2 (2020): 135–151. https://doi.org/10.1080/17504902.2019.1578452

Rees, Laurence. *The Holocaust: A New History*. New York: Public Affairs, 2018.

Trachtenberg, Barry. *The United States and the Nazi Holocaust*. London: Bloomsbury, 2018.

United Nations. Outreach Programme on the Holocaust. Accessed June 13, 2022. https://www.un.org/en/holocaustremembrance/

United States Holocaust Memorial Museum. "Introduction to the Holocaust." Holocaust Encyclopedia. Accessed March 1, 2020. https://encyclopedia.ushmm.org/content/en/article/introduction-to-the-holocaust

United States Holocaust Memorial Museum. "Kristallnacht: How Did Religious Leaders in the US Respond?" Accessed March 1, 2020. https://www.ushmm.org/research/about-the-mandel-center/initiatives/ethics-religion-holocaust/articles-and-resources/kristallnacht-how-did-religious-leaders-in-the-us-respond

Wiesel, Elie. *Night*. New York: Hill and Wang, 2006.
Wyman, David S. *The Abandonment of the Jews: American and the Holocaust, 1941–1945*. Hinsdale, MA: Plunkett Lake Press, 2018.

# Human Rights

The relationship between religion and human rights in the 21st century is complex and plays out differently in every country and every religion. Religious traditions are often supportive of national and international standards of specific rights and rights in general. The legal traditions of Christianity, Judaism, and Islam have contributed much to contemporary struggles for the recognition of human rights as a whole as well as specific rights. However, there are also many instances of religious dissent and challenges to specific human rights and their implementation. Such instances occur when the doctrine, beliefs, and practices of a religious tradition or community are in disagreement with broader or secular norms of human rights.

Most religious traditions have histories of supporting violence and the violation of human rights at some point. However, most religious traditions have also supported the growth, development, and recognition of human rights—especially since the mid-20th century and the end of World War II. One specific religious concern is that of religious freedom as a human right and its denial in increasing instances of religious persecution wherein human rights are violated on the basis of an individual's or group's religious beliefs. With respect to war and peace, one of the greatest issues in human rights is that of genocide.

Much of the contemporary political concern with human rights is a result of the tragedies of World War II, especially the Holocaust. The intent, intensity, and scale of the actions of the Nazi regime against Jews and other minorities resulted in the deaths of millions of people. "Guilty of crimes against humanity" was the verdict used to condemn the atrocities of the Nazi defendants in Nuremburg, Germany, and Japanese leaders in Tokyo at their post–World War II trials and became a foundation of much contemporary thought on human rights. The nature and extent of human rights is highly debated, but it is not a new idea in Western history.

Recognition of the need to protect human freedom and the dignity of individuals is found in the sacred texts of the world's major religions as well as in other ancient texts, such as the Code of Hammurabi from Babylon (ca. 1780 BCE). In the West, in addition to religious concepts, the idea of rights was built upon Greek and Roman notions of *jus gentium* (law for all peoples).

Many contemporary social and political issues concern human rights. The spectrum is enormous—race relations, torture, religion, abortion, euthanasia, international trade, status of women, immigration, treatment of aboriginal and native peoples, medicine, health care, legal and court procedures, political processes and voting, housing, animals, the environment, sexual orientation, education, water and natural resources, slavery and human trafficking, and many others. Human rights is a global subject, and many of the rights are directly tied to matters of war and peace, especially with respect to civilians and other noncombatants who are frequently caught in the midst of war zones. Rights issues touching on war and peace include torture, refugees, genocide, religious persecution, and religious freedom. In the 21st century, one thinks of conflict in the Middle East and Afghanistan and the many human rights issues, including torture and genocide; Myanmar (Burma) and the Rohingya crisis; western China and the Uyghur crisis; and struggles for political freedom in Hong Kong.

The term *rights* has many meanings, depending on who is using the word and in what context it is being used. Rights may refer to needs required by humans to make life easier or to preserve life or liberty. Others use the word to mean the things humans desire to make life easier. Still others consider rights to be entitlements conferred by the state. Since 1948, when the Universal Declaration of Human Rights (UDHR) was created by the United Nations, governments have defined human rights at the global level via various declarations and the United Nations system. Thus, though *rights* means different things to different people and within different religious traditions, there is a shared framework of meaning or understanding at the intergovernmental level, even though not all governments have ratified all human rights treaties and not all religious traditions agree.

In contemporary rights thought, there are four basic characteristics of human rights. The first is that regardless of the origin or justification (secular or religious), human rights represent individual or group claims for the shaping and sharing of things such as power, wealth, resources, and other human goods. The second is that *human rights* refers to things that are essential rather than nonessential claims (although what is considered essential varies, with some lists very long and others very short—perhaps the right to life or the right to equal freedom of opportunity). The third is that human rights are usually qualified by restrictions so that the rights of one individual or group do not negate the rights of others. The final characteristic is that if something is determined to be a human right, it is considered universal in character, equally possessed by all people.

In political theory and human rights literature and discussions as well as in international law, there are also distinctions between what are known as first-, second-, and third-generation rights. Additionally, there are arguments over categories of rights, such as economic and social rights versus civil and political rights. When framed within political processes, there are debates as to whether rights should be understood as means of defining the goals of state policy or as means of providing jurisdictional limits on state policy.

First-generation rights are rights that were formulated several centuries ago and are considered rights possessed by an individual that the state cannot usurp. They are prepolitical rights that antedate the state and international relations, and the purpose of government and public authority is to secure these rights. They are reflected in documents such as the English Magna Carta (1215), the American Declaration of Independence (1776), the French Declaration of the Rights of Man (1789), and the U.S. Bill of Rights in the 1791 U.S. Constitution (though there are significant differences in these documents). These rights are primarily derived from 17th- and 18th-century revolutions in Britain, France, and the United States. First-generation rights are rights that the government cannot take away and are dominated by political and civil rights. These include freedom of speech, freedom of assembly, freedom of the press, and freedom of religion. Because they are rights that cannot be taken away by government ("freedom from"), they are also sometimes referred to as "negative rights" (although some require affirmative government action).

It is first-generation rights that are articulated in Articles 2–21 of the UDHR (1948). Specific articles address matters of war and religion, or both:

- Freedom from racial, gender, ethnic, religious, national, and other equal forms of discrimination (Art. 2)
- Right to life, liberty, and security of person (Art. 3)
- Freedom from slavery or involuntary servitude (Art. 4)
- Freedom from torture or cruel, inhuman, or degrading treatment or punishment (Art. 5)
- Right to asylum from persecution (Art. 14)
- Right to a nationality (Art. 15)
- Freedom of thought, conscience, and religion (Art. 18)

- Freedom of opinion and expression (Art. 19)
- Freedom of peaceful assembly and association (Art. 20)

Each of these rights has a long history behind its articulation, and as stated in the UN declaration, these are considered universal. Some theorists argue that these are the only true or recognized human rights.

Second-generation rights are rights that pertain to social and economic welfare and were generated in the 19th and early 20th centuries, largely under socialist thinkers such as Karl Marx. These rights pertain to things for which the state is considered to be responsible and must provide its citizens. They are minimum social benefits of living in an industrialized and modern society and are considered to include the rights to housing, education, health care, and social security. In each instance, the amount guaranteed is unspecified. Many of these second-generation rights are a major part of contemporary American political discourse. Second-generation rights are largely "rights to" and are also referred to as "positive rights," though the term itself can be broad and confusing depending on its usage. These rights seek to minimize national and economic exploitation and are articulated in the Universal Declaration of Human Rights in Articles 22–27.

Third-generation rights emerged in the latter half of 20th-century political thought. When one speaks of these rights, the focus is more on groups than individuals; individuals are considered to possess them because a person is a member of the group. Particular attention has been given to groups such as women, children, and ethnic or Indigenous minorities in a specific area. Some theorists also add group rights to individual rights and argue for things such as the right to human security, the right to peace, the right to a good environment, and the right to live in a democracy. There has been considerable debate in the last fifty years over the priority that should be given to each category of right as well as which rights are truly in each category. Debate over the universality of rights versus culturally conditioned rights has also been prominent.

Which generations of rights one accepts (if any) as well as whether one accepts some or all the rights in a specific generation becomes a complex and intricate matter—especially when one adds the religious dimension.

***See also:*** Evangelicalism; Genocide; Holocaust; Protestant Denominations; Religious Freedom and Religious Persecution; Responsibility to Protect; Roman Catholicism; Torture; United Nations

## Further Reading

Griffiths, Martin, and Terry O'Callaghan. *International Relations: The Key Concepts*. London: Routledge, 2002.

May, Larry. *Crimes against Humanity: A Normative Account*. Cambridge, UK: Cambridge University Press, 2005.

Nichols, Joel A. "Evangelicals and Human Rights: The Continuing Ambivalence of Evangelical Christians' Support for Human Rights." *Journal of Law and Religion* 24, no. 2 (2008–2009): 629–692.

Turek, Lauren Francis. *To Bring the Good News to All Nations: Evangelical Influence on Human Rights and U.S. Foreign Policy*. Ithaca, NY: Cornell University Press, 2020.

Witte, John, and M. Christian Green. *Religion and Human Rights: An Introduction*. New York: Oxford University Press, 2011.

Witte, John, and Johan D. van der Vyver, eds. *Religious Human Rights in Global Perspective: Religious Perspectives*. Dordrecht, Netherlands: Martinus Nijhoff Publishers, 1996.

# I

## Iraq War

A little more than ten years separated the American presence in Iraq in the Gulf War (August 1990–February 1991) and the Iraq War (2003–2011), and Iraq and turmoil in the Middle East were never far from being headline news. Known in the West by its military name, Operation Iraqi Freedom, the war had two phases. The first phase, March–April 2003, was the coalition of military forces of the United States, Great Britain, and small contingents from other allied nations fighting the Iraqi military of the regime of Iraqi president Saddam Hussein (1937–2006). The second and much longer phase (2003–2011) involved a U.S.-led occupation of Iraq, attempts at establishing a stable democratic government, and an insurgency that lasted several years.

In the aftermath of the September 11, 2001, terrorist attacks, the George W. Bush administration became concerned that Iraq's support for terrorist groups, its alleged ongoing production and stockpiling of weapons of mass destruction (United Nations inspections during the 1990s found evidence of WMD violations of the cessation of hostilities agreement from the Gulf War), and its belligerence toward inspectors from the United Nations made regime change through military action in Iraq desirable and necessary. The idea was controversial in the United States and internationally, but with the failure of Iraq to follow UN resolutions, the U.S.-led coalition prevailed and preemptively struck Iraq on March 20, 2003, after Saddam Hussein rejected the Bush administration's ultimatum of forty-eight hours to leave Iraq.

In the months before the war, many influential religious leaders and groups had spoken about the war, and the majority of them opposed it. Globally, the Vatican, Eastern Orthodox patriarchs, the archbishop of Canterbury, and the World Council of Churches issued statements of opposition. Similarly, the World Evangelical Alliance urged restraint and supported seeking a peaceful path to resolution. Traditional American peace churches such as Mennonites and Quakers likewise opposed the war.

Surveys during the week before the hostilities of the war commenced found that only about 10 percent of Americans cited their religious values or religious leaders as shaping their views on Iraq. Almost 60 percent of those attending religious services said that their priest, minister, rabbi, or religious leader had spoken about the war, but of those who spoke, only 21 percent had expressed an opinion (Pew Research Center, "Survey," 2003). Interestingly, even though personal religious values were not a major factor in American support or opposition to the war, 15 percent of Americans thought religious leaders were saying too much about the war, and 32 percent believed they were saying too little. For Americans opposing the war, 42 percent wanted religious leaders to say more, and for Americans supporting the war, 28 percent wanted religious leaders to be more vocal. The majority of Muslim and Jewish Americans opposed the war.

Even with strong religious opposition to the war overall, Americans initially favored the war by a ratio of two to one (Pew Research Center, "Different Faiths," 2003, 1, 11). Support for the war diminished over several years such that by 2007 support and opposition were more balanced, though the majority of Americans opposed the war. Support for the war diminished when the expectation of finding weapons of mass destruction (WMDs) in Iraq was not realized and also in the aftermath of revelations of torture being used to gain intelligence. The torture debate was not limited to events in Iraq; it extended to actions in Afghanistan and the treatment of enemy combatants being held at the U.S. military facilities in Guantanamo Bay, Cuba, and other undisclosed sites globally in allied nations.

Just as U.S. citizens were religiously divided on the war, they were also divided politically. Some argued that the war was legitimate as a continuation of the Gulf War and was morally justified within the framework of the just war tradition. Others dissented and argued that war in Iraq was not justified and should not be linked ideologically, politically, or strategically to the war in Afghanistan and the larger U.S. military response to terrorism.

The extent to which President Bush and, to a lesser extent, Prime Minister Tony Blair of the United Kingdom were influenced by personal religious values is debated. However, religious language was prevalent in President Bush's statements about the war, and religious rhetoric was used by the administration.

The aftermath of the war has been as significant and more challenging than the war itself for all concerned. Although the religious and political dynamics in the United States of support for and opposition to the war were complex, there was (and remains) much greater religious and political complexity in Iraq, especially between Sunni and Shia Muslims. An oft-overlooked residual effect of the war and ongoing concern in Iraq (and elsewhere in the Middle East) is the oppression and persecution of religious minorities, including Yazidis, Baha'is, Christians, Jews, and others. The future of each of these religious traditions in the region remains uncertain. Little understood by the American public and many U.S. political leaders, the centuries-old religious split and shifting and evolving Iraqi political allegiances and dynamics created violence and political instability that continues to affect the nation and the region. This instability has been exacerbated by the presence and involvement of other nations, such as Iran and Syria, as well as other Western powers. Further, the postwar rise of the so-called Islamic State (IS) and the conflict it generated fueled instability. The 21st-century tragedy and uncertainty of Iraq remains a poignant reminder of the destructive power of the combination of politics and religion with respect to war.

*See also:* Afghanistan War; American Peace Churches; Christianity and War; Ecclesiastical Statements on War and Peace; Evangelicalism; Gulf War; Islam and War; Judaism and War; Just War Tradition; Middle East Conflict; Pacifism; Presidential Faith and War; Protestant Denominations; Religion, Conflict, and Geopolitics; Roman Catholicism; Terrorism; Torture; Weapons of Mass Destruction

## Further Reading

Cole, Darrell. "The First and Second Gulf Wars." In *America and the Just War Tradition*, edited by Mark David Hall and J. Daryl Charles, 251–270. Notre Dame, IN: University of Notre Dame Press, 2019.

Froese, Paul, and F. Carson Mencken. "A U.S. Holy War? The Effects of Religion on Iraq War Policy Attitudes." *Social Science Quarterly* 90, no. 1 (March 2009): 103–116.

Gardner, Frank. "Iraq's Christians 'Close to Extinction.'" BBC News, May 23, 2019. https://www.bbc.com/news/world-middle-east-48333923

Jacobsen, Gary C. "A Tale of Two Wars: Public Opinion on the U.S. Military Interventions in Afghanistan and Iraq." *Presidential Studies Quarterly* 40, no. 4 (December 2010): 585–610.

Johnson, James Turner. *The War to Oust Saddam Hussein: Just War and the New Face of Conflict*. New York: Rowman & Littlefield, 2005.

Jones, Jeffrey M. "Among Religious Groups, Jewish Americans Most Strongly Oppose War." Gallup News Service, March 23, 2007. https://news.gallup.com

/poll/26677/among-religious-groups-jewish-americans-most-strongly-oppose-war.aspx
Patterson, Eric. *Just American Wars: Ethical Dilemmas in U.S. Military History.* New York: Routledge, 2019.
Pew Research Center. "Different Faiths, Different Messages." March 19, 2003. https://www.pewresearch.org/politics/2003/03/19/different-faiths-different-messages/
Pew Research Center. "Religious Groups Issue Statement on War with Iraq." Compiled by Religious News Service, March 19, 2003. https://www.pewforum.org/2003/03/19/publicationpage-aspxid616/
Pew Research Center. "Survey: Americans Hearing about Iraq from the Pulpit, but Religious Faith Not Defining Opinions." March 19, 2003. https://www.pewforum.org/2003/03/19/survey-americans-hearing-about-iraq-from-the-pulpit-but-religious-faith-not-defining-opinions/
Preston, Andrew. *Sword of the Spirit, Shield of Faith: Religion in American War and Diplomacy.* New York: Alfred A. Knopf, 2012.
Rasche, Stephen M. *The Disappearing People: The Tragic Fate of Christians in the Middle East.* New York: Bombardier Books, 2020.
Ricks, Thomas E. *Fiasco: The American Military Adventure in Iraq 2003–2005.* New York: Penguin, 2007.
Roy, Oindrila. "Religious Roots of War Attitudes in the United States: Insights from Iraq, Afghanistan, and the Persian Gulf." *Foreign Policy Analysis* 12, no. 3 (July 2016): 258–274. https://academic.oup.com/fpa/article/12/3/258/1751230
Steinfels, Peter. "Beliefs; Churches and Ethicists Loudly Oppose the Proposed War on Iraq, but Deaf Ears Are Many." *New York Times*, September 28, 2002, A-15.
Tucker, Spencer C., and Paul G. Pierpaoli Jr., eds. *U.S. Conflicts in the 21st Century: Afghanistan War, Iraq War, and the War on Terror.* 3 vols. Santa Barbara, CA: ABC-CLIO, 2016.
Volker, Kurt. "Bush, Chirac, and the War in Iraq." *Foreign Policy*, November 15, 2016. https://foreignpolicy.com/2016/11/15/bush-chirac-and-the-war-in-iraq/

# Islam and War

The convergence of religion, war, and politics in the 21st-century United States has largely related to conflicts in nations with a majority Muslim population and against Islamist nonstate actors such as al-Qaeda, the so-called Islamic State in Iraq and the Levant (ISIL or ISIS), Boko Haram, Abu Sayyaf, and other Islamist terrorist organizations. As with all religions,

Islam has a long history of traditions and teachings on matters of war and peace. There is no single Islamic perspective, and the spectrum of teachings and belief is diverse, including contemporary manifestations of radical and apocalyptic expressions of war.

Within and between the two major traditions of Islam—Sunni and Shia—one finds a variety of understandings of war and peace arising out of complex historical and political contexts. Since the 1970s, there has been a renewal of politicized Islam that is driven by economics and the political failures of Arab governments, often repressive, to meet citizens' needs and expectations. Seeking strength in religion, some Muslims have accepted radicalized interpretations of Islam that expound and support violence, terrorism, and warfare. Islamic perspectives on warfare vary widely, and as with views of warfare in other religious traditions, they are frequently influenced by political, cultural, and national identities.

Demographically, though increasing, Islam in the United States is not a large religion. Yet, there are Muslims in Congress and serving in numerous state and local political positions of power and authority. Further, American Muslims have served in the U.S. military since the American Revolution. American Muslims represent a little over 1 percent of the total U.S. population and are politically diverse. They also represent the spectrum of belief and diversity within Islam.

While some U.S. citizens who are Muslim have been radicalized or self-radicalized such that their beliefs have manifested in violent acts, these instances have been isolated cases and condemned by American Muslim leaders and Muslim citizens. For example, the *fatwa* (religious ruling) from an Islamic juristic body known as the Fiqh Council of North America has condemned religious extremism and violence. Even so, there have been instances of anti-Muslim violence in the United States as well as misinformation and misunderstanding regarding Islam. Conversely, there have been several incidents of violent attacks and numerous deaths by self-radicalized American Islamists.

Although the history of warfare in Islam is centuries old, significant American awareness of it, especially in connection with Islamic political thought, did not emerge until the 1979–1981 Iran hostage crisis, when fifty-two American diplomats and citizens from the U.S. embassy in Tehran, Iran, were held captive by supporters of the Iranian Revolution. In its aftermath, there were terrorist acts with strong ties to militant Islam (Sunni and Shia) during the 1980s and 1990s, primarily in the Middle East and Africa. However, it was the September 11, 2001, terrorist attacks and the subsequent U.S.-led coalition invasions of Afghanistan and Iraq that brought Islam's history and teachings regarding war to the forefront of American religious and political discussion and debate. Twenty-first-century American support for and antagonism against Islam is unprecedented in U.S. political and religious history.

The major teaching with respect to war in Islam surrounds the concept of *jihad*, which literally means "struggle" or "striving." The term and its derivatives occur about forty times in the Qur'an. In Islam, *jihad* has a connotation of something that is good and an endeavor that is praiseworthy. It may be a personal and spiritual struggle against one's evil inclinations, or it may be a struggle that is pursued for the sake of Islam and the *umma* (the entire global community of Islam brought together by common beliefs). A secondary meaning of *jihad* is that of regulating warfare with divine sanction in defense of Islam.

Within the Qur'an, the understanding and usage of *jihad* has two dimensions. The first is *sabr*, which connotates "patient forbearance" by Muslims toward the challenges of life they face and those who wish them harm. The second term, *qital*, or "fighting," is the one normally associated with warfare. As in other religions, terminology in sacred texts has lexical histories and nuances as well as the application of those texts in cultural practice and history. Beyond the Qur'an, in later Islamic texts known as the Hadith, the two dimensions of *sabr* and *qital* came to be known as "*jihād al-nafs* (the internal spiritual struggle against the lower self) and *jihād al-sayf* (the physical combat with the sword), respectively. They were also respectively called *al-jihād al-akbar* (the greater jihad) and *al-jihād al-aṣghar* (the lesser jihad)" (Afsaruddin 2020).

Historians of Islam and Qur'anic interpretation divide the doctrine of jihad into four phases, and all of them date from the early history of Islam and the Prophet Muhammad's ministry (ca. 622–632 CE). The phases are the following: 1. Nonconfrontation (Qur'an 15:94–95); 2. Defensive fighting (Qur'an 22:39–40); 3. Initiating attack allowed but within strictures (Qur'an 2:217); and 4. Unrestricted warfare against all pagans (and perhaps against all unbelievers) at all times (Qur'an 9:5) (Firestone 1999, 47–66). In the fourth phase, Qur'an 9:29 is understood to be applicable: "Fight those who believe not in Allah nor the Last Day, nor hold that forbidden which hath been forbidden by Allah and His Messenger, nor acknowledge the religion of Truth, (even if they are) of the People of the Book [Jews and Christians], until they pay the Jizya [annual tax on non-Muslims] with willing submission, and feel themselves subdued" (Ali

1937). "People of the Book" may come under the political rule of Islam, but other religious traditions or those with no tradition must convert to Islam or fight Islam should the circumstances arise.

Jihad is legitimate only when sanctioned by a recognized and authoritative religious leader (i.e., the imam, caliph, or representatives of him). In recent years, Islamist terrorist groups have claimed the right to pronounce jihad, but such attempts and pronouncements are rejected within the larger Muslim population and religious divisions as invalid. Once jihad is declared, there are specific guidelines, regulations, and prohibitions in Sunni and Shia law that govern Muslim warfare and are meant to protect noncombatants and others.

As in all religious traditions, what is written in religious texts must be interpreted and applied to its followers. It is in the interpretation and application of the Islamic texts through the centuries that a spectrum of action based on the texts has occurred. In the 19th, 20th, and 21st centuries, there have been added geopolitical dimensions that have created national and international instability in many countries with a majority Muslim population.

Radical and aggressive interpretations of jihad and Islamic teachings on war in the last several decades, especially in the Afghan wars of the late 20th and early 21st centuries, generated significant debate within Islam with respect to jihad and support for those who were fighting against the Soviet Union's presence in Afghanistan and later against the United States and its allies. Additionally, those within Islam who supported jihad in these instances (including the terrorists acts of 9/11 and other attacks) argued that Muslims they deemed apostate and Muslim political regimes deemed apostate and corrupt were also legitimate targets of jihad. Such a view created what has been termed by them to be either jihad against "the near enemy" (Muslim governments refusing to implement sharia—Islamic law) or "the far enemy" (non-Muslim governments that support "the near enemy") or occupy Muslim territory (such as U.S. and allied troops and bases in Muslim countries). For these groups, the ultimate goal of jihad is the unification of all Muslims globally into a Islamic state upheld by sharia. Although this is a common desire among radical Islamists, there is not unanimity with respect to the best strategy for achieving this goal.

As in other religious traditions, American Muslims represent a spectrum of involvement in politics. Some have resisted it based on a religious distinction between what is termed *dar-al-Islam* (political governance that is based on Islamic norms) and *dar-al-Kufr* (non-Islamic governance). In the United States, Muslims have historically been hesitant to enter public politics, although that has changed (with hesitation by some) since the events of 9/11, and there has been more public political participation. Two prominent American Muslim political organizations addressing U.S. domestic and foreign policy matters are the United Muslims of America (UMA), established in 1982, and the Muslim Political Affairs Council (MPAC), founded in 1988 and representing a broad group of national Islamic organizations.

*See also:* Afghanistan War; Apocalypticism; Christianity and War; Contemporary Non-U.S. Conflicts; Gulf War; Hinduism and War; Iraq War; Judaism and War; Just War Tradition; Middle East Conflict; Religious Texts; Terrorism; September 11, 2001, Terrorist Attacks

## Further Reading

Afsaruddin, Asma. "Jihad." *Encyclopedia Britannica*, February 28, 2020. https://www.britannica.com/topic/jihad

Ali, A. Yusuf, trans. "The Holy Qur'an." April 4, 1937. https://quranyusufali.com

Considine, Craig. *Islam in America: Exploring the Issues*. Santa Barbara, CA: ABC-CLIO, 2019.

Cook, David. *Contemporary Muslim Apocalyptic Literature*. Syracuse, NY: Syracuse University Press, 2005.

Cook, David. *Understanding Jihad*. 2nd ed. Berkeley, CA: University of California Press, 2015.

DeRose, Jason. "U.S. Muslim Scholars Issue Edict against Terrorism." National Public Radio, July 28, 2005. https://www.npr.org/templates/story/story.php?storyId=4775588

Diamant, Jeff. "American Muslims Are Concerned—but Also Satisfied with Their Lives." Pew Research Center, July 26, 2017. https://www.pewresearch.org/fact-tank/2017/07/26/american-muslims-are-concerned-but-also-satisfied-with-their-lives/

Firestone, Reuven. *Jihad: The Origin of Holy War in Islam*. Oxford, UK: Oxford University Press, 1999.

Johnson, James Turner. *The Holy War Idea in Western and Islamic Traditions*. University Park: Pennsylvania State University Press, 1997.

Kelsay, John. *Arguing the Just War in Islam*. Cambridge, MA: Harvard University Press, 2007.

Khadduri, Majid. *War and Peace in the Law of Islam*. Baltimore: Johns Hopkins University Press, 1955.

Khan, M. A. Muqtedar. "American Muslims as Allies in the War on Terrorism." In *A Practical Guide to Winning the War on Terrorism*, edited by Adam M. Garfinkle, 117–129. Stanford, CA: Hoover Institution Press, 2004.

McCants, William. *ISIS: The Apocalypse: The History, Strategy and Doomsday Vision of the Islamic State*. New York: Palgrave Macmillan, 2015.

Mohamed, Besheer. "New Estimates Show U.S. Muslim Population Continues to Grow." Pew Research Center, January 3, 2018. https://www.pewresearch.org/fact-tank/2018/01/03/new-estimates-show-u-s-muslim-population-continues-to-grow/

The Pluralism Project and Harvard University. "Muslims and American Politics." 2020. https://pluralism.org/files/pluralism/files/muslims_and_american_politics.pdf

Reichberg, Gregory M., Henrik Syse, and Nicole M. Hartwell, eds. *Religion, War, and Ethics: A Sourcebook of Textual Traditions*. New York: Cambridge University Press, 2014.

# J

## Judaism and War

Jewish teachings regarding war and peace are centuries old, but they are extremely significant in the 21st century. The religious and political demographics of the United States in the 21st century are changing faster than many observers expected, but there remains in the political parties and religious traditions a core of individuals who constitute a significant population within each party and tradition. Similar to evangelicals and Roman Catholics within American Christianity, Jewish participation in American politics and public life remains a vibrant voice with respect to domestic and foreign policy—especially with respect to support for Israel and concern for the involvement of the United States and other nations in conflict in the Middle East. In the United States, approximately 2 percent of the total population is Jewish, and yet the voice of Jewish Americans (secular and religious) is a strong presence in American politics and has been growing since the mid-20th century.

American Jews have served in the U.S. armed forces and participated in every war in which the United States has engaged since before the American Revolution. Orthodox, Conservative, and Reformed Jewish military members serve in all branches of the U.S. military, and rabbis representing each of the three traditions serve as military chaplains.

The great textual sources of Judaism have been instrumental in creating a body of literature on war and peace within Judaism. Texts such as the Bible, the Talmud, the Mishnah, midrash, and other later codes and commentaries have multiple passages and discussions of war and peace. The commentaries and rabbinical writings through the centuries are not monolithic in their interpretations of war and peace. However, there are broad trends and categories that one finds in them, such as distinctions between obligatory wars, optional wars, and preventive or preemptive wars.

Principles of conduct in warfare and distinctions between combatants and noncombatants are also found within the texts.

Historically and experientially, there are many events that have shaped contemporary American Jewish attitudes regarding war, peace, and politics. Among these are centuries of anti-Semitism and expulsion from the regions and homes in which European Jews lived, pogroms in eastern Europe and Russia, the experience and memories of the Holocaust, the creation and international recognition of the nation of Israel in 1948, the 20th-century wars of Israel, especially the Israeli war of independence (1947–1949), the Suez Crisis (October 1956), the Six-Day War (June 1967), the Yom Kippur War (October 1973), and the First Intifada (1987–1993). During the Gulf War (1991), Israel did not respond to missile attacks against it from Iraq, but the event gained international attention and concern.

In 2015, almost three-fourths (73%) of American Jews responding to a Pew Research Center survey stated that remembering the Holocaust is an essential aspect of their personal Jewish identity. In part, this also explains why there is strong support for Israel among American Jews. Further, 43 percent of respondents stated that caring for Israel was essential to their Jewish identity. These responses reflect the deep historical and theological elements of the identity with the land and geographic region of Israel as well as support for Israel as a nation. They also demonstrate the significance of the meaning and memory of the Holocaust—an event that affected every realm of Jewish life and belief, regardless of one's national citizenship. Commitments that the Holocaust will not be repeated are also linked to contemporary Jewish thought on war and peace.

More recently, in the 21st century, the Second Intifada, also known as the Al-Aqsa Intifada in Israel and disputed territories (2000–2005); the Lebanon War (2006); the Gaza War (2008–2009); the September 11, 2001, terrorist attacks; the wars in Afghanistan and Iraq; continued political unrest in the Middle East; and concern regarding Iran as a potential nuclear weapons power provide ongoing headlines for religious and political commentary and action. Each of these affects American Jewish political interests, even when American forces are not involved.

As found in Christianity, Islam, and other major religious traditions, there is also a long history of addressing issues of war and peace in Judaism. Throughout the centuries, there have been principles and practices regarding war and peace that are considered normative within Judaism, but they have not received universal acceptance by its practitioners. Every religious tradition has a spectrum of belief and practice within. Within contemporary Judaism, issues of war and peace are made more complex in application when they are spoken of with respect to or applied to the secular political nation of Israel (by Israeli Jews and non-Israeli Jews).

Judaism has 3,000 years of written and oral tradition upon which it draws for issues of war and peace. With respect to Jewish texts on war and peace, there are deep roots in the Hebrew scripture (the Christian Old Testament), especially Deuteronomy 20, which gives biblical legislation for conduct in war (*jus in bello*) but not the conditions for going to war (*jus ad bellum*). Verses regarding war and the environment and exemption from military service are also found in this passage. Interpretations formulated by rabbis of this text and other narratives of war in the Hebrew scriptures are recorded in the Babylonian Talmud. With the Bible and Talmud as a reference point and starting point, there has been continuous discussion and development of war and peace in Judaism through the centuries and extending to the present.

By the time of the compilation of the Babylonian Talmud around 500 CE, Jews no longer had a political state or independence and were in a centuries-long diaspora. However, the rabbis speak of war in the Talmud, and their discussions may be grouped into three broad categories: *milhemet hova* (obligatory war), *milhemet reshut* (optional war), and preemptive, or perhaps preventive, war. Unlike the Christian and now secular just war tradition in which one asks whether a war is just or unjust, rabbinic discussions focus on whether a war is obligatory or optional. A defensive war *is* obligatory (just); preemptive action *may* or *may not* be obligatory.

Within the biblical text, concepts of proportionality and self-defense are found in Exodus 21 and 22, and the concept of protecting a third party is found in Deuteronomy 22. Although these passages were written in the context of criminal justice, later rabbinic interpretations extrapolated principles of war from them.

Observant Jewish citizens in the United States (or any country) balance religious values and national values and actions. Within Judaism, there is much that addresses issues of 21st-century warfare, human rights, and international law. The overlap between principles in secular ethics and religious ethics finds much common ground within Judaism. In concerns of war and peace, there are strong principles within Judaism, but the application of those principles in contemporary international relations and conflicts remains a challenge. However, when prudently and appropriately applied, the principles uphold a major tenet of Jewish thought and practice—*tikkun olam* ("repair the world"). The Hebrew term dates to the Mishnaic period in the first two centuries of the Common Era and teaches that Jews have a responsibility to engage in acts that enhance the world. Such ethical actions, when necessary, may include violent acts of war. In the 21st century, secular and religious American Jews agree that there is much in the world needing repair. For them, active engagement in the American political system is one tool for making such repairs and supporting justice—locally, nationally, and internationally.

*See also:* Gulf War; Holocaust; Iraq War; Islam and War; Just War Tradition; Middle East Conflict; Religious Texts; Rhetoric, Sermons, and Prayers; Terrorism; Wars of Israel; Weapons of Mass Destruction

## Further Reading

Adams, Peter. *Politics, Faith, and the Making of American Judaism*. Lansing: University of Michigan Press, 2014.

Afterman, Adam, and Gedaliah Afterman. "'Rise Up and Kill Him First': On Modern Attempts to Create a Jewish Ethics of War." *Nova et Vetera* 10, no. 4 (Fall 2012): 1183–1213.

Dorff, Elliot N., and Danya Ruttenberg, eds. *Jewish Choices, Jewish Voices: War and National Security*. Philadelphia: Jewish Publication Society, 2010.

Eisen, Robert. *The Peace and Violence of Judaism: From the Bible to Modern Zionism*. New York: Oxford University Press, 2011.

Firestone, Reuven. *Holy War in Judaism: The Fall and Rise of a Controversial Idea*. New York: Oxford University Press, 2012.

Goldberg, Edwin C. *Swords and Plowshares: Jewish Views on War and Peace*. New York: URJ Press, 2006.

Kimelman, Reuven. "Judaism, War, and Weapons of Mass Destruction." *Conservative Judaism* 56 (Fall 2003): 36–56.

Krasner, Jonathan. "The Place of Tikkun Olam in American Jewish Life." *Jewish Political Studies Review* 25, nos. 3/4 (Fall 2013): 59–98.

Lipka, Michael. "A Closer Look at Jewish Identity in Israel and the U.S." Pew Research Center, March 16, 2016. https://www.pewresearch.org/fact-tank/2016/03/16/a-closer-look-at-jewish-identity-in-israel-and-the-u-s/

Moore, Deborah Dash. *GI Jews: How World War II Changes a Generation*. Cambridge, MA: Belknap Press, 2006.

Pew Research Center. "Religious Landscape Study." 2014. https://www.pewforum.org/religious-landscape-study/

Schiffman, Lawrence, and Joel B. Wolowelsky. *War and Peace in the Jewish Tradition*. New York: Yeshiva University Press, 2007.

Solomon, Norman. "Judaism and the Ethics of War." *International Review of the Red Cross* 87, no. 858 (June 2005): 295–309.

Wald, Kenneth D. "The Choosing People: Interpreting the Puzzling Politics of American Jewry." *Politics and Religion* 8 (2015): 4–35.

Wilkes, George. "Judaism and Justice in War." In *Just War in Comparative Perspective*, edited by Paul Robinson, 6–23. Burlington, VT: Ashgate Publishing, 2003.

# Just War Tradition

The just war tradition is a centuries-old Western moral, ethical, legal, and philosophical framework for political leaders, diplomats, and policymakers to consider when thinking about and making decisions regarding war and peace. Religious and secular proponents of it have used it to support and reject recent American wars. The tradition seeks to address the rights and wrongs of warfare and does so by drawing upon a considerable history of thought—much of it originally informed by Christianity (although in contemporary society, there are secular and religious models of the just war tradition).

Historically, just war moral reasoning is the normative and mediating position for understanding issues related to war, peace, and the use of force. It has a long and rich history in the Western cultural and intellectual tradition and has received renewed attention from secular as well as religious advocates in the last fifty years. It promotes consensual thinking about justice as that which is due all individuals (as per the thought of Aristotle and Aquinas) based on our shared humanity. In part, its purpose is to provide moral rationale to help undergird a vision of responsible policy, statecraft, and use of military force when necessary to secure the protection, public good, and flourishing of civil society in a nation. The tradition deals with considerations of events occurring before war, activities in war, and activities and responsibilities after war. In recent American religious history and military history, it has informed the responses of many denominations and religious groups, especially with respect to conflict in the Balkans, Afghanistan, and Iraq.

Throughout its development since the era of Plato and Aristotle in the 5th and 4th centuries BCE, the just war tradition has served three important functions. First, its proponents have sought to minimize the occurrence and devastation of war. Global eradication of war may not ever become a reality, but it is realistic to work toward the progressive limitation of war. Second, the tradition provides a common moral framework and language for discussing issues of war in the public and private arenas, including religious contexts. Third, the tradition continues to provide moral guidance to individuals in the development of their consciences, responsibilities, and responses to issues of war. It is not a static tradition. Rather, through the ages, it has demonstrated flexibility to adapt to new circumstances and technologies. Nor is the tradition a monolithic one. It is instead a multiplicity of closely related voices that constitute a unified field of inquiry and judgment that can be applied practically to matters of war when they arise.

Heavily influenced by Christian history and theology, early proponents of the just war tradition also drew from Greek philosophy and Roman law, looking to thinkers such as Plato (428/427 or 424/423–348/347 BCE), Aristotle (384–322 BCE), and Cicero (106–43 BCE). Within Christianity, just war thought emerges in the writings of Ambrose (ca. 330–397 CE) and Augustine (354–430 CE). Both writers discuss the moral criteria for the use of coercive force and argue that Christian love requires the protection and defense of innocent third parties. Their thought, especially Augustine's, dominated Western theology and philosophy throughout the Middle Ages.

In the 13th century Thomas Aquinas (1225–1274) continued the thought of Augustine and the tradition, arguing that justice and charity are not at odds with one another. Justice is the right ordering of society for the sake of social peace, and because it is possible for a just peace or an unjust peace to exist, the former is the goal even if it involves going to war to gain such a final state of peace. Because a tyrant or dictator can have peace, the goal in the just war tradition is not simply peace, but just peace.

In the centuries following Aquinas, through the Renaissance, Reformation era, Enlightenment, and in the late 19th and 20th centuries, the tradition continued to develop with numerous thinkers and proponents. With the rise of the nation-state after the Treaty of Westphalia (1648) and the rise of international law, international relations, and the increasing separation of religion and the state in the West, the just war tradition became separate from Christian theology as a functional model in international affairs. Therefore, presently, although the tradition has a Christian heritage as part of its intellectual genealogy, it is possible to speak of both a Christian just war perspective and a secular just war perspective. The tenets of the latter remain firmly embedded in international law, especially the law of armed conflict.

Within the Christian just war tradition, and building upon the thought of Augustine, Aquinas, and many others, ideas of war and peace are a subset of the idea of citizenship and the concern that Christians not abdicate civic responsibilities. The structure of the tradition developed such that categories were derived for governing whether, ethically, a nation should to go to war—"justice on the way to war" (*jus ad bellum*)—and, if so, how a government should proceed in the midst of war with respect to the employment of military force such that there is "justice in war" (*jus in bello*). In the late 20th and 21st centuries, there has arisen an emphasis on a third stage, or stage three category, of just war known as "justice after war" (*jus post bellum*).

Within the first two categories of *jus ad bellum* and *jus in bello*, there are usually seven principles or components required for the war to be considered a just war: just cause, right intention, last resort, formal declaration, limited objectives, proportionate means, and noncombatant immunity. The first five apply as a nation is "on the way to war" (*jus ad bellum*), and the final two apply to military forces "in the midst of war" (*jus in bello*). In the justice "after war" (*jus post bellum*) component, there is a recognition and understanding that once hostilities stop, there is a desired end state in which there is security and a just peace. To achieve this, there is the need for order, justice, and conciliation, and these may require a considerable amount of time and various activities.

There is no universally agreed-upon definition, interpretation, and application of just war principles by its proponents. There is also no guarantee that the principles will receive strict adherence. The intent of the principles and tradition is to limit the occurrence of war and contain it when it does occur. The principles of the just war tradition are for the containment of war, not the conflagration of war. It is a fluid intellectual tradition.

Four presuppositions provide the foundation of the just war tradition: first, some evil in the world is unavoidable; second, just war principles are ethically normative for all people (even if they do not subscribe to them); third, the tradition is an attempt to confine war within the limits of justice such that if all nations were guided by its principles, there would be a significant reduction in war; and fourth, only governments have the right to declare war and use military force. The fourth presupposition is one that significantly affects the religious values of individuals. It does so in that it contends that the key issue is not whether an individual can fight in war. Rather, it is whether a government has the right to engage in armed conflict. Once the government determines that it may do so, it then becomes a matter of conscience and religious view as to whether a citizen (religious or not) should participate as an agent of the government. According to the just war tradition, a person's individual participation in any conflict is always a matter of conscience (informed by religious or other values).

Throughout the centuries, the just war tradition has never been a monolithic viewpoint with unanimous assent to all of it aspects by proponents. Rather, it has been a consensual perspective that has undergone continuous refinement.

With respect to religion and the wars of the United States, the just war tradition, in part and as a whole, has significantly affected how Americans have viewed and participated or refused to participate in the conflicts of the United States. Some religious groups have looked to the tradition to provide guidance for whether to support American wars. Other religious groups, among them Mennonites and Quakers, have rejected the tradition and upheld pacifism. Still other groups have been divided on the issue of war.

As an ethical, philosophical, and political construct (with theological history) that addresses the problems and practices of war, the just war tradition acknowledges that there is no more compelling and enduring problem in human existence than war. War is morally awful, politically problematic, and legally contentious, and it is in the tragic and traumatic experience of these realities that religious traditions have sought to provide individual, corporate, and national guidance—at times using the just war tradition.

*See also:* American Civil War; American Peace Churches; American Revolution; Christianity and War; Cold War; Ecclesiastical Statements on War and Peace; Gulf War; Human Rights; Korean War; Pacifism; Peacemaking; Presidential Faith and War; Protestant Denominations; Responsibility to Protect; Roman Catholicism; Vietnam War; Weapons of Mass Destruction; World War I; World War II

## Further Reading

Biggar, Nigel. *In Defence of War*. New York: Oxford University Press, 2013.
Brunstetter, Daniel R., and Cian O'Driscoll, eds. *Just War Thinkers: From Cicero to the 21st Century*. London: Routledge, 2018.

Burkhardt, Todd. *Just War and Human Rights: Fighting with Right Intention.* Albany: State University of New York Press, 2017.

Charles, J. Daryl, and Timothy J. Demy. *War, Peace, and Christianity: Questions and Answers from a Just-War Perspective.* Wheaton, IL: Crossway Publications, 2010.

Hall, Mark David, and J. Daryl Charles, eds. *America and the Just War Tradition: A History of U.S. Conflicts.* Notre Dame, IN: University of Notre Dame Press, 2019.

Johnson, James Turner. *Morality and Contemporary Warfare.* New Haven, CT: Yale University Press, 1999.

O'Donovan, Oliver. *The Just War Revisited.* Cambridge, UK: Cambridge University Press, 2003.

Orend, Brian. *The Morality of War.* 2nd ed. Peterborough, ON: Broadview Press, 2013.

Patterson, Eric. *Ending Wars Well: Order, Justice, Conciliation in Contemporary Post-Conflict.* New Haven, CT: Yale University Press, 2012.

Patterson, Eric. *Just American Wars: Ethical Dilemmas in U.S. Military History.* New York: Routledge, 2019.

Patterson, Eric. "Just War Theory & Terrorism." *Providence: A Journal of Christianity & American Foreign Policy,* no. 4 (Summer 2016): 38–44.

Patterson, Eric D., and Marc LiVecche, eds. *Responsibility and Restraint: James Turner Johnson and the Just War Tradition.* Middletown, RI: Stone Tower Press, 2020.

Settje, David E. *Faith and War: How Christians Debated the Cold and Vietnam Wars.* New York: New York University Press, 2011.

Smylie, James H. "American Religious Bodies, Just War, and Vietnam." *Journal of Church and State* 11, no. 3 (Autumn 1969): 383–408.

Walzer, Michael. *Just and Unjust Wars: A Moral Argument with Historical Illustrations.* 5th ed. New York: Basic Books, 2015.

# K

## King, Martin Luther, Jr. (1929–1968)

In recent U.S. history the name that stands above all others in relation to civil disobedience is that of American Baptist minister and civil rights leader Martin Luther King, Jr. During the 1960s, his pronounced opposition to American involvement in the Vietnam War became a defining event and position in the anti-war movement. It also set a pattern that others would use in their religious and political opposition to future wars. By linking the 1960s American civil rights movement and the American anti-war movement with respect to Vietnam, King created an ideological linkage that continues to the present. His combining of the two disparate movements received wide criticism in the media, including from the *Washington Post* and *New York Times*. Additionally, opposers included civil rights leaders such as Ralph Bunche and the National Association for the Advancement of Colored People (NAACP). Despite the criticism, King continued to attack the Vietnam War as economically unviable and morally reprehensible. His denunciation of the war and U.S. foreign policy reverberates in American politics more than fifty years later.

King was born in Atlanta, Georgia, and received his education at Morehouse College, Crozier Theological Seminary, and Boston University. In 1955, King led the Montgomery bus boycott and subsequently became the first president of the Southern Christian Leadership Conference (SCLC), and African American civil rights organization. In 1963, he helped organize the August 28 March on Washington for Jobs and Freedom event, where he delivered his famous "I Have a Dream" speech on the steps of the Lincoln Memorial. Almost five years later, on April 4, 1968, King was assassinated in Memphis, Tennessee.

Already a national and international figure due to his leadership in the civil rights movement and as a 1964 recipient of the Nobel Peace Prize,

King's public opposition to the war emerged in early 1965. For example, on March 9, 1965, at a civil rights march in Selma, Alabama, King said in a speech that "millions of dollars can be spent every day to hold troops in South Vietnam and our country cannot protect the rights of Negroes in Selma" (Stellato 2012, 250).

King's public objection to and criticism of the war effort continued, and on April 4, 1967, he spoke to more than 3,000 people at the historic Riverside Church in New York City. King called the speech, drafted with the assistance of Vincent Harding, a history professor at Spelman College in Atlanta, "Beyond Vietnam: A Time to Break Silence." The title was somewhat of a misnomer, as his vocal opposition to the war had been growing for two years. However, this speech gained national attention and occurred at time when the anti-war movement was growing. In the speech, King saw poverty, racism, and war as interrelated. (He was assassinated a year to the day later.) King's speech on April 4 was followed on April 30 by a sermon titled "Why I Am Opposed to the War in Vietnam." Between the two presentations at Riverside Church, King appeared on the television news program *Face the Nation* on April 16, 1967, where he discussed his opposition to the war.

Although some of the anti-war protests were violent, King promoted nonviolent and peaceful protest of the war. Violence was being used against Americans promoting civil rights in the South, and King was adamantly opposed to the use of violence in protesting war. The social injustice that King's movement opposed also included a growing critique of capitalism, imperialism, and American militarism. King's leadership, inspiration, and example became pivotal in the civil rights movement of the 1960s. Probably more than any other individual in American history, King used the ideas of nonviolent civil disobedience to shape a movement, challenge a government, and mobilize thousands to a cause for justice and social equality. Using a blending of ideas from Henry David Thoreau (1817–1862), Mahatma Gandhi (1869–1948), and the Bible that emphasized love for one's enemies, King created a doctrine of nonviolent disobedience. Tragically, like Gandhi, King was also assassinated.

King's view of law was that just laws are in conformity with his Christian understanding of the laws of God and elevate the dignity of all humans. Unjust laws discriminate against the minority, deny constitutional rights, and are enacted by undemocratically elected legislatures. Just laws should be obeyed; unjust laws should be disobeyed—but disobeyed nonviolently. For King, such disobedience extends to participation in unjust wars.

The weakness in the movement King led was not in the courage and determination of those who bravely worked for civil rights through nonviolence; it was perhaps in a philosophy and theology that may have been too optimistic about human nature and its propensity toward evil. Dr. King's tragic murder cut short a life that invigorated millions with hope and determination. The decades since his death have brought forth significant progress in his cause, but no one has yet risen to his stature in the realm of the practice of civil disobedience or in vocal opposition to war in such a way that it mobilizes enough dissenters to change or significantly influence U.S. foreign policy. This is not to discount the enormous influence of leaders and movements outside the United States, such as those led by people such as Nelson Mandela (1918–2013) in South Africa, Lech Walesa (1943–) in Poland, students protesting in Tiananmen Square in China in 1989, protesters in Hong Kong in 2019, and others.

Some of these were successful and others not; some had Christian underpinnings as voiced by King, and others did not. Though they are beyond the scope of this work, studies of each of these movements (and others) show the enormous influence of religion on political processes as well as the importance of religious freedom as a key component of liberty. There have been voices of opposition to war and American military operations in the decades since King's death that have applied his principles to anti-war protests, and many of his concerns remain and are expressed in 21st-century opposition to U.S. military operations and conflicts.

*See also:* Christianity and War; Cold War; Conscientious Objection; Pacifism; Vietnam War

## Further Reading

Ansbro, John. *Martin Luther King, Jr.: The Making of a Mind.* New York: Orbis Books, 1983.

Fairclough, Adam. "Martin Luther King, Jr. and the War in Vietnam." *Phylon* 45, no. 1 (1st qtr. 1984): 19–39.

Hanes, Walton, Jr. *The Political Philosophy of Martin Luther King.* Westport, CT: Greenwood Publishing, 1971.

Hedin, Benjamin. "Martin Luther King, Jr.'s Searing Antiwar Speech, Fifty Years Later." *New Yorker*, April 3, 2017. https://www.newyorker.com/culture/culture-desk/martin-luther-king-jr-s-searing-antiwar-speech-fifty-years-later

King, Martin Luther, Jr. *Stride toward Freedom.* New York: Harper and Brothers, 1958.

King, Martin Luther, Jr. *A Testament of Hope: The Essential Writings of Martin Luther King, Jr.* Edited by James Melvin Washington. San Francisco: Harper & Row, 1986.
Lischer, Richard. *The Preacher King: Martin Luther King, Jr. and the Word That Moved America.* Rev. ed. New York: Oxford University Press, 2020.
Shelby, Tommie, and Brandon M. Terry, eds. *To Shape a New World: Essays on the Political Philosophy of Martin Luther King, Jr.* Cambridge, MA: Belknap Press, 2018.
Stellato, Jesse, ed. *Not in Our Name: American Antiwar Speeches, 1846 to the Present.* University Park: Pennsylvania State University Press, 2012.

# Korean War

Twenty-first-century concerns regarding geopolitical events on the Korean Peninsula are directly linked to the Korean War (1950–1953). Although an armistice agreement was signed on July 27, 1953, the two separate nations of North Korea and South Korea continue to occupy the Korean Peninsula, and each nation essentially occupies the same territory it held when North Korea attacked South Korea on June 25, 1950. The agreement stopped military action but was not a peace treaty and thus left the region in a tenuous military and political environment that remains highly volatile in the 21st century.

Arising in the first decade of the Cold War, the conflict in Korea became a rallying point for religious and political conservatives who framed the war as an ideological conflict between the Judeo-Christian United States and its allies from the United Nations and the atheism of the North Korean regime supported by communist China and the Soviet Union. For many Christians and political conservatives in the United States, the conflict became a symbol of the need to contain communist expansion. The war was understood in terms of the domino theory of containing communism—the belief that if one nation fell, others nearby or in the region would also succumb to communist control. This theme continued throughout the Cold War and was very prominent in U.S. attitudes regarding participation in the Vietnam War. For many, the containment of communism and the upholding of Judeo-Christian values were seen as necessary and complementary endeavors.

Before the war began, in the aftermath of World War II, President Truman's Cold War strategy of containment of global communism was set into motion in August 1947. From his perspective, economic and military prowess were insufficient to defeat communism. He believed that there must also be a moral and spiritual component. He subsequently sought to mobilize global religious leaders such as Pope Pius XII as well as other faith leaders to combat the communist threat. In the same way that the United States was taking a significantly increased leadership role in postwar global politics, it also encouraged the garnering of religious fervor against communism and the Cold War Soviet Union and its satellite nations and allies. Interestingly, Truman met with significant political opposition from liberal Protestants of the Federal Council of Churches.

Whereas most religious groups generally supported the war effort (e.g., evangelist Billy Graham went to South Korea to visit and preach to troops—something he would do again during the Vietnam War), many conservative Protestants opposed Truman's military strategy of not seeking a unified Korea. Instead, Truman aimed to defend the territory south of the 38th parallel (latitude 38° north) in a limited war. Their opposition intensified after Truman relieved General Douglas MacArthur for insubordination. MacArthur vocally opposed the president's strategy and sought to expand the war into Manchuria and possibly use nuclear weapons. Similarly, many liberal Protestants opposed the president's larger desire to use ecumenism to fight communism ideologically. For many, such opposition arose out of fear that the Vatican would become too powerful in global politics. One thing that arose out of this religious division was competing religious views of how the United States should fight the Cold War and how and which religious values should shape American foreign policy.

One of the greatest religious and ethical debates of the war was whether nuclear weapons should be used against the Chinese and North Korean forces, as they had been in 1945 against the Japanese forces, to end the war. Such weapons were not used, but in the decades since the armistice, North Korea has sought to become a nuclear power. That desire continues in the 21st century and has been a source of great tension on the peninsula.

One often overlooked dimension of the war was the presence of Christians in North Korea and in the war zone. Korean Christians and Christian missionaries influenced activities on the ground and were also instrumental in the relocation of refugees. In the 21st century, a third of

South Koreans identify as Christian, and the religion plays a prominent role in Korean culture and politics. This has also been a 21st-century flashpoint in that North Korea continues to persecute Christians among its own population as well as imprison Christians who are citizens of other nations but come to North Korea on humanitarian relief missions. One notable case is that of Korean American Christian pastor Kenneth Bae, who was detained, tried, and imprisoned for two years (2012–2014).

When one considers some of the religious responses to conflict in the 21st century, as well as responses to dictatorial and oppressive regimes such as North Korea's, much of it can be traced to the latter half of the 20th century. Further, the roots of contemporary religiopolitical divisions in the United States can be found in the early years of the Cold War and the Korean War.

***See also:*** American Exceptionalism; American Peace Churches; Cold War; Graham, William Franklin, Jr. ("Billy"); Just War Tradition; Literature; Music; Pacifism; Presidential Faith and War; Protestant Denominations; Rhetoric, Sermons, and Prayers; Roman Catholicism; United Nations; Vietnam War; Weapons of Mass Destruction; World War II

## Further Reading

Bandow, Doug. "North Korea's War on Christianity: The Globe's Number One Religious Persecutor." *Forbes*, October 31, 2016. https://www.forbes.com/sites/dougbandow/2016/10/31/north-koreas-war-on-christianity-the-globes-number-one-religious-persecutor/#7f5db78156e3

Clouse, Robert C. "Korean War and Vietnam Wars." In *The Wars of America: Christian Views*, edited by Ronald A. Wells, 227–264. Macon, GA: Mercer University Press, 1991.

Hall, Mark David, and J. Daryl Charles, ed. *America and the Just War Tradition: A History of U.S. Conflicts*. Notre Dame, IN: University of Notre Dame Press, 2019.

Inboden, William C. *Religion and American Foreign Policy, 1945–1960*. Cambridge, UK: Cambridge University Press, 2010.

Kirby, Diane, ed. *Religion and the Cold War*. New York: Palgrave Macmillan, 2013.

Mojzes, Paul. *North American Churches and the Cold War*. Grand Rapids, MI: Eerdmans, 2018.

Muehlenbeck, Philip. *Religion and the Cold War: A Global Perspective*. Nashville, TN: Vanderbilt University Press, 2012.

Padgett, Timothy D. *Swords & Plowshares: American Evangelicals on War, 1937–1973*. Bellingham, WA: Lexham Press, 2018.

Preston, Andrew. *Sword of the Spirit, Shield of Faith: Religion in American War and Diplomacy*. New York: Alfred A. Knopf, 2012.

Settje, David E. *Faith and War: How Christians Debated the Cold and Vietnam Wars*. New York: New York University Press, 2011.

## Literature

Literature in the form of novels and poetry regarding the United States' 21st-century conflicts and wars is emerging and following the pattern of such literature from other wars. The writing of poetry, memoirs, and novels usually increases in publication during and after a war. This period of increase is then followed by a slow but steady flow of literature in the first decade after the conflict and then more widely acclaimed literature ten years or so after the conflict and beyond. The exception to significant works being produced long after a conflict is the poetry that is written during the conflict. Such poetry may utilize religious language, religious images, and scriptural texts and allusions as part of its content and message. In part, the sequence of significant literary works arising from war may be attributed to the distance and lapse of time from the war that is needed for critical reflection, analysis, and multidimensional healing, which is necessary from the experiences of war on the home front and the battlefront.

Unlike previous war literature, one finds in these 21st-century writings more direct references to and confrontations of the traumas and injuries of war as pertaining directly to post-traumatic stress disorder (PTSD) and moral injury in veterans and serving members of the military.

In much of the poetry of the wars in Afghanistan and Iraq, the religious imagery and allusion are written by veterans. Contemporary examples include "Transubstantiation" by Dwight A. Gray, "You Can Seek Redemption on Route 66" by Matthew Oudbier, and "Call to Prayer" and "Pre-Deployment Chaplain's Brief" by Graham Barnhart.

What one often finds in war literature is not poetry and novels that are written from a deeply religious perspective or to convey religious content. Rather, works draw from religious history, language, and beliefs to entertain, instruct, and enable the reader to enter the world of the characters or speakers (who are not always the same as the poet or author) and observe, experience, and reflect upon the content or story. In so doing, the reader may then bring his or her own religious and political views and values, as well as life experiences, to the work for entertainment, education, and enrichment. Beyond contemporary literature, the carrying and reading of religious texts by warriors has been commonplace and well documented through the centuries and in every American conflict. The use of religious texts is also common in popular culture in times of war. Religious texts are also found on memorials and used during services of commemoration and memorialization.

War literature is a popular format that dates to the ancient Near East, including the Greek epic poem *The Iliad* of Homer, the Roman saga *The Aeneid* of Virgil, and the Old English *Beowulf* and Arthurian legends and literature. In *The Trojan Women* tragedy of Euripides and Shakespeare's *Henry V*, there are also strong religious and political themes that continue to resonate with readers in the 21st century.

In the 20th century, war literature and films derived from conflict captivated readers and audiences during, between, and after two global wars and many regional ones. It was on the eve of World War II that British prime minister Neville Chamberlain (1869–1940) sought to avoid war with Germany and Adolf Hitler (1889–1945) with the Munich Agreement and returned to England on September 30, 1938, declaring in a speech that his efforts gained "peace for our time." The phrase was recognizable to Britons based on the petitionary prayer phrase "The Order for Morning Prayer" in the *Book of Common Prayer* (1662): "Give us peace in our time." The phrase in the *Book of Common Prayer* was translated from the 7th-century hymn "Da pacem Domine," with lyrics of the same wording that translate as follows: "Give peace in our time, O Lord; because there is none other that fighteth for us, but only thou, O God."

Although it was a 20th-century political event and usage, the citation of a religious literary text shows how deeply ingrained religious and political words and images can be in a culture and the citizens of a nation. Even in an increasingly secular 21st-century context, religion matters in the thoughts and lives of millions of Americans. Although Americans are proud of the First Amendment of the U.S. Constitution and the separation of religion and the state, literary works make use of both, especially in times of war.

*See also:* Art; Music; Religious Texts; Rhetoric, Sermons, and Prayers; September 11, 2001, Terrorist Attacks

## Further Reading

Barnhart, Graham. *The War Makes Everyone Lonely*. Chicago: University of Chicago Press, 2019.
Brosman, Catharine Savage. "The Functions of War Literature." *South Central Review* 9, no. 1, Historicizing Literary Contexts (Spring 1992): 85–98.
Cohen, Allen, and Clive Matson, eds. *An Eye for an Eye Makes the Whole World Blind: Poets on 9/11*. Oakland, CA: Regent Press, 2002.
Goldensohn, Lorrie, ed. *American War Poetry: An Anthology*. New York: Columbia University Press, 2006.
Gray, Dwight A. "Transubstantiation." *Sewanee Review* 123, no. 4 (Fall 2005): 639. https://muse.jhu.edu/article/602000
McGuire, Matt. "When the War Is Over, Literature Can Help Us Make Sense of It All." The Conversation, October 5, 2014. https://theconversation.com/when-the-war-is-over-literature-can-help-us-make-sense-of-it-all-32424
Molin, Peter. "39 American Iraq-and-Afghanistan War Poets." Acolytesofwar.com, April 12, 2017. https://acolytesofwar.com/2017/04/12/22-american-iraq-and-afghanistan-war-poets/
"The Order for Morning Prayer." In *The Book of Common Prayer*. Church of England, 1662.
Oudbier, Matthew. "You Can Seek Redemption on Route 66." *O-Dark-Thirty: A Literary Journal* 5, no. 4 (Summer 2017): 85–87. https://odarkthirtydotorg.files.wordpress.com/2017/09/odt_5-4_web.pdf

## Middle East Conflict

The 21st-century Middle East has been an area of continuous major and minor conflicts and remains a focal point of international attention. Combined, two dozen countries comprise the Middle Eastern and North African regions in which there is much overlapping and interlocking of economic, political, and religious history. Situated in a geographically strategic position, the Middle East has been a battleground for thousands of years (though historically it is not more prone to conflict and war than many other regions). The birthplace of the world's three great monotheistic religions (Judaism, Christianity, Islam), the region has never lacked religious fervor or intense political dynamics.

Prominent conflicts in the Middle East in the 21st century include the following:

- Iraq War (2003–2011)
- Second Palestinian Intifada (2005–2010)
- Israel-Hezbollah War (2006)
- ISIS regional conflict (2006–present)
- Gaza Strip Fatah-Hamas conflict (2006–present)
- Gaza and Post-Intifada conflict (2010–present)
- Egyptian Crisis (2011–2014)
- Iran–Saudi Arabia proxy conflict (2011–present)
- Syrian Civil War (2011–present)
- Iraqi Civil War (2014–2017)
- Yemeni Civil War (2015–present)

In each of these, American religious and political voices, organizations, and denominations have worked to diminish the conflicts either in support of or in opposition to American policy and proposed or actual military engagement. Other conflicts of lower international visibility have occurred as well as political unrest, uprisings, and revolts throughout the Middle East and North Africa in what has been termed the Arab Spring (2010–2012).

American religious and political awareness of and interest in the region can be traced to the earliest years of the American experience in the New World. This continued throughout the early decades of the new American nation and grew significantly after World War I and World War II as the United States became a global superpower.

Economically, much of this was due to the vast petroleum resources in the region and the growing global market for them. From a religious perspective, many Americans, especially Protestants and Jews, had strong desires that a permanent Jewish state be established in what is commonly called the Holy Land. This occurred with the creation of the nation of Israel through action by the United Nations in 1948 in the aftermath of World War II and the Holocaust. The United States was among the first countries to formally recognize Israel, and in the decades since, it has become one of Israel's staunchest political, military, and economic allies. Though beneficial to Israel, this relationship and other U.S. actions have often placed the United States in the middle of fragile and volatile Middle Eastern politics and conflict.

To date, the 2003–2011 Iraq War was the largest conflict in the Middle East in which the United States was among the direct belligerents. Among the most protracted recent conflicts in the region, the Syrian Civil War (2011–present) has destroyed much of the country, created hundreds of thousands of refugees and displaced persons, and killed more than 400,000 persons.

Exacerbated by the rise and violence of the so-called Islamic State in Iraq and the Levant (ISIL or ISIS), the civil war is a tragic and gruesome example of complex and intractable conflicts in the Middle East. Further, it exemplifies the reality that every conflict and war in the Middle East has multiple national, regional, and international entities involved. Frequently among these nations are the United States, Iran, Saudi Arabia, and Russia. All of this also has been complicated by regional and international terrorism from nonstate entities supported by nations as proxy instruments of political power. Groups such as al-Qaeda, Hezbollah, Hamas, the Islamic State (IS), and others continue to foment regional violence and instability, often in the name of religion.

It is not only nations that are involved in Middle East conflicts. Humanitarian and religious nongovernmental organizations (NGOs) are routinely present in efforts to alleviate suffering and foster conflict resolution and peace. Religious leaders such as the pope, Orthodox patriarchs, rabbis, imams, and denominational leaders are often visible and vocal in Middle Eastern concerns. Additionally, faith groups spanning the spectrum of religious belief (and political perspective) have been a part of U.S. domestic politics in attempts to influence U.S. foreign policies in the region. Perhaps most vocal and visible have been the American evangelicals, whose strong support for Israel is grounded in part in their theology and interpretation of biblical texts, many of which are considered apocalyptic. American religious and secular Jewish support for Israel also remains a prominent factor in U.S. interactions with and policy in the Middle East. The growing American Muslim population's political voice is also increasing.

One aspect that is often overlooked in conflict, and is often a by-product of it, is ethnic or religious persecution. This also occurs in authoritative regimes where political dissent is stifled. Beyond ongoing Sunni and Shia Muslim violence against each other, there has been a steady increase in the Middle East in the persecution of Jews (outside of Israel), Christians, and other religious minorities. Highlighting one aspect of this, in March 2021, Pope Francis made a historic visit to Iraq in support of the plight of the diminishing Christian population there and elsewhere in the Middle East. During the visit, he was vocal against hostility, extremism, and violence, contending that such things were contrary to true spirituality.

The Middle East is not the only region of the world where conflict continues, but for many Americans, it is the region that repeatedly draws their religious and political interest, attention, and action.

*See also:* Apocalypticism; Christianity and War; Contemporary Non-U.S. Conflicts; Ecclesiastical Statements on War and Peace; Evangelicalism; Gulf War; Human Rights; Iraq War; Islam and War; Judaism and War; Peacemaking; Religion, Conflict, and Geopolitics; Religious Freedom and Religious Persecution; Terrorism; United Nations; Wars of Israel

## Further Reading

Ahram, Ariel I. *War and Conflict in the Middle East and North Africa*. Cambridge, UK: Polity Press, 2020.

Amstutz, Mark R. *Evangelicals and American Foreign Policy*. New York: Oxford University Press, 2014.

Bunton, Martin. *The Palestinian-Israeli Conflict: A Very Short Introduction*. New York: Oxford University Press, 2013.

Cook, David. *Contemporary Muslim Apocalyptic Literature*. Syracuse, NY: Syracuse University Press, 2008.

Fraihat, Ibrahim. *Iran and Saudi Arabia: Taming a Chaotic Conflict*. Edinburgh, UK: Edinburgh University Press, 2020.

Mearsheimer, John. *The Israel Lobby and U.S. Foreign Policy*. New York: Farrar, Strauss and Giroux, 2007.

Oren, Michael B. *Power, Faith, and Fantasy: America in the Middle East 1776 to the Present*. New York: W. W. Norton & Co., 2007.

Rasche, Stephen M. *The Disappearing People: The Tragic Fate of Christians in the Middle East*. New York: Bombardier Books, 2020.

Roy, Oindrila. "Religious Roots of War Attitudes in the United States: Insights from Iraq, Afghanistan, and the Persian Gulf." *Foreign Policy Analysis* 12, no. 3 (July 2016): 258–274. https://academic.oup.com/fpa/article/12/3/258/1751230

Tucker, Spencer C., and Paul G. Pierpaoli Jr., eds. *U.S. Conflicts in the 21st Century: Afghanistan War, Iraq War, and the War on Terror*. 3 vols. Santa Barbara, CA: ABC-CLIO, 2016.

# Military Chaplains

Military chaplains in the United States have served since the American Revolution and the founding of the nation. Chaplains across the religious spectrum are endorsed for service to the U.S. Department of Defense by their respective denominations. Although they represent their faith tradition and denomination, they work in a religiously pluralistic environment not unlike other institutional ministry settings. In recent decades, as the nation has become more religiously diverse, so too has the composition of chaplains within the services—U.S. Army, U.S. Air Force, and U.S. Navy (the navy provides chaplains to the U.S. Marine Corps and U.S. Coast Guard).

Military chaplains are commissioned officers and employed by the government. However, they represent their respective religious traditions and function within religious boundaries of those traditions and the legal and constitutional boundaries of the U.S. Constitution. Balancing the demands required of these two domains necessitates skill and sensitivity. In an era and national culture that increasingly emphasizes secularism, diversity, and individualism, maintaining the balance and providing meaningful service remains a persistent challenge. Throughout American history, there have been several legal challenges to the chaplain services with respect to the validity of the separation of the church and state. The courts have ruled in favor of government-funded chaplaincy services as the best way of ensuring the First Amendment rights of every person in the military.

Historically, the magnitude of World War II and the number of men and women in uniform created the need for a large number of Protestant, Roman Catholic, and Jewish military chaplains. Prior to the war, most Protestant chaplains came from what are known as "mainline denominations," such as Presbyterians, Lutherans, Episcopalians, and Methodists. The need for chaplains and the circumstances under which they were recruited changed such that there was a broadening of the spectrum of chaplain representation—though still limited to Protestants, Roman Catholics, and Jews. This broadening continued in the late 20th and 21st century such that in addition to more diversity among Protestants and other denominations, in the 21st century, there were other religious traditions, such as Islam and Buddhism, represented by U.S. military chaplains. Over the decades, as the religious demographics within the service chaplaincies changed, there arose concerns of denominational discrimination by some chaplains and the chaplaincy structure within the services. In the U.S. Navy, this resulted in several federal lawsuits regarding policies, promotions, and other personnel matters.

As the religious, social, and political dynamics within the United States have continued to change in recent decades, some religious groups and denominations have, of necessity or choice, reduced the number of clergy they have endorsed for military chaplaincy. This has resulted in shortages of chaplains available to serve the First Amendment rights of service members. Some groups, such as historic peace churches, have continued opposition to U.S. policies and wars. Others, such as the Roman Catholic Church, have experienced significant decreases in the number of priests being ordained. Such shortages then reduce the number of clergy available for military chaplaincy. One result of this is an increase in the number of serving chaplains who were born outside of the United States. In 2020, 19 percent of the U.S. Army chaplains and 10 percent of the U.S. Navy chaplains were born elsewhere (Gütting 2020).

By international law as well as Department of Defense policy, military chaplains, like medical personnel, are noncombatants. This unique status, coupled with recognition as religious leaders who share humanitarian concerns and impulses, allows chaplains to serve as mediators and facilitators of humanitarian relief efforts in times of war and disaster. While not all chaplains have expertise in such endeavors, there is often the opportunity to engage in these missions. Similarly, increasingly since the early 1990s, some military chaplains have provided area and regional expertise regarding religious dynamics in areas of operation. This often entails working with local religious leaders for common goals of humanitarian assistance, stability, and peace.

Military chaplains in the 21st century have had to respond with the rest of the nation and military to the increasing religious diversity within the military and United States. Further, the religious dynamics of the so-called global war on terrorism and the rise of militant Islam have created new challenges for all concerned. Chaplains have continued to serve on American battlefields in Iraq and Afghanistan as well as other locations around the globe where the U.S. military is deployed.

Like other members of the armed forces, chaplains span the spectrum of ideological and political perspectives. Although military chaplains bring a uniquely religious attitude toward their service, they are representative of the larger American society. In an era when religious values are often a factor in international headlines, military chaplains give a unique voice to American democracy and the promotion of religious freedom.

*See also:* American Peace Churches; Cold War; Just War Tradition; Protestant Denominations; Religious Identity in the Armed Forces; Rhetoric, Sermons, and Prayers; Roman Catholicism; World War II

## Further Reading

Dorsett, Lyle W. *Serving God and Country: U.S. Military Chaplains in World War II*. New York: Dutton Caliber, 2013.

Gütting, Tonia. "They're Not from the US. But They're Ministering to the Nation's Soldiers." *Christianity Today*, March 17, 2020. https://www.christianitytoday.com/ct/2020/april/born-abroad-born-again-and-born-to-serve.html

Hansen, Kim Philip. *Military Chaplains and Religious Diversity*. New York: Palgrave Macmillan, 2012.

Hutcheson, Richard G., Jr., and Mark A. Jumper. *The Churches and the Chaplaincy*. Rev. ed. Middletown, RI: Stone Tower Press, 2021.

Johnson, Douglas M. "U.S. Military Chaplains: Redirecting a Critical Asset." *Review of Faith and International Affairs* 7, no. 4 (2009): 25–32.

Laing, John D. *In Jesus' Name: Evangelicals and Military Chaplaincy*. Eugene, OR: Resource Publications, 2012.
Padgett, Timothy D. *Swords & Plowshares: American Evangelicals on War, 1937–1973*. Bellingham, WA: Lexham Press, 2018.
Stahl, Ronit Y. *Enlisting Faith: How Military Chaplaincy Shaped Religion and State in Modern America*. Cambridge, MA: Belknap Press, 2017.

# Music

Every major American conflict or war has generated music. It was during the War of 1812 that the lyrics to the national anthem, "The Star-Spangled Banner," were written by Francis Scott Key on September 14, 1814, as he witnessed the bombardment of Fort McHenry by British ships in Baltimore Harbor. Originally titled by Key as "The Defense of Fort McHenry," the fourth verse speaks of national trust in God and American exceptionalism, declaring, "Praise the Power that hath made and preserved us a nation! Then conquer we must, when our cause it is just, And this be our motto: 'In God is our trust.'" Probably the best-known American song combining politics, war, and religion is the 1861 Civil War song "Battle Hymn of the Republic," with lyrics written by Julia Ward Howe (1819–1910) in which every phrase contains biblical imagery and wording. On September 14, 2001, at the 9/11 memorial service at the Washington National Cathedral, the song was sung, with five presidents (Gerald Ford, Jimmy Carter, George H. W. Bush, Bill Clinton, and George W. Bush) singing with other attendees.

With respect to music that combines politics, religion, and war, the political aspect is often found not so much in the lyrics as in the reason for the music's composition—either in support of a war effort or in opposition to it. In 20th-century American history, World War II and the Vietnam War generated a significant amount of pro-war and protest music, with both themes found in popular music. For example, during World War II, the popular songs "Praise the Lord and Pass the Ammunition" (1942) and "Comin' in on a Wing and a Prayer" (1943), both based on combat events of the war, topped the music charts, and the titles became part of American popular culture and language throughout the last half of the 20th century and to the present day. Pop music rising to the top of the music charts that contained overwhelming religious themes would not occur again in the

United States until the Vietnam War and the song "Sky Pilot" (1968), performed by the musical group Eric Burdon & the Animals, which refers to a military chaplain blessing troops.

At times, music has been strongly supportive of the war or the memory of it. Counterbalancing this music, there also have been music and songs of protest. Examples of music with religious themes and imagery protesting war include the Civil War–era spiritual "Down by the Riverside," with the refrain lyrics "ain't gonna study war no more" being derived from the biblical quotation of Isaiah 2:4: "nation shall not lift up sword against nation, neither shall they learn war any more" (KJV). The song was very popular as a protest song performed by folk singer Pete Seeger (1919–2014) during the Vietnam War. Folk composer and singer John McCutcheon (1952–present) is well known for his ballad "Christmas in the Trenches" (1984), which tells the story of the World War I Christmas Truce of 1914, and his 1987 general peace and anti-war song "Alleluia, the Great Storm Is Over."

With respect to religious music and war, many Christian hymns have been frequently sung and performed throughout the 20th century and into the 21st century during times of war. The hymn "Onward Christian Soldiers" (lyrics 1865, tune 1871) was a favorite of Prime Minister Winston Churchill and was sung at worship services in 1941 aboard the battleship HMS *Prince of Wales* during the meeting agreeing to the Atlantic Charter by Churchill and President Franklin Roosevelt.

The famous hymn "Jerusalem," written in 1916 at the height of World War I by Sir Charles Hubert Hastings Parry (1848–1918), drawing from the preface of the 1803 work *Milton: A Poem in Two Books* by William Blake (1757–1827), is the most popular hymn in the United Kingdom in the 21st century. Similarly, the hymns "Eternal Father Strong to Save," "Abide with Me," "Leaning on the Everlasting Arms," and "O God Our Help in Ages Past" continue to be favorite hymns among military personnel in times of conflict and are frequently used in military funerals and public services of remembrance and commemoration. Secular and religious music written during and after World War II commemorating the Holocaust also evokes strong emotional and national responses. Among the frequently used compositions for commemoration is Henryk Górecki's (1933–2010) Symphony no. 3, *Symphony of Sorrowful Songs* (1977).

The power of music is such that compositions created during one conflict often become part of larger national and international canons. Music is also composed and performed after conflicts and war as part of memory and commemoration (e.g., *War Requiem*, Op. 66, by Benjamin Britten, written and performed at the consecration of the new Coventry Cathedral after the destruction of the original 14th-century structure during World War II). Beyond music as religious and commemorative during war, it can also be used as a weapon of war and in psychological warfare.

The list of popular music about 9/11 is extensive; many artists have composed and performed music about the event. From the more conservative political and cultural perspective, many listeners in the 21st-century United States have found appreciation and resonance with country and western music. Within this genre, songs such as "Arlington" (2005) by Trace Adkins, "Soldiers and Jesus" (2010) by James Otto, and "Angel Flight" (2009) by Radney Foster blend religion and recent American conflicts. Also popular is the 1984 Lee Greenwood song "God Bless the U.S.A.," which gained prominence during the 1990–1991 Gulf War.

A similar song of long-standing popularity is "God Bless America," written by Irving Berlin in 1939 and popularized by singer Kate Smith (1907–1986) during World War II. It has become a mainstay of American patriotic music in the decades since its composition. Though also used as a song sung by labor workers on strike, it is frequently sung and heard during times of national crisis and conflict. In 2001, the song's title was the name of a charity album of patriotic and spiritual songs. *God Bless America* was released in October 2001, and proceeds were for the Twin Towers Fund, benefiting families of those lost in the September 11, 2001, terrorist attacks. The album included songs written or performed by Celine Dion ("God Bless America"), Bruce Springsteen ("Land of Hope and Glory"), Bob Dylan ("Blowin' in the Wind"), Gloria Estefan ("Coming Out of the Dark"), Mariah Carey ("Hero"), Lee Greenwood ("God Bless the U.S.A."), Mahalia Jackson ("We Shall Overcome"), Tramaine Hawkins ("Amazing Grace"), and others. The album debuted at number one on the Billboard 200 its first week of release and received wide praise across the political and music spectrum. Its success showed the powerful influence of music as a comfort, prioritizing patriotism, ideology, and spirituality regardless of one's cultural, political, or religious background or preferences.

Although pop music is often the most well-known genre of music, every major conflict inspires music across the spectrum of genres—religious, classical, folk, country, pop, and so on. The same has occurred in the post-9/11 years with a broad variety of national and international musical responses to 9/11, war, and the dynamics of memory and meaning.

*See also:* Afghanistan War; American Civil War; American Exceptionalism; Art; Holocaust; Iraq War; Literature, Peace Movements; Religious Texts; September 11, 2001, Terrorist Attacks; Vietnam War; World War I; World War II

## Further Reading

Botstein, Leo. "Why Music in a Time of War?" *New York Times*, March 3, 1991. https://www.nytimes.com/1991/03/03/arts/classical-music-why-music-in-a-time-of-war.html

Brown, Kellie D. *The Sound of Hope: Music as Solace, Resistance and Salvation during the Holocaust and World War II*. Jefferson, NC: McFarland, 2020.

Classic FM. "Classical Music Inspired by 9/11." Accessed June 13, 2022. https://www.classicfm.com/discover-music/occasions/memorial/classical-music-inspired-911/

Ferris, Marc. *Star-Spangled Banner: The Unlikely Story of America's National Anthem*. Baltimore, MD: Johns Hopkins University Press, 2014.

Gamble, Richard M. A. *Fiery Gospel: The Battle Hymn of the Republic and the Road to Righteous War*. Ithaca, NY: Cornell University Press, 2019.

Kashkowitz, Sheryl. *God Bless America: The Surprising History of an Iconic Song*. New York: Oxford University Press, 2013.

Key, Francis Scott. "The Star-Spangled Banner, 1814." https://web.archive.org/web/20130126153519/http://www.thenationalanthemproject.org/lyrics.html

Klugewicz, Stephen M. "Music of War and Remembrance: Ten Classical Music Pieces." The Imaginative Conservative, November 15, 2011. https://theimaginativeconservative.org/2015/11/music-war-remembrance-ten-great-classical-music-works-stephen-klugewicz.html

Pareles, Jon. "Pop Music and the War: The Sound of Resignation." *New York Times*, January 2, 2007. https://www.nytimes.com/2007/01/02/arts/music/02songs.html

Potter, Pamela M., Christina L. Baade, and Montemorra Marvin, eds. *Music in World War II: Coping with Wartime in Europe and the United States*. Bloomington: Indiana University Press, 2020.

Ritter, Jonathan, and J. Martin Daughtry, eds. *Music in the Post-9/11 World*. New York: Routledge, 2013.

Ross, Alex. "When Music Is Violence." *New Yorker*, June 27, 2016. https://www.newyorker.com/magazine/2016/07/04/when-music-is-violence

Shevory, Thomas. "All We Are Singing: Popular Musical Responses to the Iraq War." *Poroi: An Interdisciplinary Journal of Rhetorical Analysis and Invention* 5, no. 1 (2008): 1–38. https://doi.org/10.13008/2151-2957.1018

Stauffer, John, and Benjamin Soskis. *The Battle Hymn of the Republic: A Biography of a Song That Marches On*. New York: Oxford University Press, 2013.

Tierney, Dominic. "'The Battle Hymn of the Republic': America's Song of Itself." *The Atlantic*, November 4, 2010. https://www.theatlantic.com/entertainment/archive/2010/11/the-battle-hymn-of-the-republic-americas-song-of-itself/66070/

# N

## Nongovernmental Organizations

The desire to provide assistance to civilians caught in the crossfire of war and conflict regardless of ethnicity, nationality, or religion has initiated the work of many secular and religious organizations. Collectively, these organizations are known as nongovernmental organizations (NGOs). Probably the best-known NGO in the world is the nonreligious International Committee of the Red Cross (ICRC). Its founding in 1859 arose out of European warfare. Similarly, Doctors without Borders (Médecins Sans Frontières), a French NGO founded in 1971, often works in war zones. Founded in 1844 in London, the YMCA remains a visible NGO whose work during World War I is especially noteworthy.

There are NGOs for almost any cause one may consider, and these causes are supported in war and peace. However, during wartime and in war zones, the needs are accentuated and the suffering magnified to levels only surpassed by natural disasters.

Many religious groups, faith traditions, and denominations have NGOs as official entities within the group or denomination. Their work is viewed as an application of their faith commitments and values—putting faith into action. Such efforts are centuries old. For example, within Christianity, the rise of the idea of hospitals can be traced to the era of the Crusades, and the idea of helping the sick and poor is grounded in biblical texts and exhortations. Within Jewish NGOs, who find in biblical texts the concept of *tikkun olam* ("repair the world"), there is also the idea of necessary human effort to alleviate suffering regardless of spiritual or physical boundaries.

Within the realm of NGOs, entities that derive their existence and mission from faith traditions of religious groups are called faith-based organizations (FBOs). For example, about 10 percent of the organizations given "observer" status by and working with the United Nations are FBOs. NGOs provide humanitarian assistance and relief on a daily basis in thousands of locations. Their efforts are seen in such things as medical aid, education, community development, human rights, agricultural assistance, disaster relief, famine relief, and a score of other types of endeavors. The work they perform in peacetime becomes much more dangerous in regions where there is conflict and war. Postwar relief is also an essential aspect of the work of many NGOs. Without their assistance and efforts, the traumas and devastation of war for individuals and communities would be greatly exacerbated.

The term *NGO* has various meanings in different contexts. It is a generic term used to reference the work of thousands of organizations whose mission is derived from secular and religious commitments to humanitarian assistance. Invariably, these definitions include a form of citizen organization to achieve a common purpose and represent the concerns of the public and stakeholders external to governments. They are typically nonprofit organizations, although recent NGOs also include organizations that lobby their government in representation of specific interests.

Within the broader context of NGOs, humanitarian service, and the United Nations, NGOs—and often specifically faith-based NGOs—perform humanitarian relief functions that the United Nations as an organization is unwilling or unable to fulfill. Religious NGOs come alongside as co-problem-solvers to address needs of the poor, marginalized, and persecuted in conflict and postconflict areas and in response to natural disasters. These NGOs are active in the same geosocial realms as the United Nations, serving the international public good with vital complementary purpose.

Although religious NGOs arise from specific faith commitments, recipients of their work are not limited to specific religious values or commitments. Religious NGOs provide aid regardless of one's religious or secular values and faith. The largest and most well-known religious NGOs that provide aid to victims of war include American Friends Service Committee (Quaker), Catholic Relief Services (Roman Catholic), World Vision International (Christian), Mercy Ships (Christian), Samaritan's Purse (Christian), the Islamic Relief (Muslim), the Adventist Relief and Development Agency (Christian), Lutheran World Relief (Christian), and the Hebrew Immigrant Aid Society (Jewish).

Providing services that address health, education, and religious freedoms, faith-based NGOs have acquired a high level of public trust and are able to collaborate at the international level. Other organizations, such as the World Bank, recognize that religious NGOs provide value to bridge gaps in resources and staff to achieve their goals and mission. The collaboration is aided by religious NGO coordination with the United Nations' Interagency Task Force on Religion and Development. Religious NGOs operate on many levels—local, regional, national, and international—to provide resources, capabilities, and assets.

Faith-based NGOs perform critical functions in both humanitarian and human rights work. Secular NGOs usually specialize in only one of these two areas, as human rights work often involves advocacy and awareness campaigns, while humanitarian work meets needs while staying out of any political or controversial publicity that may interfere with the provision of aid. Unlike secular NGOs, FBOs working locally usually do not make a distinction between these two areas and engage in both humanitarian aid and human rights advocacy.

As faith-based NGOs often provide aid to local populations on an ongoing basis, they provide a useful monitoring function to protect refugees, the marginalized, and the persecuted from human rights abuses. Reporting from local church councils can provide early warnings of emergencies, such as famine, as in the case of the Dutch Interchurch Aid (DIA) warning in 1983 of impending famine in Ethiopia. After eleven years of reporting and urging for action, DIA was finally able to engage European and other countries to mobilize a large-scale response to avert further catastrophe.

Every major religious tradition supports or has its own NGOs, and every faith tradition promotes humanitarian assistance, development, and human security as efforts of faith in action. Faith-based NGOs are frequently combined with missionary activities and often include a focus on protecting religious freedoms (something the UN Universal Declaration of Human Rights considers a fundamental right). These groups provide services to populations in times of war and peace, often at the cost of the lives of NGO workers, and provide assistance to all individuals regardless of religious affiliation or nonaffiliation.

Contemporary humanitarian crises addressed by NGOs are myriad. Prominent examples include displacement of populations due to climate emergencies such as drought; aid to victims of conflict and violence, including in Syria, Afghanistan, South Sudan, and the Central African Republic; help for refugees in crisis, including victims of conflict and those displaced from Myanmar; the provision of aid and assistance for victims of pandemic and disease, including COVID-19, Ebola, and diphtheria; and help in feeding the poor and averting famine in war-torn countries such as Yemen.

Some religious NGOs, such as the American Friends Service Committee (Quaker), have a long history of service in war zones. This is true even though the Quakers are pacifists and are one of the denominations identified with American peace churches. The efforts of such NGOs show that even though an individual or a religious group may not support a war politically or may be in vocal political opposition to it, such opposition does not preclude humanitarian assistance to the victims of war regardless of their faith or nationality. Regardless of one's political or religious values, the efforts of NGOs to curtail human suffering as a result of war are seen by most people as laudatory and a sincere demonstration of faith commitments. Such efforts around the globe are tangible evidence of faith in action.

*See also:* American Peace Churches; Christianity and War; Genocide; Human Rights; Pacifism; Responsibility to Protect; United Nations

## Further Reading

Abrams, Elliott. *The Influence of Faith: Religious Groups and U.S. Foreign Policy*. New York: Rowman & Littlefield, 2002.

Barnett, Michael, and Janice Gross Stein. *Sacred Aid: Faith and Humanitarianism*. Oxford, UK: Oxford University Press, 2012.

The Committee of Religious NGOs at the United Nations. "About." Accessed March 1, 2020. rngos.wordpress.com/

Ferris, Elizabeth. "Faith-Based and Secular Humanitarian Organizations." *International Review of the Red Cross* 87, no. 858 (2005): 311–325.

The Inter-Agency Standing Committee. "The Inter-Agency Standing Committee." Accessed March 1, 2020. interagencystandingcommittee.org/the-inter-agency-standing-committee

Penner, Glenn B. "A Framework for NGO-Military Collaboration." *Small Wars Journal*, July 9, 2004. https://smallwarsjournal.com/jrnl/art/a-framework-for-ngo-military-collaboration

Short, Elliot, and Milt Luenstein. "International NGOs Dedicated to Reducing Armed Conflict." 2018. http://www.miltlauenstein.com/uploads/8/5/5/9/85599410/international_ngos_dedicated_to_reducing_armed_conflict.pdf

The World Bank. "Faith Based and Religious Organizations." Accessed June 13, 2022. www.worldbank.org/en/about/partners/brief/faith-based-organizations

# P

## Pacifism

Pacifism is the philosophical or religious belief that it is always morally and ethically wrong for individuals and nations to participate in war. Although the idea is centuries old, the word *pacifism* was first used in 1902 at the Tenth International Peace Conference. There are varieties of pacifism, but all hold that violence and war are unjustifiable and that all differences, political and otherwise, should be resolved peacefully. This idea may be grounded in religious beliefs, in nonreligious beliefs of the sanctity of life, or in a practical belief that war is wasteful and ineffective as a means of resolving national and international issues.

For many pacifists, pacifism must be more than nonparticipation in war and conflict. It must also include constructive acts of promoting justice, peace, and human rights. It is more than just a rejection of war. When considering and discussing pacifism, one must also make a distinction between individual morality and pacifism and the application of those principles to the actions of the nation-state and international political order. There have been strong voices of pacifism, religious and secular, during the 21st century that have called for the cessation and avoidance of military operations by the United States in Afghanistan, Iraq, Syria, and elsewhere.

Pacifists contend that it is always wrong to go to war—all wars everywhere under all conditions are morally and ethically wrong. Pacifists may have secular or religious foundations upon which they construct their ideas of pacifism. One need not be religious to be a pacifist (or a conscientious objector). Pacifist beliefs transcend religious boundaries such that, for example, one may be Buddhist, Jewish, Roman Catholic, Protestant, or some other faith tradition, and be a pacifist. In American religious history, Christian pacifism has been the most prevalent of the pacifist perspectives.

Throughout American history, there have been voices of pacifism for every conflict and war. However, this has been a minority viewpoint and never the prevailing perspective of American citizens. Yet, it has been a strong voice, and there are religious groups and denominations that are historically pacifist in their beliefs and practices. Often known as *peace churches*, denominations such as the Brethren, Mennonites, Moravians, Friends (Quakers), and others have long supported pacifism and nonresistance. They have also actively worked to create organizations such as the Mennonite Central Committee and the American Friends Service Committee to provide religious and humanitarian assistance to those caught in the tragedy of war. During World War I, pacifists who refused to fight were known as *conscientious objectors*, a term that is now commonplace. Some religious groups are pacifists by doctrine, and other denominations have strong pacifist segments within the denomination, but the denomination does not espouse pacifism by doctrine or creedal statement. Arising from the termination of World War II and the history of the Cold War, there are strands of pacifist thought within Protestantism, Roman Catholicism, Eastern Orthodoxy, and Anglicanism. Pacifist strands are especially evident with respect to the issues of nuclear weapons and, to a lesser extent, other weapons of mass destruction, such as chemical and biological weapons.

Pacifism in Christian theology, spirituality, and practice has a long history. Strands of Christian pacifism can be traced to the early Christian era, certainly by the 2nd century. They were often textually grounded in the interpretations of specific biblical texts, such as Matthew 5:9, 38–42. There are two dominant strands of argumentation (with some variations) set forth in the Christian pacifist position. The first argues that nonviolence is preferable to violence because, ultimately, nonviolence always produces better results than war. This is the pragmatic argument for pacifism. The second strand contends war and violence are incompatible with a Christian understanding of God, God's desires for humanity, and what is entailed in being a follower of Jesus. This is the Christian witness argument for pacifism. There are recognized strengths and weaknesses of each strand.

Among the strengths of the pragmatic argument, it recognizes a wide array of effective means and methods of political engagement and action. In many circumstances, nonviolence can be more effective than violence in promoting and attaining a group's goals. Also, the argument is a reminder of the enormous human and social costs of violence. Among the strengths of the Christian witness argument, it acknowledges that an acceptance of or a judgment about pacifism is, in its most basic form, a theological judgment about what ought to be and how people ought to act ethically. The argument does not rely on any valuation or judgment about whether nonviolence is or is not an effective peace mechanism. Additionally, the Christian witness argument takes with great seriousness dedication to Christian spirituality and the practice of it in the daily life of the individual and the Christian community.

Critics of religious pacifism contend that it does not adequately or fully recognize and acknowledge the depravity of humanity due to sin. It is argued that this weakness in position effectively gives a moral and political preference to tyranny rather than war. Further, some critics of pacifism posit that the decentralized structure of and number of nations involved in international politics make occurrences of war likely despite efforts to limit war or prevent it. Finally, critics argue that the pacifist pragmatic argument dogmatically asserts and overstates the effectiveness of nonviolence.

Similarly, critics argue that there are weaknesses in the witness argument of pacifism. The witness argument rests on a minority interpretation of the concept of Christian love (*agape*), and that *agape* is not the only type of love taught in the Bible and in Christianity. Further, the witness argument denies Christian responsibility for attempts to prevent unjustifiable and violent attacks on other individuals, groups, or nations. Finally, critics argue that the position completely separates the Christians and church and the world (temporally and spiritually). For critics of pacifism, the principal problem with pacifism is that it misidentifies the morality of the individual as justification for (or morality of) the behavior of the state.

Secular and Christian pacifists believe that violence and coercive force are *never* justifiable under any circumstances and that war must be avoided at *any and all* costs. To its great credit, pacifism is sensitive to the violent tendencies that permeate human nature and society. Additionally, it recognizes diverse avenues for political and social action. Also, in its religious form, the pacifist position takes seriously both the commitment to neighbor love and the requirements of a strong Christian faith. Pacifism is sensitive to and presents an alternative to what it considers distortions of religious belief and commitment that arise amid an uncritical view of the state. Pacifists help sensitize nonpacifists and provide spiritual and political antidotes to an all-too-human tendency to rationalize violence in the service of nationalism.

Yet, because of pacifist commitment to nonviolence and consequent refusal to resist evil directly through action entailing the use of force, critics argue that, in practice, pacifism bestows upon evil and tyranny an advantage in the present life. A further prominent feature of the pacifist position is its excessively pessimistic view of governing authorities and related detachment from civil affairs. Consequently, it severs meaningful ways of constructively contributing to statecraft and, specifically, security issues, whether in domestic or foreign affairs.

Though it is a minority position, pacifism remains a strong presence and vibrant voice in American religious life with respect to American foreign policy and the use and deployment of military forces around the globe. Its emphasis on human rights, arms limitation, and the destructive nature of war provides citizens, religious leaders, and political leaders with much to consider when developing and implementing policies and practices that are grounded in deeply held religious convictions in a democratic society.

*See also:* Afghanistan War; American Civil War; American Peace Churches; American Revolution; Cold War; Conscientious Objection; Ecclesiastical Statements on War and Peace; Gulf War; Human Rights; Iraq War; Judaism and War; Just War Tradition; Peace Movements; Peacemaking; Presidential Faith and War; Protestant Denominations; Religious Texts; Rhetoric, Sermons, and Prayers; Roman Catholicism; Weapons of Mass Destruction; World War I; World War II

## Further Reading

Charles, J. Daryl, and Timothy J. Demy. *War, Peace, and Christianity*. Wheaton, IL: Crossway Publishers, 2010.

Clouse, Robert G., ed. *War: Four Christian Views*. Downers Grove, IL: InterVarsity Press, 1981.

Holmes, Arthur F., ed. *War and Christian Ethics: Classic and Contemporary Readings on the Morality of War*. 2nd ed. Grand Rapids, MI: Baker Books, 2005.

Preston, Andrew. *Sword of the Spirit, Shield of Faith: Religion in American War and Diplomacy*. New York: Alfred A. Knopf, 2012.

Settje, David E. *Faith and War: How Christians Debated the Cold and Vietnam Wars*. New York: New York University Press, 2011.

# Peace Movements

In the 21st-century United States, peace movements have primarily arisen in response to conflicts in Afghanistan and Iraq, especially with the U.S.-led coalition during Operation Iraqi Freedom (2003–2011). More dispersed and secular than religious, the 21st-century movement was not as broad and intense as earlier movements, such as protests against the Vietnam War.

Christian peace activists have drawn inspiration from the application of religious texts, such as "Blessed are the peacemakers, for they shall be called children of God" (Matthew 5:9 KJV), as well as the nonviolent teaching of Mahatma Gandhi (1869–1948), which was adopted by U.S. religious leaders such as Martin Luther King, Jr. (1929–1968) during the civil rights movement of the 1950s–1960s. The religious dimensions of American peace activism in the last one hundred years have often had strong ties to broader issues of social concerns, such as civil rights, ecology, feminism, and the labor movement. American religious peace activists have also been prominent in issues beyond national politics. Concerns such as Israeli-Palestinian violence, issues of genocide, and other international social and political concerns have become part of peace movement issues.

Peace movements have had a long and unique role in American political, military, and religious history. At times, the various movements have arisen as a voice of citizens calling for the United States to be part of global efforts for peace and the avoidance of war. In this regard, efforts such as the unsuccessful League of Nations after World War I and the more vibrant United Nations, founded in the aftermath of World War II, are international examples. At other times, peace movements have been more narrow in emphasis and arisen in protest to specific wars, such as the Vietnam War and low-intensity conflict in Central America, or to the development, stockpiling, and use of specific weapons, such as nuclear weapons. The latter arose in the aftermath of the bombing of Hiroshima and Nagasaki by the United States in 1945 and the subsequent arms race and Cold War that arose after World War II. Sometimes peace movements in the United States are short-term and single-issue movements; at other times, the movements have had a decades-long life.

In both of these categories of single-issue and long-form movements, global peace, anti-war, and religious advocates across many faith traditions have provided strong voices of assent and dissent. Historically in the West, one can trace religious promotion of peace and opposition to war to two movements in Europe during the late Middle Ages: the Peace of God (*Pax Dei*) and the Truce of God (*Treuga Dei* or *Treva Dei*). These movements, centered in France and arising within Western Christianity, were attempts to regulate and reduce Christian-on-Christian violence in the aftermath of the fall of the Carolingian dynasty. Although they arose more than a thousand years ago, these two movements set the foundations for later peace movements in Europe.

Several strands of Protestant traditions arose out of the 16th-century Reformation in Europe, of which the Anabaptist tradition had a strong pacifist and nonpolitical stance due in part to its persecution by other Protestants and Roman Catholics. It is from this strand that "peace churches" evolved, such as the Church of the Brethren, the Religious Society of Friends (Quakers), and the Mennonites. Other groups in the peace tradition include the Amish, Old Order Amish, Moravians, and Hutterites. All of these have a centuries-old theological and political stance of pacifism, and they have been a core element of American Protestant peace movement involvement. In the 20th century, and especially during and after the Vietnam War, growing segments of "mainline" Protestant denominations, such as Methodists, Lutherans, Presbyterians, and the United Church of Christ, became more liberal theologically and politically and provided strong voices in peace movements.

While shifts were occurring in 20th-century U.S. Protestantism, within Roman Catholicism, there arose in the early 20th century the Catholic Worker Movement, which emphasized social justice issues and support for workers and the labor movement, especially during the Great Depression of the 1930s.

Throughout the 20th century, there were strong individual and group voices protesting war and U.S. participation in it, including World War I and World War II. During the Cold War, some peace movement activists (religious and secular) refused to participate in air raid drills designed to prepare citizens for nuclear attacks. Under the Federal Civil Defense Act (1950) such refusal was illegal. Later, during the Vietnam War, religious groups, especially from the peace churches, were active in assisting young men in resisting the draft (Selective Service Act).

In the 21st century, the concept of *peacemaking*, negotiated settlements to end conflict, and conflict transformation focused on reconciliation have become dimensions of peace activism that go beyond protest and become involved in the difficult issues of postconflict social and cultural rebuilding.

***See also:*** Conscientious Objection; Ecclesiastical Statements on War and Peace; Genocide; Iraq War; Pacifism; Peacemaking; Vietnam War

## Further Reading

Chatfield, Charles, with Robert Kleidman. *The American Peace Movement: Ideals and Activism*. New York: Twayne Publishers, 1992.

Chiba, Shin, and Thomas J. Schoenbaum. *Peace Movements and Pacifism after September 11*. Cheltenham, UK: Edward Elgar Publishing, 2008.

Cortright, David. *Peace: A History of Movements and Ideas*. Cambridge, UK: Cambridge University Press, 2008.

Duffey, Michael K., and Irfan A. Omar. *Peacemaking and the Challenge of Violence in World Religions*. Malden, MA: Wiley-Blackwell, 2015.

Joustra, Robert J. "A Just and Durable Peace? American Evangelicals and the Quest for Peace after WWII." *Review of Faith & International Affairs* 17, no. 3 (2019): 68–79.

Koziol, Geoffrey. *The Peace of God*. Leeds, UK: ARC Humanities Press, 2018.

McNeal, Patricia. *Harder Than War: Catholic Peacemaking in Twentieth-Century America*. New Brunswick, NJ: Rutgers University Press, 1992.

Nepstad, Sharon Erickson. *Religion and War Resistance in the Plowshares Movement*. New York: Cambridge University Press, 2008.

Stellato, Jesse, ed. *Not in Our Name: American Antiwar Speeches, 1846 to the Present*. University Park: Pennsylvania State University Press, 2012.

Tobey, Kristen. *Plowshares: Protest, Performance, and Religious Identity in the Nuclear Age*. University Park: Pennsylvania State University Press, 2016.

# Peacemaking

Peacemaking entails an array of practical actions that seek to transform conflict from violence to the cessation of hostilities and, ultimately, to full reconciliation among adversaries. It seeks to move belligerent parties from violence to dialogue and entails the use of diplomatic efforts to end violence. Among the many tools used by those implementing the peacemaking process are negotiation, arbitration, judicial settlement, sanctions, blockading, and forceful intervention (United Nations 1945, Article 33). This may be done by local, regional, national, or international groups or forces depending on the circumstances.

Peacemaking falls within the realm of several terms and activities. It often intertwines and overlaps with activities such as preventive diplomacy, peacekeeping, and peacebuilding. When considered within the framework of the just war tradition, it falls under the third phase of *jus post bellum* ("justice after war"). The peacemaking testimony or witness goes beyond negative peace (the absence of war among nations) to positive or structural peace that includes the many dimensions of social justice.

Peacemaking entails conflict resolution and active endeavors toward peace and stability locally, nationally, and internationally; however, it is also preemptive in accepting pacifism and nonviolence as the best course of conflict resolution. It builds strongly on the leadership and teachings of historic voices such as Mahatma Gandhi (1869–1948) and Martin Luther King, Jr. (1929–1968).

Work begun by religious organizations in peacemaking pre-2001 included activities in Sudan in 1972 and Mozambique during its civil war in 1992. In the post-2001 environment, the role of religious organizations in diminishing hostilities has continued in places such as North and South Sudan, Northern Ireland, Syria, Iraq, Afghanistan, and the Balkans. In places where religious organizations provide peacemaking services, among other things, such trusted organizations bring credibility, the ability to mobilize services from the local to international levels, and a commitment to the long-term process that is often necessary.

Peacemaking organizations, religious and secular, build upon centuries of rejecting violence and seeking peaceful resolution and reconstruction when violence and conflict are present. In an era where religion is often a major component of conflict, the work of peacemaking organizations recognizes that every religious tradition also has values, beliefs, and practices that promote peace and nurture the well-being and vitality of individuals and communities. As such, religious peacemaking can serve as a beacon of hope to all who observe and experience the tumultuous seas of national and international violence.

*See also:* American Peace Churches; Genocide; Human Rights; Just War Tradition; King, Martin Luther, Jr.; Pacifism; Peace Movements

## Further Reading

Chiba, Shin, and Thomas J. Schoenbaum. *Peace Movements and Pacifism after September 11*. Cheltenham, UK: Edward Elgar Publishing, 2008.

Duffey, Michael K., and Irfan A. Omar. *Peacemaking and the Challenge of Violence in World Religions*. Malden, MA: Wiley-Blackwell, 2015.

Johnston, Douglas, and Cynthia Sampson, eds. *Religion, the Missing Dimension of Statecraft*. Oxford, UK: Oxford University Press, 1995.

Kern, Kathleen. *In Harm's Way: A History of Christian Peacemaker Teams*. Eugene, OR: Cascade Books, 2009.

McNeal, Patricia F. *Harder Than War: Catholic Peacemaking in Twentieth-Century America*. New Brunswick, NJ: Rutgers University, 1992.

Omar, Irfan A., and Michael K. Duffey, eds. *Peacemaking and the Challenge of Violence in World Religions*. Oxford, UK: Wiley-Blackwell, 2015.

Ouellet, Julian. "Peacemaking." *Beyond Intractability*. Posted September 2003. Edited by Guy Burgess and Heidi Burgess. Conflict Information Consortium, University of Colorado, Boulder. http://www.beyondintractability.org/essay/peacemaking

Patterson, Eric, ed. *Ethics Beyond War's End*. Washington, DC: Georgetown University Press, 2012.

Patterson, Eric D. *Ending Wars Well: Order, Justice, and Conciliation in Contemporary Post-Conflict*. New Haven, CT: Yale University Press, 2012.

Rasmussen, J. Lewis. "Peacemaking in the Twenty-First Century: New Rules, New Roles, New Actors." In *Peacemaking in International Conflict: Methods and Techniques*, edited by I. William Zartman and J. Lewis Rasmussen, 23–50. Washington, DC: United States Institute of Peace Press, 1997.

Schmid, Muriel, ed. *Religion, Conflict, and Peacemaking: An Interdisciplinary Conversation*. Salt Lake City: University of Utah Press, 2017.

Smock, David, and Qamar-ul Huda. "Islamic Peacemaking Since 9/11." Special Report 218. United States Institute for Peace, January 2009. https://www.acommonword.com/downloads/USIP_Report_1_2009.pdf

Smock, David R., ed. *Interfaith Dialogue and Peacebuilding*. Washington, DC: United States Institute for Peace, 2002.

Smock, David R. "Religious Contributions to Peacemaking: When Religion Brings Peace, Not War." Peaceworks No. 55. United States Institute for Peace, January 1, 2006. https://www.usip.org/publications/2006/01/religious-contributions-peacemaking-when-religion-brings-peace-not-war

Stassen, Glen H. *Just Peacemaking: The New Paradigm for the Ethics of Peace and War*. Cleveland, OH: Pilgrim Press, 2008.

Thistlethwaite, Susan Brooks, ed. *Interfaith Just Peacemaking: Jewish, Christian, and Muslim Perspectives on the New Paradigm of Peace and War*. New York: Palgrave Macmillan, 2012.

United Nations. "United Nations Charter." June 26, 1945. https://www.un.org/en/about-us/un-charter/full-text

# Presidential Faith and War

Presidential faith and warrior faith are part of the legacy of American civil religion. In times of war, American presidents throughout the nation's history have relied on their personal faith and the religious values of the American people to encourage and unify them in a common cause of victory. Presidential prayers and religious statements have been commonplace during American wars. For presidents with strong religious values and faith, such public commitments have been a sincere public display of private faith. Presidents without strong professions of faith have still acknowledged the faith of Americans as a source of individual and community strength. Further, American presidents have used the religious values and words of earlier presidents.

Many American presidents served in uniform during wartime prior to their election as president. In the 20th century, presidents such as Theodore Roosevelt (Spanish-American War), Harry S. Truman (World War I), and Dwight D. Eisenhower (World War I) served before World War II. Later, Dwight D. Eisenhower, John F. Kennedy, Lyndon B. Johnson, Richard M. Nixon, Gerald R. Ford, Jimmy Carter, Ronald Reagan, and George H. W. Bush all served in uniform during World War II. Prior to the 20th century, George Washington, Andrew Jackson, and Ulysses S. Grant are prominent presidents who experienced wartime service before rising to elected office, although several others also served in uniform.

During wartime, serving presidents have publicly and privately voiced religious commitments, sought divine guidance, and expressed prayers of petition and thanks. Such statements and prayers have become part of American political history and American civil religion. Two of the best-known incidents involve two of the nation's most prominent leaders—George Washington and Abraham Lincoln.

During the American Revolution (1775–1783), before becoming president, General George Washington was said to have prayed for help before victory and during the harsh winter of 1777–1778, as indicated by the image and story of a praying Washington while the Continental Army was encamped at Valley Forge. While there is no eyewitness account, letter, or diary of the prayer incident, it has become part of American lore. The first reference to this prayer entered American culture with the publication of *The Life of George Washington* (1800), which was the first biography of Washington published after his death. Authored by Mason Locke Weems (1759–1825), the work did much to popularize the life of Washington and was filled with apocryphal and embellished stories of Washington's life. (The prayer story was added to a later edition of the 1800 publication.) Late 19th- and 20th-century paintings and engravings of the alleged event further popularized it.

During the American Civil War (1861–1865), Abraham Lincoln stated of the warring sides in his Second Inaugural Address (March 4, 1865), "Both read the same Bible, and pray to the same God; and each invokes His aid against the other" (Lincoln 1865). On another occasion, Lincoln was asked about God and war and stated, "My concern is not whether God is on our side; my greatest concern is to be on God's side, for God is always right" (Lincoln n.d.). This quote was used by other wartime presidents in the 20th century, including George H. W. Bush during the Gulf War (1990–1991), using it and referencing President Lincoln and the Civil War. President Bush firmly believed that American actions in defense of Kuwait and against Iraq were morally acceptable and firmly within the framework of the just war tradition.

Presidential calls for divine favor and prayer were not always a part of American political history. President Thomas Jefferson refused to call for a national day of prayer, arguing that for him to do so would violate the First Amendment of the U.S. Constitution. Presidents followed his lead for almost fifty years, until Abraham Lincoln called for a national day of prayer in 1861. Such days have often been called for by presidents since then.

In the 20th century, the most prominent displays of presidential faith and war came during World War II (although World War I president Woodrow Wilson was very devout in his personal Presbyterian faith). On December 24, 1941, seventeen days after the Japanese attack on Pearl Harbor, President Roosevelt (Episcopalian) hosted the United Kingdom's prime minister, Winston Churchill, at the White House for a Christmas tree lighting ceremony and a declaration of January 1, 1942, as a National Day of Prayer for the United States. President Roosevelt continued public displays of faith and prayer throughout the war, including a prayer he read over the radio in a national broadcast on the evening of the D-Day invasion, June 6, 1944.

President Roosevelt died in office on April 12, 1945, before the war came to an end, and he was succeeded by Harry S. Truman (Baptist). After the dropping of the atomic bombs on Hiroshima and Nagasaki, ending the war in the Pacific theater of operations and bringing World War II to a conclusion, President Truman called for Sunday, August 19, 1945, to be National Day of Prayer, giving thanks for victory. He had called for a similar day of prayer on May 13, 1945, in the aftermath of victory in Europe. Truman also stated in diaries and speeches that prayer was a part of the decision-making process in the use of the atomic bombs.

During the Cold War, American presidents frequently relied on private and public pronouncements of faith. It was also during this era that references to the "Judeo-Christian" heritage of the United States came to be widely used. Throughout the Cold War and beyond, religious leaders such as Billy Graham (1918–2018) frequently provided pastoral care to American presidents (Democrats and Republicans). It was also during this era that President Harry Truman signed a bill in 1952 establishing the National Day of Prayer (the first Thursday of May) and President Dwight Eisenhower attended the first National Prayer Breakfast held by congressional leaders in 1953, which is now a presidential tradition.

In the 21st century, the United States has been in continuous conflict since the terrorist attacks of September 11, 2001, and every American president since then has dealt with terrorism and conflict. Religiously motivated terrorism as well as conflict in Iraq and Afghanistan have brought religious ideology and warfare to the forefront of issues of war and peace. American presidents since the 9/11 attacks have repeatedly declared that the United States was not at war with Islam but, instead, with militant Islamists. President George W. Bush (Episcopal) often referred to his personal faith and belief in divine guidance during his presidency. Expressions of faith and religious language were repeatedly part of his comments and speeches with respect to the events of 9/11 and the subsequent conflicts in Afghanistan and Iraq. Presidents Barack Obama and Donald Trump spoke of faith but were less vocal about religion and personal religious views. President Joe Biden, a Roman Catholic, faced none of the questions of faith and political allegiance to the Vatican that confronted John F. Kennedy in the election of 1960. With respect to war, Biden's Roman Catholic faith has not been an issue for American voters, unlike Kennedy's.

None of the U.S. presidents have denied the importance of religion for the nation, especially during wartime. Regardless of their personal religious commitments, every president from the 20th century to the present has understood the power of religion to inform and shape public opinion and political discourse. Such understanding has been most prevalent since the 1970s, and although the power of religion in American politics is changing, especially with respect to religious pluralism, faith remains a significant presence that no president is willing to ignore.

***See also:*** Art; Cold War; Graham, William Franklin, Jr. ("Billy"); Gulf War; Iraq War; Just War Tradition; Rhetoric, Sermons, and Prayers; September 11, 2001, Terrorist Attacks; World War II

## Further Reading

American Rhetoric: Rhetoric of 9-11. "George W. Bush: Remarks at the National Day of Prayer & Remembrance Service." September 14, 2001. https://www.americanrhetoric.com/speeches/gwbush911prayer&memorialaddress.htm

Balmer, Randall. *God in the White House: How Faith Shaped the Presidency from John F. Kennedy to George W. Bush.* New York: HarperOne, 2008.

Beschloss, Michael. *Presidents of War: The Epic Story, from 1807 to Modern Times.* New York: Crown Publishing, 2018.

Burnidge, Cara Lee. *A Peaceful Conquest: Woodrow Wilson, Religion, and the New World Order.* Chicago: University of Chicago Press, 2016.

Franklin D. Roosevelt Presidential Library and Museum. "A 'Mighty Endeavor': D-Day." Accessed June 13, 2022. https://www.fdrlibrary.org/d-day

*The Guardian* (U.S. Edition). "George Bush: 'God Told Me to End the Tyranny in Iraq.'" October 7, 2005. https://www.theguardian.com/world/2005/oct/07/iraq.usa

Guelzo, Allen C. *Abraham Lincoln: Redeemer President.* Grand Rapids, MI: Eerdmans, 2002.

Haberski, Raymond J. *God and War: American Civil Religion since 1945.* New Brunswick, NJ: Rutgers University Press, 2012.

Hankins, Barry. *Woodrow Wilson: Ruling Elder, Spiritual President.* New York: Oxford University Press, 2016.

Harris, Christopher. "Mason Locke Weems's *Life of Washington:* The Making of a Bestseller." *Southern Literary Journal* 19, no. 2 (Spring 1987): 92–101.

Heimbach, Daniel R. "The Bush Just War Doctrine: Genesis and Application of the President's Moral Leadership in the Persian Gulf War." In *From Cold War to New World Order: The Foreign Policy of George H. W. Bush*, edited by Meena Bose and Rosanna Perotti, 441–464. Westport, CT: Greenwood Press, 2002.

Junker, Detlef. "America, God, and War since 1945." HCA Graduate Blog, January 29, 2020. https://hcagrads.hypotheses.org/2770

Lincoln, Abraham. "Abraham Lincoln Quotes." Historynet. Accessed June 13, 2022. https://www.historynet.com/abraham-lincoln-quotes

Lincoln, Abraham. "Second Inaugural Address." March 4, 1865. https://www.theatlantic.com/past/docs/issues/99sep/9909lincaddress.htm

Masefield, Stephen. *The Faith of George W. Bush.* New York: Penguin, 2003.

McGready, Blake. "Revisiting the Prayer at Valley Forge." *Journal of the American Revolution*, October 15, 2018. https://allthingsliberty.com/2018/10/revisiting-the-prayer-at-valley-forge/

O'Connell, David. *God Wills It: Presidents and the Political Use of Religion.* New York: Routledge, 2015.

Pierard, Richard V., and Robert D. Lindner. *Civil Religion & the Presidency.* Grand Rapids, MI: Zondervan Publishing House, 1988.

Smith, Gary Scott. *Religion in the Oval Office: The Religious Lives of American Presidents*. New York: Oxford University Press, 2015.

## Protestant Denominations

Because Protestantism is a very broad term and encompasses so many groups and denominations, there is no single political ideology, perspective, or sociopolitical position that dominates Protestantism. There are scores of Christian groups, networks, and denominations in the 21st-century United States. Broadly speaking, Protestant denominations refer to non-Catholic and non-Orthodox churches. Further, some Episcopal churches and Anglican churches consider themselves Protestant, and some do not, contending that as Episcopalians and Anglicans, they constitute a category separate from Protestant, Orthodox, and Catholic Christians. Every Christian group has a history, theology, and practice unique to its denomination or entity. There are also doctrines, rituals, and practices that are shared or overlap with other denominations. These variations exist among Protestant, Catholic, and Orthodox Christian faiths as well as internally within each of the three.

Many observers have noted that the United States in the 21st century is the most religiously diverse nation in the world from both a Christian and non-Christian perspective. Among Christians in the United States, Protestantism is the largest grouping, representing about 43 percent of the population in 2019, though Christianity overall is in decline in the country (Pew Research Center 2019).

With respect to religion and the nation, some Protestant denominations and their members are active in the political process (e.g., Baptist, Lutheran, Reformed, Presbyterian, Methodist), while others (e.g., Quaker, Brethren, Pietist, Mennonite, Anabaptist) have doctrinal beliefs that eschew or limit political participation. Likewise, some Protestant denominations have a strong unified tradition of pacifism rooted in their history and theology; others do not, but they may have pacifist groups within the denomination. For example, the extent to which one may or may not serve in the military or hold public office varies widely among Protestants.

With respect to humanitarian efforts, conflict resolution, and peacemaking, almost all denominations support such endeavors. Many also have denominational agencies or commissions that either encourage favorable government policies toward such ends or actively send representatives and aid to war-torn regions of the globe.

American Protestants are far from monolithic in their politics. Broadly speaking, Protestants who are conservative in theology are also conservative in politics, and those who are liberal in theology tend to be liberal in their politics. However, there are also single-issue voters who span the theological spectrum. Further, Protestants who identify as evangelicals inside and outside of many Protestant denominations and their theological and political beliefs may not align with denominational positions. This is especially true of evangelicals in the "mainline" Protestant denominations, such as those denominations associated with the National Council of Churches of Christ in the USA (NCC).

With respect to war and conflict, since the Vietnam War in the 1960s and early 1970s, there has been a decline in support among mainline Protestant denominations for wars and conflicts in which the United States was a belligerent. Protestant denominations that are more conservative politically and theologically, such as various Baptists, Pentecostals, and Independent Bible Churches, have generally been more supportive of military actions. The post-9/11 days brought a brief resurgence of religious activity and worship attendance, as is often the case in a national crisis, but within a few months, the attendance level at worship services had declined.

In the last two decades, Protestant denominations have not been uniform in their support of presidential candidates, the wars in Afghanistan and Iraq, or in their views of other events in the Middle East, such as the civil war in Syria, civil war in Yemen, Palestinian-Israeli conflict, or the moving of the U.S. embassy in Tel Aviv, Israel, to Jerusalem. This affirms that the breadth of Protestant beliefs and values is such that one cannot speak of the "Protestant vote" on any foreign policy issue or matter of war and peace.

*See also:* Afghanistan War; American Peace Churches; Human Rights; Iraq War; Pacifism; Peacemaking; Religious Texts; Roman Catholicism

## Further Reading

Bottum, Joseph. "The Death of Protestant America: A Political Theory of the Protestant Mainline." *First Things*, August 2008. https://www.firstthings.com/article/2008/08/the-death-of-protestant-america

Djupe, Paul A., and Christopher P. Gilbert. *The Political Influence of Churches*. New York: Cambridge University Press, 2009.

Goldman, Samuel. "Protestant Rivalries and American Foreign Policy." *Providence*, April 18, 2018. https://providencemag.com/2018/04/protestant-rivalries-american-foreign-policy-michael-doran/

Mead, Walter Russell. "God's Country?" *Foreign Affairs* (September/October 2006). http://www.foreignaffairs.org/20060901faessay85504-p20/walter-russell-mead/god-s-country.html

Newport, Frank. "Americans' Views of Israel Remain Tied to Religious Beliefs." Gallup, March 19, 2019. https://news.gallup.com/opinion/polling-matters/247937/americans-views-israel-remain-tied-religious-beliefs.aspx

Newport, Frank. "Protestants and Frequent Churchgoers Most Supportive of Iraq War." Gallup, March 16, 2006. https://news.gallup.com/poll/21937/protestants-frequent-churchgoers-most-supportive-iraq-war.aspx

Olson, Roger E., Frank S. Mead, et al. *Handbook of Denominations in the United States*. 14th ed. Nashville, TN: Abingdon Press, 2018.

Pew Research Center. "In U.S., Decline of Christianity Continues at a Rapid Pace." October 17, 2019. https://www.pewforum.org/2019/10/17/in-u-s-decline-of-christianity-continues-at-rapid-pace/

Pew Research Center. "Religious Groups Issue Statement on War with Iraq." Compiled by Religious News Service, March 19, 2003. https://www.pewforum.org/2003/03/19/publicationpage-aspxid616/

# R

## Religion, Conflict, and Geopolitics

Religious entities, religious leaders, and religious values are a prominent presence in the 21st-century world. Nationally and internationally, religious influence varies from nation to nation and region to region, but it is an ever-present reality. Religion can promote peace and stability, but at times, it can also be a force that supports, and sometimes initiates, conflict.

The combination of religion, conflict, and geopolitics as a destructive force rather than a constructive force was manifested and experienced in the United States during the terrorist attacks of September 11, 2001. Just as politics can be constructive or destructive in the experiences and lives of individuals, societies, and nations, so too can religion have the same effects. When coupled together, religion and politics can be a powerful force for doing good or for doing harm. Most conflicts are not religious conflicts at their source, but most conflicts have religion as a factor in the same way that economics, history, politics, ethnicity, and resources may be factors.

Every religion has teachings regarding war and peace as well as a spectrum of beliefs about conflict. Similarly, in every nation and region of the globe, there exists a relationship between religion and politics and between religion and the state. In some nations, there is great overlap between religious and political dynamics (e.g., Iran). In other more secular nations, there is less influence, formally or informally. In totalitarian nations, there is often the repression of religion and the persecution of people of faith and religious institutions. In the United States, the relationship between religion and the state is one of formal separation that is grounded in the First Amendment of the U.S. Constitution. However, religion has been a significant force in American politics and culture and has always been a dynamic in American conflicts. This dynamic has been evidenced in the lives of members of the American military, in the support or opposition of American war efforts, and in the influencing of domestic and foreign policies.

The concept of political theology is that of how religious people and groups think and further their values with respect to others and the state. For example, they may call for a political regime that upholds human rights and religious freedom or for a regime that suppresses them. Similarly, it matters whether a government tends to lean toward independence of religion and the state or interdependence.

The last quarter of the 20th century was one in which secularism and the demise of established religion increased in Europe and, to a lesser extent, in North America. From the 1960s onward, many observers believed that religion would diminish as a presence in international relations, especially with respect to conflict and war. A premise of secularization, globalization, and postmodernity was that religion was no longer relevant to contemporary life and would no longer play a defining role in the national and global arenas.

While this debate was occurring in some parts of the world, other regions, such as Africa, South America, and the Middle East, were experiencing a resurgence of religious fervor. At times, this renewal, which often addressed the political and economic frustrations of many, was coupled with militancy and violence against existing governments and their allies. Whether religion was at the center of desires for social and political change or was used as an instrument to assist in creating change varies in each instance. What is not disputed is that the presence of religion has been a critical factor.

In every conflict in which a nation participates, there are three entities that influence the course of the nation's fighting: the people (citizens), the government, and the military. In each of the three entities, religion may be either a major or minor influencing factor. For example, support for or against a war by a nation's citizens may be influenced by religious values.

Every major conflict of the 21st century has had a significant religious component or dynamic in at least one of the belligerent state or nonstate actors. And in every conflict in which the United States has participated, there have been religious groups and denominations that expressed support or opposition to the war effort in attempts to influence U.S. government policies and actions. Similarly, on an international level, religious leaders with global influence, such as Popes John Paul II, Benedict XVI, and Francis; the Dalai Lama; and patriarchs of the Orthodox churches, have encouraged the peaceful resolution of conflicts and the upholding of human rights and religious freedom.

One of the most visible violent manifestations of religion in the 21st century is that of terrorism. Religious terrorist attacks have persisted since the attacks of September 11, 2001. Though not limited to a single religion, the majority of attacks have been carried out by Islamist terrorist groups such as al-Qaeda, Boko Haram, the Islamic State (ISIL or ISIS), Abu Sayyaf, and self-radicalized individuals. Beyond attacks in the United States, there have been hundreds of large and small attacks globally. For example, in Europe, major attacks include the Madrid train bombing (2004), the London Underground and bus bombings (2005), the Paris bomb and shooting attack (2015), the Brussels airport bomb (2016), the Istanbul Airport bomb and shooting attack (2016), the Berlin Christmas market truck attack (2016), the Manchester Arena bombing (2017), and the Barcelona van attack (2017). Each of these was initiated by individuals claiming religion as justification for their acts. Similarly, in India, the 2001 Indian Parliament attack and the 2008 Mumbai attack at the Taj Mahal Palace hotel were both carried out by the Islamist terrorist organization Lashkar-e-Taiba, which is based in Pakistan.

The quest for national and international peace and stability is something for which the majority of people of faith and religious institutions around the globe work and pray to realize. Some religious groups and denominations have representatives or agencies whose function is to observe or interact with the government or other agencies to foster peace and security and to influence national and international policies.

The presence and influence of religion in 21st-century national and global affairs remain visible and viable. Although the future of the union of religion and politics with respect to conflict is unknown, for the present, the words of former U.S. secretary of state Madeleine Albright are prescient: "Religion counts" (Albright 2006, 42).

*See also:* Contemporary Non-U.S. Conflicts; Human Rights; Middle East Conflict; Peacemaking; Religious Freedom and Religious Persecution; Responsibility to Protect; United Nations

## Further Reading

Albright, Madeleine. *The Mighty and the Almighty: Reflections on America, God, and World Affairs*. New York: HarperCollins, 2006.

Berger, Peter L., ed. *The Desecularization of the World: Resurgent Religion and World Politics*. Grand Rapids, MI: Eerdmans, 1999.

Bettiza, Gregorio. *Finding Faith in Foreign Policy: Religion and American Diplomacy in a Postsecular World*. New York: Oxford University Press, 2019.

Fraihat, Ibrahim. *Iran and Saudi Arabia: Taming a Chaotic Conflict*. Edinburgh, UK: Edinburgh University Press, 2020.

Juergensmeyer, Mark. *Terror in the Mind of God*. 4th ed. Berkeley: University of California Press, 2017.

McDougall, Walter A. "The Myth of the Secular: Religion, War, and Politics in the Twentieth Century." Templeton Lecture on Religion and World Affairs, Foreign Policy Research Institute, October 17, 2019. https://www.fpri.org/article/2019/10/the-myth-of-the-secular-religion-war-and-politics-in-the-twentieth-century/

Toft, Monica Duffy, Daniel Philpott, and Timothy Samuel Shah. *God's Century: Resurgent Religion and Global Politics*. New York: W. W. Norton, 2011.

Wade, Francis. *Myanmar's Enemy Within: Buddhist Violence and the Making of a Muslim "Other."* London: Zed Books, 2019.

## Religious Freedom and Religious Persecution

Religious freedom and religious persecution may be viewed as the affirmation and denial of a core human right. When the right is upheld and promoted, religious freedom is affirmed. When the right is denied, there is active or passive religious persecution.

Religious freedom has a long history in the West and is closely tied to ideas of democracy, justice, and political freedom. As stated by the United Nations in the promulgation and adoption of the Universal Declaration of Human Rights (UDHR; 1948), religious freedom is a fundamental human right: "Everyone has the right to freedom of thought, conscience and religion; this right includes freedom to change his religion or belief, and freedom, either alone or in community with others and in public or private, to manifest his religion or belief in teaching, practice, worship and observance" (United Nations 1948, Article 18). The concept of religious freedom entails several things, among them the freedom to have or adopt a religion or belief of one's choosing; the freedom to change one's beliefs or religion; freedom from coercion with respect to one's beliefs or religion; and the freedom to publicly display or practice religion or belief in worship, observance, and teaching.

Religious freedom is frequently a barometer of other human rights in a society. Religious freedom is not an insignificant concern or human right for an individual or a society. Rather, as a human right, it is one of the central strands woven through the fabric of an individual's and society's daily life and experience. A nation, culture, and political structure that supports religious freedom understands and appreciates the linkages between religious freedom and national and human security. In such support, there is the realization that national security must incorporate a commitment to civil and political liberties—inclusive of religious freedom.

Religious persecution is the opposite of religious freedom. It is the systematic and intentional persecution of individuals or groups *because of* their religious faith and their religious practices. Religious persecution or religious discrimination occurs where religion is a significant or a defining aspect or component of the injustice that is directed at and suffered by an individual or group. It can be instigated and promulgated by individuals or groups attacking others, or it can be sponsored by governments and carried out directly or indirectly by them. It can happen in secular states or religious states and even in democracies. Ideologically, there is a direct connection between the concepts of religious pluralism, religious tolerance, and freedom of religion. Additionally, there is linkage between the establishment and disestablishment of national religion (just as there is linkage with other core democratic values and rights, such as freedom of speech and the right of assembly). Religious persecution can be subtle or aggressive—active or passive. It can involve intentional acts of violence against citizens by a government and its representatives, or it can involve the intentional lack of intervention by the government as violence is committed against its citizens by other citizens or groups either inside or outside national geographic boundaries.

When a nation and its leaders and citizens intentionally persecute individuals and groups because of the faith of those individuals or groups, there are several possible responses, reactions, and outcomes that may occur by and for those who are persecuted. They may choose acquiescence, or they may choose cobelligerence with others of similar beliefs or others being persecuted. Or, they may go underground or resist by becoming holy warriors with some enduring martyrdom. Another potential for the persecuted is that there will be ideological and institutional restructuring of the persecuted. Finally, especially in a globalized world of rapid communications, there may be an international alliance and allegiance to gain support and resources. Any single response or combination of them is possible when there is religious persecution. And there are current and historical examples of each. Often, these accompany rebellion and conflict within a nation's borders and also regional warfare that transcends the boundaries of a single nation.

Within American religious communities, international religious freedom (IRF) has long been recognized as a right that transcends religious beliefs and political ideologies. In 1998, the U.S. Senate passed the International Religious Freedom Act (IRFA). The bill passed with a bipartisan vote of 98–0 by the Senate and was signed into law by President Bill Clinton. The IRFA provided for an ambassador-at-large position. Recognizing that there is linkage between religious freedom and national and human security, the IRFA requires that the ambassador produce an annual State Department Report on International Religious Freedom that evaluates nations, country by country, and designates violating nations as "Countries of Particular Concern." Additionally, the act created the independent and bipartisan U.S. Commission on International Religious Freedom (USCIRF) to advise on foreign policy.

A third component of the act was the creation of an advisory position on international religious freedom on the National Security Council. That position was unfilled by presidential administrations until 2018. In 2016, an amendment to the IRFA was added to strengthen it by having the ambassador-at-large report directly to the secretary of state. In 2020, President Donald Trump signed Executive Order 13926—Advancing International Religious Freedom. In part, the document states, "Religious freedom for all people worldwide is a foreign policy priority of the United States, and the United States will respect and vigorously promote this freedom" (Trump 2020).

Examples of 21st-century religious freedom restriction or persecution have been documented in more than fifty countries and include the persecution and imprisonment of Uyghur Muslims in China; the persecution of Christians, Baha'is, Yazidis, and Jews in Iraq and elsewhere in the Middle East; the persecution of Christians and Muslims in Afghanistan; the persecution of Rohingya in Myanmar; and Christian persecution in Nigeria, to name but a few. Unfortunately, denial of religious freedom and ongoing religious persecution will likely remain a subject of U.S. bipartisan concern and international headlines.

***See also:*** Genocide; Holocaust; Human Rights; Responsibility to Protect; United Nations

## Further Reading

Bosco, Robert M. *Securing the Sacred: Religion, National Security, and the Western State*. Ann Arbor: University of Michigan Press, 2016.

Farr, Thomas. "What in the World Is Religious Freedom?" Religious Freedom Institute, November 1, 2019. https://www.religiousfreedominstitute.org/blog/what-in-the-world-is-religious-freedom

Farr, Thomas. *World of Faith and Freedom: Why International Religious Liberty Is Vital to American National Security*. New York: Oxford University Press, 2008.

Green, Emma. "The Impossible Future of Christians in the Middle East." *The Atlantic*, May 23, 2019. https://www.theatlantic.com/international/archive/2019/05/iraqi-christians-nineveh-plain/589819/

Johnson, Noel. *Persecution & Toleration: The Long Road to Religious Freedom*. Cambridge, UK: Cambridge University Press, 2019.

Lindkvist, Linde. *Religious Freedom and the Universal Declaration of Human Rights*. Cambridge, UK: Cambridge University Press, 2020.

Pew Research Center. "A Closer Look at How Religious Restrictions Have Risen around the World." July 15, 2019. https://www.pewforum.org/2019/07/15/a-closer-look-at-how-religious-restrictions-have-risen-around-the-world/

Rasche, Stephen M. *The Disappearing People: The Tragic Fate of Christians in the Middle East*. New York: Bombardier Books, 2020.

Seiple, Robert A., and Dennis R. Hoover, eds. *Religion & Security: The New Nexus in International Relations*. Oxford, UK: Rowman & Littlefield, 2004.

Trump, Donald J. "Executive Order on Advancing International Religious Freedom." June 2, 2020. https://trumpwhitehouse.archives.gov/presidential-actions/executive-order-advancing-international-religious-freedom/

United Nations. "Universal Declaration of Human Rights." December 10, 1948. https://www.un.org/en/universal-declaration-human-rights/

U.S. Department of State. "International Religious Freedom Reports." https://www.state.gov/international-religious-freedom-reports/

Wilken, Robert Louis. *Liberty in the Things of God: The Christian Origins of Religious Freedom*. New Haven, CT: Yale University Press, 2019.

## Religious Identity in the Armed Forces

The relationship between religion and the U.S. military dates to the era of the American Revolution and Continental Congress, when the Continental Congress authorized the funding of chaplains for the Continental Army.

As the nation has become more diverse in the last few decades, that diversity has also become part of the American military experience. Religion and religious dynamics have been a part of the military since then.

The American military went to an all-volunteer force on July 1, 1973, ending the Selective Training and Service Act of 1940, commonly known as "the draft," that was started on September 16, 1940. The 21st-century American military forces represent the economic, political, educational, and religious spectrum of American society, though it does not necessarily mirror the same demographics.

The U.S. Department of Defense does not track specific faith group demographics for service members, nor does it collect information on the political parties or preferences of members of the military. However, a limited voluntary study in 2009 by the Defense Equal Opportunity Management Institute (DEOMI) examined the religious self-identification, beliefs, and practices of military personnel. The study found that self-reported religious identity that was more than 10 percent of those surveyed was 23.9 percent Roman Catholic, 17.2 percent Baptist, and 12.1 percent no religious preference. All other faith traditions were less than 10 percent (e.g., Jewish 1.7%, Muslim 0.6%). From that survey, a total of 78.5 percent self-identified as within the Christian tradition (Military Leadership Diversity Commission 2010, 2). The study also found that there was more religious diversity among younger service members as well as more members choosing "No religious preference." Nonbelief of religion in the military service also reflects the growing secular trend in American society as a whole.

There are more than 200 religious groups and faith traditions that are recognized by the Department of Defense with respect to groups that are recognized as eligible for endorsing clergy for military chaplaincy. With respect to politics and religion in the military, the two most personal matters are (1) the upholding of the establishment clause of the First Amendment rights of all service members, such that they maintain their right to freedom of religion and the ability to practice or not practice their faith (no faith) while in the military, and (2) religious accommodation with respect to religious practices and the wearing of religious apparel. All members of the U.S. military are encouraged to vote in local, state, and national elections. Registration is accomplished in the member's home of record, which is typically the state from which the individual joined the service.

Each of the branches of the U.S. military continues to wrestle with ways of affirming the diversity of the individuals within the services and upholding the rights of each member. At the same time, the services must maintain unit cohesion, readiness, the core values of each service, and the ability to successfully complete missions they are called upon to perform by the nation. The balancing of sacred and secular and individual and institutional needs and rights remains a persistent challenge. It is, however, one that is readily accepted by the U.S. military in furtherance of individual and national freedom.

*See also:* Military Chaplains; Protestant Denominations; Roman Catholicism

## Further Reading

Military Leadership Diversity Commission. "Religious Diversity in the U.S. Military." Issue Paper 22 (June 2010). https://www.hsdl.org/?view&did=716143

Pew Research Center. "Accommodating Faith in the Military." July 3, 2008. https://www.pewforum.org/2008/07/03/accommodating-faith-in-the-military/

Pew Research Center. "U.S. Religious Landscape Survey." June 1, 2008. https://www.pewforum.org/dataset/u-s-religious-landscape-survey/

Reynolds, George M., and Amanda Shendruk. "Demographics of the U.S. Military." Council on Foreign Relations, April 24, 2018. https://www.cfr.org/article/demographics-us-military

Sandhoff, Michael. "Religious Diversity in the U.S. Military." In *Inclusion in the American Military: A Force for Diversity*, edited by David E. Rondall, Morten G. Ender, and Michael D. Matthews, 169–188. Lanham, MD: Lexington Books, 2017.

U.S. Department of Defense. "Are Service Members Permitted to Freely Practice Their Religious Beliefs." March 29, 2019. https://www.defense.gov/ask-us/faq/Article/1774638/are-service-members-permitted-to-freely-practice-their-religious-beliefs/

U.S. Department of Defense. "DoD Instruction 1300.17: Religious Liberty in the Military Services." September 1, 2020. https://www.esd.whs.mil/Portals/54/Documents/DD/issuances/dodi/130017p.pdf

# Religious Texts

Sacred texts have often been used to justify or oppose the use of armed force as well as to give guidance on how to relate to the state and whether to participate in the political process and state matters. Some religious traditions, such as Jainism, eschew all violence and war, but most religions have a spectrum of belief and practice with respect to war and peace. For the person of faith, sacred texts may provide authoritative guidance for how matters of war, peace, and politics are viewed within the individual's faith tradition and community. The importance of sacred texts in life, spirituality, and decision-making processes should not be ignored or minimized.

The definition of *scripture* and what constitutes a religious text also differ across the religious spectrum. The Abrahamic faith traditions (Judaism, Christianity, and Islam) have set compilations or canons that are considered authoritative for religious guidance and practice. The Tanakh (Hebrew Bible) in Judaism, the Bible (Old Testament and New Testament) in Christianity, and the Qur'an in Islam are the primary texts, though each tradition also has secondary texts for guidance. In other traditions, such as the Indic and Asian religions of Hinduism, Buddhism, and Shinto, there is more diffusion of religious texts, and the purpose of them and authority given to them differ from the weight and authority given in Abrahamic faith traditions. Similarly, the role of oral tradition rather than written tradition is important in many religions, such as African tribal and Caribbean religions. Religious texts are also composed of a variety of types of literature, including history, letters, wisdom statements, prophetic statements, parables, law, ceremonial procedures, and other genres. Each of these can have material pertaining to war, peace, and community or state obligations.

Further compounding the challenge of identifying texts regarding war, peace, politics, and the state is the fact that most religious texts are centuries or even millennia old, predating contemporary understanding and history of the nation-state that emerged after the 1648 Treaty of Westphalia. Yet, the texts are still looked to for guidance on matters of war, peace, and the political order.

Many religious texts recount battles of actual and mythic wars that are deemed significant in the history of a particular faith tradition. But for contemporary warfare and the political dimensions surrounding it and the balancing of the responsibilities of one's citizenship and one's religious beliefs, the process of observation, interpretation, and application of religious texts becomes important. In the process of reading a scriptural text, an individual or community must ask the question, "What does the text say?"

The next step is the interpretation of the text wherein this question is asked and studied: "What does the text mean?" This is a step that may be very complex and for which different readers of the text will arrive at different interpretations. The discipline of interpreting literary texts (sacred or secular) is known as *hermeneutics*. A faith tradition's sacred texts as a whole as well as individual verses and texts very often have a history of interpretation. Such histories are often long and complex, but they inform contemporary understandings of sacred texts.

The final question in the process after observation and interpretation involves application of the text: "How should the text be applied in the present in the life of the individual or group?" Every reader of a text, secular or religious, undergoes this process, consciously or subconsciously, when reading anything. When a person of faith of any religious tradition looks to that tradition's sacred texts, questions of the texts that arise with respect to war, peace, and citizenship include the following:

- To what extent may or should an individual participate in the political process?
- Is it ever permissible for a nation, a person of faith, or both to go to war?
- If it is permissible to go to war, when is it permissible?
- Who has the right to authorize war?
- What are the limitations, if any, on the use of force with respect to people and places?
- How should wars be fought with respect to codes of conduct?
- What is the peace process, and how is peace to be upheld?

Most religious traditions have a mixture of peace texts and war texts with different emphases accorded to particular texts. The same is true for texts that pertain to social and political issues and how and whether the person of faith is to participate in the political process. What must be studied within each religious tradition and religious text is whether a particular text is to be understood as applying to the individual believer, the religious community, or the larger political entity or state. In the same way that Americans determine when to apply federal tax laws to individuals and when to apply them to businesses or other entities, people of faith also seek to understand the scope of application of specific religious texts. Which sacred texts apply to the ethics and morality of the individual, and which texts apply to ethics and morality of the state—and is there any textual overlap?

Religiously, the overwhelming majority of American citizens are from the monotheistic religions of Christianity, Judaism, and Islam. Within those traditions, some of the most common verses about war and peace from sacred texts are cited below. (This is a very limited sampling of the rich textual traditions within each faith.)

## JUDAISM

- "He [God] makes wars cease to the end of the earth; he breaks the bow and shatters the spear; he burns the chariots with fire." Psalm 46:9 (ESV)
- "For everything there is a season, and a time for every matter under heaven . . . a time to love, and a time to hate; a time for war, and a time for peace." Ecclesiastes. 3:1, 8 (ESV)
- "He [God] shall judge between the nations, and shall decide disputes for many peoples; and they shall beat their swords into plowshares, and their spears into pruning hooks; nation shall not lift up sword against nation, neither shall they learn war anymore." Isaiah 2:4 (ESV)

One of the central (and lengthy) scriptural texts of war within Judaism is Deuteronomy 20:1–20, which sets forth extensive guidelines for the Israelites after they were freed from slavery in Egypt.

## CHRISTIANITY

- "Blessed are the peacemakers, for they shall be called sons of God." Matthew 5:9 (ESV)
- "You have heard that it was said, 'An eye for an eye and a tooth for a tooth.' But I say to you, Do not resist the one who is evil. But if anyone slaps you on the right cheek, turn to him the other also." Matthew 5:38, 39 (ESV)
- "Jesus said to them, 'Render to Caesar the things that are Caesar's, and to God the things that are God's.'" Mark 12:17 (ESV)
- "If possible, so far as it depends on you, live peaceably with all." Romans 12:18 (ESV)
- "Let every person be subject to the governing authorities. For there is no authority except from God, and those that exist have been instituted by God. Therefore whoever resists the authorities resists what God has appointed, and those who resist will incur judgment. For rulers are not a terror to good conduct, but to bad. Would you have no fear of the one who is in authority? Then do what is good, and you will receive his approval, for he is God's servant for your good. But if you do wrong, be afraid, for he does not bear the sword in vain. For he is the servant of God, an avenger who carries out God's wrath on the wrongdoer. Therefore one must be in subjection, not only to avoid God's wrath but

also for the sake of conscience. For because of this you also pay taxes, for the authorities are ministers of God, attending to this very thing. Pay to all what is owed to them: taxes to whom taxes are owed, revenue to whom revenue is owed, respect to whom respect is owed, honor to whom honor is owed." Romans 13:1–7 (ESV)
- "First of all, then, I urge that supplications, prayers, intercessions, and thanksgivings be made for all people, for kings and all who are in high positions, that we may lead a peaceful and quiet life, godly and dignified in every way." 1 Timothy 2:1–2 (ESV)
- "Remind them to be submissive to rulers and authorities, to be obedient, to be ready for every good work." Titus 3:1 (ESV)

In addition to the many texts of the New Testament, Christians also consider the Old Testament (Hebrew Bible) to be a part of their canon.

## ISLAM

- "Fight in the cause of Allah those who fight you, but do not transgress limits; for Allah loveth not transgressors." Qur'an 2:190 (Abdullah Yusuf Ali)
- ". . . to save a life would be as great a virtue as to save all of mankind." Qur'an 5:32 (Muhammad Sarwar)
- "Take not life, which Allah hath made sacred, except by way of justice and law . . . ." Qur'an 6:151 (Abdullah Yusuf Ali)
- ". . . if the enemy incline towards peace, do thou (also) incline towards peace, and trust in Allah: for He is One that heareth and knoweth (all things)." Qur'an 8:61 (Abdullah Yusuf Ali)

The decision of a nation to go to war or to apply armed force is always a political decision that usually requires strong justification if a nation's citizens and allies are going to support the war effort and, eventually, the cessation of hostilities and the peace process. The taking of life by armed force is always a serious act, and unless one is a pacifist, it can only be warranted under certain circumstances and only for significant causes. An individual's participation or nonparticipation in violent acts of the state is a matter of conscience. Persons of faith will often use sacred texts for making decisions about participation or nonparticipation and support of war efforts. Values have consequences, and for many people, personal values and public actions are informed by the reading, interpreting, and applying of religious texts to their private, public, and political lives.

**See also:** Buddhism and War; Christianity and War; Ecclesiastical Statements on War and Peace; Hinduism and War; Judaism and War; Islam and War

## Further Reading

Dorn, A. Walter. "The Justification for War and Peace in World Religions. Part III: Comparison of Scriptures from Seven World Religions." Contract Report, CR 2010-036. Defence R&D Canada. Toronto, March 2010. https://apps.dtic.mil/dtic/tr/fulltext/u2/a535552.pdf

Goldberg, Edwin C. *Swords and Plowshares: Jewish Views on War and Peace.* New York: URJ Press, 2006.

Reichberg, Gregory M., Henrik Syse, and Endre Begby, eds. *The Ethics of War: Classic and Contemporary Readings.* Oxford, UK: Blackwell Publishing, 2006.

Reichberg, Gregory M., Henrik Syse, and Nicole M. Hartwell, eds. *Religion, War, and Ethics: A Sourcebook of Textual Traditions.* New York: Cambridge University Press, 2014.

# Responsibility to Protect (R2P)

All American religious traditions value human life and its protection. In politics, international relations, and war, this concern is manifested in the desire to protect innocent civilians, which is expressed explicitly in religious texts and practices. It is also grounded in international law in the United Nations Universal Declaration of Human Rights (UDHR). When national leaders either attack or cannot protect the citizens they govern, the international community has debated the need and legal and moral obligation to intervene, a requisite "Responsibility to Protect." As an international norm, the responsibility to protect rests on three pillars of equal standing: "the responsibility of each State to protect its populations (pillar I); the responsibility of the international community to assist States in protecting their populations (pillar II); and the responsibility of the international community to protect when a State is manifestly failing to protect its populations (pillar III)" (Šimonović 2016). The need for an international policy or doctrine arose in the late 1980s and the 1990s in the aftermath of events such as the 1989 chemical gas attack on Kurdish civilians in Halabja, Iraq; the 1994 genocide in Rwanda; and other attacks by leaders on their citizens or instances in which leaders were unable to protect their citizens.

In 2001, the International Commission on Intervention and State Sovereignty panel (ICISS), an ad hoc commission of participants from members of the UN General Assembly, published a report and doctrine to fulfill a United Nations mandate to propose guidelines for humanitarian intervention. The Canadian-led panel titled the report "The Responsibility to Protect" (commonly referred to as "R2P"). The doctrine was formally codified due to numerous precipitating events, the key highlights of which will be discussed below. Despite the need for a unified international armed force that might exercise R2P intervention in specific cases of human rights violations and attempts by the International Criminal Court (ICC) to recognize and stop "crimes against humanity" (a concept grounded in post–World War II international human rights), it took ten years of debate before the international community finally invoked the doctrine: a coalition including the United States used the doctrine to justify the bombing of Benghazi, Libya, in 2011.

A sovereign's responsibility (a sovereign is the nation-state or state in contemporary international relations) for the good of the people over which they rule is rooted in the classical just war tradition, the medieval origins of which can be traced back to Thomas Aquinas (1225–1274). Aquinas established Christian theological interpretations of Greek, Roman, Jewish, and other Christian canonistic just war thinking in his work *Summa Theologica*, published in 1485. Adaptations of this classic tradition in subsequent centuries included both secular and religious interpretations. In recent decades, one of the most influential of these is the 1983 pastoral letter by the United States Conference of Catholic Bishops (USCCB), "The Challenge of Peace," which applies just war concepts to a pacifist stance against a deemed immoral use of nuclear weapons. The iterations of the pastoral letter were significant to the concept of a responsibility to protect, especially the 1993 document known as "The Harvest of Justice Is Sown in Peace," stating, "Force may be used only to correct a grave, public evil, i.e., aggression or massive violation of the basic rights of whole populations" (USCCB 1993). Critics such as James Turner Johnson argue that the USCCB has never adequately applied positive use of force to protect innocent populations harmed by their ruling governments as stated; rather, they have used the interpretation to encourage restraint and to prohibit the use of force as immoral (Trinity Forum 2015).

Thus, whereas during conflicts in previous centuries sovereigns mainly used military force in their interests to gain territory or resources or to defend their countries against acts of aggression by another, some leaders in contemporary times have considered the obliged use of military force to protect human rights of a populace through intervention. In such instances, the doctrine of the responsibility to protect is understood to overrule the standing international norm of sovereign national borders. The NATO-led action in Libya in 2011 is the culmination of this trend. Article 138 of the 2005 UN summit outcome document "acknowledges the responsibility of individual sovereign states to protect their population from four acts: 1) genocide, 2) crimes against humanity, 3) war crimes, and 4) ethnic cleansing." It is worth noting that, although the 2005 UN summit outcome language is an ongoing effort supported by UN deliberation since 1945, the statements are political and not legal in nature. The explicit intent of the doctrine—as stated by Kofi Annan (b. 1938, the seventh secretary-general of the United Nations who mandated guidelines for R2P in 2001)—is not to develop new law but to strengthen states' existing humanitarian obligations to its citizens.

Contemporary application of R2P doctrine is complex: if humanitarian intervention is accepted by the international community as a just cause for entering a conflict, against whom are the enforcers taking armed action? The international community, through the UN Security Council, might act to enforce global human rights, but the politics pitting communist states such as Russia and China against democratic states such as Great Britain and the United States make unified enforcement difficult, if not impossible. Yet, no single nation-state, much less the United States, desires sole risk and responsibility for intervening in interstate affairs. As stated above, the cases of Rwanda and the U.S.-led intervention in Somalia (1992–1993, culminating in the October 1993 Battle of Mogadishu) demonstrate the infeasibility of intervention even in clear cases where citizens are being tyrannized or threatened by their government. The next best option for U.S. multilateral application of the doctrine includes either NATO or, as termed in recent cases of intervention, a "coalition of the willing."

Several religious groups have affirmed R2P as aligning with their theological and religious values. Christian Protestant denominations have published various responses to the USCCB's just war arguments, including the United Methodist Church Council of Bishops' 1986 study, *In Defense of Creation*. The tragedies of genocide in Rwanda and Bosnia prompted additional statements from the USCCB (including its 1993 statement, "The Harvest of Justice Is Sown in Peace") and Protestant denominations (including a United Presbyterian 1996 statement approving humanitarian intervention). Pope Benedict XVI (b. 1927) called leaders to support R2P in his 2008 UN address. However, the USCCB declined to invoke R2P and support the UN Security Council–authorized air bombing of Libya by a "coalition of the willing" led by U.S. president Barack Obama's administration in 2011.

Care for the poor and protection of the innocent have been central practices within American religious traditions. It is questionable whether the international community can enforce R2P as a legal mandate and not just a suggested moral obligation. Such potential limitations, however, do not eradicate the religious expectations for care and protection of the weak—expectations that will be voiced by the faithful in their religious and political lives. As such, R2P will remain an issue of significant religious and political consequence, domestically and internationally.

*See also:* Contemporary Non-U.S. Conflicts; Ecclesiastical Statements on War and Peace; Genocide; Holocaust; Human Rights; Just War Tradition; Religion, Conflict, and Geopolitics; Religious Texts; United Nations

## Further Reading

Badescu, Cristina Gabriela. *Humanitarian Intervention and the Responsibility to Protect: Security and Human Rights*. London: Routledge, 2012.

BBC News. "Viewpoint: 'Overwhelming' Moral Case for Military Path." March 8, 2011. https://www.bbc.com/news/world-africa-12676248

Bellamy, Alex J., and Edward C. Luck. *The Responsibility to Protect: From Promise to Practice*. Cambridge, UK: Polity Press, 2018.

Dallaire, Roméo. *Shake Hands with the Devil: The Failure of Humanity in Rwanda*. Toronto: Random House Canada, 2003.

Gobush, Matt. "Calling All Christians: The Responsibility to Protect." *Providence*, April 28, 2016. https://providencemag.com/2016/04/calling-christians-responsibility-to-protect-r2p/

Haslett, Brighton. "No Responsibility for the Responsibility to Protect: How Powerful States Abuse the Doctrine, and Why Misuse Will Lead to Disuse." *North Carolina Journal of International Law* 40, no. 1, art. 5 (Fall 2014). https://scholarship.law.unc.edu/cgi/viewcontent.cgi?article=2030&context=ncilj

Power, Samantha. *"A Problem from Hell": America and the Age of Genocide*. New York: Basic Books, 2013.

Ross, Jeffrey Ian. *Religion and Violence: An Encyclopedia of Faith and Conflict from Antiquity to the Present*. Armonk, NY: M. E. Sharpe, 2011.

Šimonović, Ivan. "The Responsibility to Protect." UN Chronicle 53, no. 4 (December 2016). https://www.un.org/en/chronicle/article/responsibility-protect

The Trinity Forum. "Evening Conversation with James Turner Johnson (March 3, 2015)." Posted May 31, 2016. YouTube Video, 1:24:38. https://www.youtube.com/watch?v=MwAV-BngFKE

United Nations. "Universal Declaration of Human Rights." Accessed August 11, 2020. https://www.un.org/en/universal-declaration-human-rights/

United States Conference of Catholic Bishops. *The Challenge of Peace: God's Promise and Our Response: A Pastoral Letter on War and Peace by the National Conference of Catholic Bishops*. May 3, 1983. https://www.usccb.org/upload/challenge-peace-gods-promise-our-response-1983.pdf

United States Conference of Catholic Bishops. "The Harvest of Justice Is Sown in Peace." November 17, 1993. https://www.usccb.org/resources/harvest-justice-sown-peace

## Rhetoric, Sermons, and Prayers

Rhetoric, sermons, and prayers have been associated with warfare for millennia across the religious and cultural spectrum. For example, in American history, Abraham Lincoln's Gettysburg Address is infused with religious imagery and wording that is often compared to and parallels the "Funeral Oration" given by Athenian politician Pericles at the end of the first year of the Peloponnesian War (431–404 BCE).

The often-heard phrase "The pen is mightier than the sword" was written by English politician, novelist, and playwright Edward Bulwer-Lytton (1803–1873) in 1839, in his historical play *Cardinal Richelieu*. However, variations of it date as far back as classical Greece. There has also been a blending of war and words in the history, religious experiences, and politics in the United States from its earliest colonial days to the 21st century. Existing alongside the constitutional and legal aspects of the separation of religion and the state ("church and state"), the presence of this rhetoric has had a greater influence than is often realized. When used apart from places of worship and in the public square, it has formed a central pillar of American civil religion.

In every war in American history, religious leaders, political leaders, and individual citizens, soldiers, and sailors have used religious rhetoric (used here in its broadest sense and encompassing sermons and prayers) for encouragement, assurance, and hope. For many, the words were proclaimed in support of war efforts, but religious opposition to wars has also been voiced publicly and privately.

Religious rhetoric has been used by political leaders for personal spiritual strength as well as for calling the nation to a common cause. In its early history, religious rhetoric was almost exclusively Christian and Jewish. As the nation grew and the population's religious diversity broadened, especially in the last half of the 20th century and first decades of the 21st century, so too did the religious rhetoric.

In the days after the September 11, 2001, terrorist attacks, religious rhetoric in many forms was once again used by religious and political leaders. This continued as Americans again went to war in Afghanistan and Iraq and served in numerous global regions of conflict. It remains a part of contemporary American religious and political life. Often the prayers were and are private or spoken, along with sermons, within houses of worship. But there have been numerous calls to public and national prayer, including national days of prayer. The latter is a centuries-old tradition that came to America in the colonial era and followed practices in England.

During the colonial era and the American Revolution, sermons were a primary means of public communication and a mechanism through which religious and political ideas were transmitted. In New England especially, the role of the minister was very powerful. More than 70 percent of New Englanders attended church, and it has been estimated that the average colonial New Englander heard more than 15,000 hours of sermons in his or her lifetime. Before and during the revolution, many ministers (though not all) were staunch advocates of the revolution and closely identified with the events leading to the colonial declaration of independence.

One example of sermonic support for the revolution is the May 17, 1776, sermon of John Witherspoon (1723–1794). Preached in New Jersey at Princeton College by its president, Witherspoon's sermon, based on the biblical text of Psalm 76:10, is titled *"The Dominion of Providence over the Passions of Men."* Many historians consider it as one of the principal sermons that prepared the way for the Declaration of Independence, which was signed two and a half months later on July 4, 1776, with Witherspoon as a signatory—the sole clergyperson to sign it. The occasion of the sermon was a General Fast Day, appointed by the congress of the American colonies for prayer in a time of uncertainty filled with the potential for war.

Religious rhetoric continued to be linked to American warfare throughout the 19th century, with the most visible instances of it during the Civil War (1861–1865). During this conflict, Americans on both sides publicly and privately sought divine favor. Moving beyond rhetoric, one of the best illustrations of the blending of war and religion is Julia Ward Howe's lyrics for the song "Battle Hymn of the Republic." Though not written in wartime, Lee Greenwood's 1984 patriotic song "God Bless the U.S.A." gained national prominence and was closely identified with the 1991 Gulf War and post-9/11 military operations in Iraq and Afghanistan.

In the years between World War I and World War II, there was a strong pacifist movement (secular and religious) in the United States. In this era, one also finds much religious rhetoric. For example, one of the most prominent advocates was the liberal Protestant minister and famous orator Harry Emerson Fosdick (1878–1969), who, on November 12, 1933, preached a famous sermon titled "The Unknown Soldier" in which he renounced war. In World War I, he had served as a military chaplain in France, but with this sermon, he firmly rejected war and participation in it. He maintained this position throughout World War II, the Korean War, the Cold War, and the Vietnam War until his death. Throughout the history of American wars there has been religious dissent, often voiced in sermons, for every conflict.

From the beginning of the American war effort during World War II, political and religious rhetoric were easily blended. President Franklin D. Roosevelt used religious terminology in his first address to the nation and to the U.S. Congress after the bombing of Pearl Harbor in December 1941. He continued usage of it throughout the war. On the evening of the Allied invasion of Europe on D-Day, June 6, 1944, President Roosevelt prayed on national radio for the safety and victory of Allied forces. Earlier, on January 1, 1942, shortly after the United States entered the war, he called for a national day of prayer—something earlier presidents had also done in wartime.

Similarly, after Roosevelt's death in office, his successor, President Harry S. Truman, called for a similar day of prayer on May 13, 1945, in the aftermath of victory in Europe. Three months later, he called for Sunday, August 19, 1945, to be a national day of prayer giving thanks for victory. National days of prayer were also called for by presidents during the Korean War, Vietnam War, the Gulf War, and after September 11, 2001.

Events such as the famous Patton "weather prayer" in early December 1944, during which he asked the Third Army chaplain for a prayer and had it distributed to all members of the Third Army became legendary. Pocket scriptures, especially New Testaments, have been carried by military members of many nations since before the founding of the United States. Very popular with service members, during World War II, many of these contained a copy of a letter written to troops and signed by President Roosevelt, commending the Bible to them and demonstrating the prevalence of civil religion and the war effort.

During the war, slogans (and music) such as "Praise the Lord and Pass the Ammunition" (based on an incident during the attack on Pearl Harbor) and "Comin' in on a Wing and a Prayer" (based on a bomber in Europe returning from a mission) became commonplace, blending patriotism, religion, and war. Sermons also remained a strong source of upholding morale on the home front (as well as on the battlefront through the work of chaplains). The sermons of nationally recognized religious leaders such as Presbyterian minister Peter Marshall (1902–1949), who was appointed chaplain of the U.S. Senate after the war, were printed in denominational periodicals as well as syndicated columns. The widespread use of radio during the era did much to promulgate news, propaganda, and other war-related messages.

Among Roman Catholics, one very popular small book of prayers was *Fulton Sheen's Wartime Prayer Book*. During the war, Fulton J. Sheen (1895–1979) was a priest who hosted the nighttime radio program *The Catholic Hour* on NBC. Many similar pocket-sized prayer books were written and distributed for Protestant and Jewish service members and civilians. Small prayer books had been distributed in previous wars and continue to circulate in the 21st century.

A very visible illustration of religious rhetoric can be seen in the World War II Victory Medal. This award was authorized by Congress to be worn by all who served in the military from December 7, 1941, to December 31, 1946. The reverse side of the medal bears the words "Freedom of Speech and Religion."

With the rise of the Cold War, religious rhetoric was not only found at the pulpit but also in schools and public places. Religious rhetoric on the broadest and most public level can be seen during the Cold War when "In God We Trust" became the official motto of the United States by means of legislation passed by the Eighty-Fourth Congress (P.L. 84–851) and signed by President Eisenhower on July 30, 1956. The two words "under God" were also added to the Pledge of Allegiance during this era. This was done and signed into law by President Eisenhower in 1954 out of a desire to differentiate the values of the United States from the official atheism of the Soviet Union.

A 1966 photo of a demonstration supporting the war in Vietnam in which a demonstrator holding a sign with the words "Kill a Commie for Christ" illustrates how religious sentiments, whether sincere or cynical, can become part of popular culture. The slogan was also utilized by the vocal Presbyterian fundamentalist minister Carl McIntire (1906–2002).

Throughout the Cold War and beyond, internationally known evangelist Billy Graham (1918–2018) frequently preached to military crowds, including trips during the wars in Korea and Vietnam. During the Gulf War and 21st-century conflict in Iraq and Afghanistan, pocket cards and bumpers stickers with references to Psalm 91 were common.

One unique aspect of sermons and warfare from the Gulf War onward for the United States was concern regarding the Friday sermons preached in mosques in the Middle East and how the content of those sermons might affect U.S. belligerents or potential belligerents. In the 21st century, the sermon or homily does not have the same prominence in American culture as it did in previous centuries. For the religious faithful, it remains a standard part of worship services. However, with increasing secularism and as participation in religious services has declined and American religious demographics have broadened, there has been a diminishing of the influence of religious rhetoric and sermons in American political and cultural life.

*See also:* American Civil War; American Exceptionalism; Cold War; Ecclesiastical Statements on War and Peace; Graham, William Franklin, Jr. ("Billy"); Gulf War; Just War Tradition; Korean War; Military Chaplains; Music; Pacifism; Protestant Denominations; Roman Catholicism; Vietnam War; World War I; World War II

## Further Reading

Bush, George W. "Remarks at the National Day of Prayer & Remembrance Service." American Rhetoric: Rhetoric of 9-11, September 14, 2001. https://www.americanrhetoric.com/speeches/gwbush911prayer&memorialaddress.htm

Byrd, James P. *Sacred Scripture, Sacred War: The Bible and the American Revolution.* New York: Oxford University Press, 2013.

Frazer, Gregg L. *God against the Revolution: The Loyalist Clergy's Case against the American Revolution.* Lawrence: University Press of Kansas, 2010.

Hatch, Nathan O. *The Sacred Cause of Liberty: Republican Thought and the Millennium in Revolutionary New England.* New Haven, CT: Yale University Press, 1977.

History on the Net. "When Patton Enlisted the Entire Third Army to Pray for Fair Weather." May 8, 2020. https://www.historyonthenet.com/when-patton-enlisted-the-entire-third-army-to-pray-for-fair-weather

Kidd, Thomas S. *God of Liberty: A Religious History of the American Revolution*. New York: Basic Books, 2010.

Lambert, Frank. *The Founding Fathers and the Place of Religion in America*. Princeton, NJ: Princeton University Press, 2003.

Larson, Mark J. *Calvin's Doctrine of the State: A Reformed Doctrine and Its American Trajectory, the Revolutionary War, and the Founding of the Republic*. Eugene, OR: Wipf & Stock, 2009.

Lischer, Richard. *The Preacher King: Martin Luther King, Jr. and the Word That Moved America*. Rev. ed. New York: Oxford University Press, 2020.

Mailer, Gideon. *John Witherspoon's American Revolution*. Chapel Hill: University of North Carolina Press, 2017.

Marshall, Peter J., ed. *The Wartime Sermons of Peter Marshall*. Geneseo, NY: Clarion Call Publishing, 2005.

Noll, Mark A. *Christians in the American Revolution*. 2nd ed. Vancouver Canada: Regent College Publishing, 2006.

Preston, Andrew. *Sword of the Spirit, Shield of Faith: Religion in American War and Diplomacy*. New York: Alfred A. Knopf, 2012.

Ruotsila, Markku. *Fighting Fundamentalist: Carl McIntire and the Politicization of American Fundamentalism*. New York: Oxford University Press, 2016.

Sandoz, Ellis, ed. *Political Sermons of the American Founding Era, 1730–1805*. 2 vols. Indianapolis, IN: Liberty Fund, 1991.

Snape, Michael. *God and Uncle Sam: Religion and America's Armed Forces in World War II*. Rochester, NY: Boydell Press, 2105.

Stout, Harry S. "War." In *The New England Soul: Preaching and Religious Culture in Colonial New England*, 2nd ed., 233–255. New York: Oxford University Press, 2011.

# Rituals and Symbolism

Rituals and symbols serve as significant items of meaning in the lives of individuals, groups, and nations. They can be intensely significant and personal, and as such, they can motivate, renew, comfort, and energize individuals who use, see, or hear them. Rituals and symbols provide visible witness of the religious or political values of an individual, a group, or a nation. Rituals and symbols may also be tied to race or ethnicity. They may become so prevalent in a person's life or culture that use and acceptance of them is almost unconscious or routine. Their use and popularity often increase significantly in times of personal or national crisis—for example, the prominence and increase of displays of the American flag after the September 11, 2001, terrorist attacks.

Religious and political commitments are deeply held values by individuals, and expressions of them are manifested in many ways, including through the use of rituals and symbols from both domains—the world of politics and the world of religion. The linking of religion, religious symbols, and religious rites to warfare has occurred for millennia. When coupled with political symbols and the linking of politics and warfare, there is often an intensity of conflict and infusing of meaning and memory that goes far beyond the physical acts of warfare.

The nexus of religion, politics, and war is often evidenced in physical objects, written texts, and verbal statements. This may occur before, during, or after conflict. Rituals may be verbal or silent gestures (individual or collective), and the symbolism may be drawn from religious traditions and religious history or be something that is created within the context of a specific conflict for use on the battlefield or the home front. Rituals and symbols also easily become part of civil religion. A symbol or ritual, political or religious, may have temporary or lasting significance. In post-9/11 America, one such instance was the World Trade Center cross, also known as the Ground Zero cross. This was a formation of steel beams found among the debris of the World Trade Center site in New York City that resembled a Christian cross (and is now preserved at the National September 11 Memorial & Museum). In the 21st-century United States, intense debates about the national anthem, Pledge of Allegiance, and the personalities and symbols of the Civil War and the Confederacy have also been prominent in private and public political discourse. There have also been debates regarding symbols and rituals and whether their use was cultural appropriation. There have often been religious dimensions to these discussions and debates.

Although many people find solace and affirmation in the use of rituals and symbols, such things may also be considered offensive or inappropriate by others. In the United States, such instances frequently provoke legal challenges with respect to the First Amendment and the expression and establishment of religion. Historically, there are also instances of religious or political symbols and rituals being co-opted by groups for purposes other than that which they were originally intended. One thinks here of the co-opting of the Hindu and Buddhist symbol of the swastika by the National Socialist Party (Nazis) in Germany before and during World War II (and presently by neo-Nazi groups).

Each of the major world religions has sacred texts pertaining to war and peace, and many of them have had or do have rituals related to war and peace. In times of war, things such as the blessing of troops, weapons, and missions have been prevalent—and also controversial. There are also gods and goddesses of war. In Christianity, there are patron saints affiliated with war, such as St. George, St. Sebastian, St. Joan of Arc, St. Barbara, St. Martin of Tours, and others. These have often been looked to for protection and assistance. Martyrdom and death are also instances where there is a fusion of religion, politics, and war.

In the 20th century, creation of trench art during World War I and subsequent wars was very common. During World War I, there was the belief in and propagation of stories of divine assistance and apparitions, such as the "Angels of Mons." There were also many stories, (usually false) such as that of the "crucified Canadian," that were infused with religious and political meaning and used for propaganda purposes. During World War II, the photographic images of the bombed Coventry Cathedral and the burning St. Paul's Cathedral were very strong symbols of destruction and defiance in England and as such had great propaganda value.

Historically, the carrying of religious relics into war was commonplace. On the individual level, the use of religious medals, pocket scriptures, and other religious items in wartime is very common. During the 1991 Gulf War, the wearing of uniform religious insignia as collar devices by chaplains became a political issue, with historically Christian nations not wanting to offend Muslims and host nation Saudi Arabia, where many of the U.S.-led coalition forces were stationed. Chaplains were required to remove the collar devices, which illustrates the power religious symbols can have over international relations and politics.

Funeral rituals and the observance of various military honors with them, such as boots with upturned weapons, the bugle call of "Taps," gun salutes, flag-draped coffins, military cemeteries, and the many roles and responsibilities, also illustrate symbols and rituals. These may occur for serving members of the military, veterans, or politicians (e.g., presidential funerals, lying in state in the U.S. Capitol). Historically, in the U.S. Navy, a Christian crewmember of a ship whose family experienced the birth of a child could have the child baptized by the ship's chaplain using the ship's bell, which was upturned and filled with water, as a baptismal font and then had the child's name engraved in the bell.

In daily political and military activities by citizens and those serving in the military, the Pledge of Allegiance, the observance of raising and lowering the national flag in the morning and evening, rituals associated with the national anthem, national days of prayer or mourning, public prayers, and moments of silence are examples of rituals and symbols where religion and politics are often blended.

In the 21st-century, the aftermath of the September 11, 2001, terrorist attacks saw much use of rituals and symbols that were political and religious. In the two decades since that historic day, aspects of many of the items mentioned above can be found in the religious and political life of the United States and its citizens. Religion and politics remain powerful instruments in promoting war and peace, as do the more concrete rituals and symbols of war and peace. They provide a tangible link between the individual and the ideologies of faith and citizenship.

*See also:* Art; Gulf War; Literature; Military Chaplains; Music; Presidential Faith and War; Religious Texts; Rhetoric, Sermons, and Prayers; September 11, 2001, Terrorist Attacks

## Further Reading

Bergen, Doris L. *Twisted Cross: The German Christian Movement in the Third Reich*. Chapel Hill: University of North Carolina Press, 1996.

Edwards, Jason, and Joseph M. Valenzano III, eds. *The Rhetoric of American Civil Religion: Symbols, Sinners, and Saints*. London: Lexington Books, 2016.

Frost, J. William. "Why Religions Facilitate War and How Religions Facilitate Peace." Lecture at Swarthmore College, June 2005. https://www.swarthmore.edu/friends-historical-library/why-religions-facilitate-war-and-how-religions-facilitate-peace

Gerteis, Joseph. "The Social Functions of Religion in American Political Culture." The Society Pages, White Paper, March 14, 2012. https://thesocietypages.org/papers/religion-and-politics/

Marshall, Tim. *A Flag Worth Dying For: The Power and Politics of National Symbols*. New York: Simon & Schuster, 2016.

Nagasaki, T. K. *The Buddhist Swastika and Hitler's Cross: Rescuing a Symbol of Peace from the Forces of Hate*. Berkeley, CA: Stone Bridge Press, 2017.

Pew Research Center. "U.S. Religious Landscape Survey: Religious Beliefs and Practices." June 1, 2008. https://www.pewforum.org/2008/06/01/chapter-1-religious-beliefs-and-practices/

# Roman Catholicism

Roman Catholicism is the largest and oldest of Christianity's three main branches, including Orthodoxy (Eastern Orthodoxy) and Protestantism. As such, understanding past and current influences of Roman Catholicism on theology, culture, and politics is fundamental to understanding the values and beliefs undergirding much of Western identity, thought, and civilization. Even in the post-Reformation era (1500–present), there have been many shared and overlapping beliefs and values, with Protestantism and Orthodoxy affecting many realms of life, including attitudes toward politics and war in the United States and globally.

Comprising roughly half of all Christians, the Roman Catholic Church has more followers than Buddhism, Hinduism, and all other branches of Christianity. According to a 2013 Pew Research Center study, Roman Catholics have comprised 16–17 percent of the world's population since at least 1910, when the Roman Catholic population was 291 million, to 2018, when the number of Roman Catholics had grown to nearly 1.2 billion (Pew Research Center 2013).

There have been Roman Catholics in the United States since its earliest days (such as the colony of Maryland, which was founded in 1632 as a safe haven for English Catholics). The largest immigration surge of Roman Catholics occurred during and after the 1880s and involved Roman Catholics from Italy, Germany, Ireland, and eastern Europe. With increased numbers also came a raised political voice, especially in the latter half of the 20th century.

Notably, in the 20th-century United States, there was a significant Roman Catholic social and political movement addressing such matters as unions, the rights of workers, and living conditions. Much of this was tied to the increase in the Roman Catholic population in the United States due to immigration. Strong Roman Catholic political voices from official statements as well as social and political activism have continued to address many issues, such as immigration, women's health and rights concerns, and social and economic disparities.

With respect to issues of war and peace, Roman Catholics, as with all religious groups, have not been monolithic in their support or nonsupport of American wars. Nor were responses predicated solely on religious values. Roman Catholics have fought and not fought American wars primarily based on social and political values as citizens rather than as Christians.

Probably the greatest present-day influence and interaction at the intersection of politics, war, and religion is that of the just war tradition. Tracing 21st-century Roman Catholic responses to events of conflict or war requires some understanding of that tradition and the structure and social education mechanisms used by the church, including underlying presuppositions, canon law, papal encyclicals, and pastoral letters. In the United States, roughly 25 percent of the population (with nearly seventy million parishioners as of 2017) is Roman Catholic. In the late 20th and 21st centuries, American Roman Catholicism has had a prominent influence on American attitudes and thinking regarding war (especially related to nuclear weapons), peace, and social justice.

The structure of the Roman Catholic Church in the United States and elsewhere is consistent with the Holy See in Rome, consisting of the ecumenical council (composed of bishops who address issues as received from the Vatican), the plenary council of bishops as organized by country, and provincial and diocesan councils with representatives divided further into provinces and diocese. Not monolithic in composition, further distinctions exist in the United States for addressing ethnic groups, including, but not limited to, Irish, Italian, Polish, and Hispanic parishes.

Built upon a centuries-long history of canon law and just war tradition, the Roman Catholic Church's teachings regarding war and peace held sway (differing little from the emerging Protestant traditions) until the Treaty of Westphalia (1648) in matters of justice before and during war (respectively, *jus ad bellum* and *jus in bello*). Such had been the case since the medieval era of Thomas Aquinas (1225–1274), when theological views were combined with political and military thinking and practice. After 1648 and a period of 300 years of lesser influence, Roman Catholic just war thinking (differentiated here from secular and other Christian just war thought) returned to public discourse in the United States with the undisputedly influential publication of the 1983 American Bishops' Pastoral Letter, "The Challenge of Peace," written in response to the use of the atomic bombs at the end of World War II, the subsequent nuclear arms race of the Cold War, and the preventive action in the Iran-Iraq War (1980–1988) and alleged production of weapons of mass destruction (WMDs). As with the 1983 pastoral letter, subsequent pastoral letters such as "The Harvest of Justice Is Sown in Peace" (1993), were also written in response to specific threats, concerns, and conflicts (whether nuclear or events of the 21st century).

When viewed collectively, the pastoral letters represent the ideological and functional position of the church at large, even though they were written by the American bishops. Roman Catholic ideology and thought manifest differently in various countries depending on unique political and historical context, but the overall position trend in matters of war and peace post-1983 has been toward pacifism rather than the just war tradition. That said, as with any religious group, Roman Catholic practitioners are not always theologically or politically aligned with the official statements.

James Turner Johnson, a prominent just war scholar, critiques contemporary Roman Catholicism's shift away from just war tradition as markedly pacifistic—with a presumption of peace supplanting a presumption of justice that at times requires the use of force. Indeed, "The Challenge of Peace" includes a prescriptive stance on the use of force as a last resort, to only be used in extreme circumstances, whereas the just war tradition presumes the use of force in cases where the management of violence may be necessary, including coming to the aid of a neighboring population, as has been addressed in contemporary discourse as a "Responsibility to Protect" (R2P).

Significant events of the 21st century that have received pronouncements from the United States Conference of Catholic Bishops include statements in response to the September 11, 2001, terrorist attacks, the Iraq War, the Afghanistan War, and the civil war in Syria. Also not to be overlooked, there are the international humanitarian efforts led by Roman Catholic organizations such as Catholic Relief Services, one of the world's largest nongovernmental organizations (NGOs). Roman Catholic organizations are also one of the biggest contributors to both education and health care worldwide.

While Roman Catholic social teaching in the 20th century did not focus as much on war and peace as it did on domestic concerns and issues in the workplace, in the late-20th and 21st centuries, Catholic social teaching has included a markedly international focus, including issues of war, peace, and human rights.

Often overlooked but of enormous international political consequence in the post–World War II era is the active role of the Vatican in undermining communism and helping to bring an end to the Cold War. The epicenter for these actions was Poland, the birthplace of Pope John Paul II (Karol Józef Wojtyla, 1920–2005). He and U.S. president Ronald Reagan

(1911–2004) formed a strong alliance and ardently worked to bring freedom and democracy to Poland, whose population at the time was overwhelmingly Roman Catholic.

While the Vatican, in concert with the United States and other nations, was steadily working to bring democracy and freedom to countries such as Poland that were part of the Soviet Eastern Bloc, there were different challenges in various nations of the West concerning political corruption, economic disparity, and systemic abuse of human rights. In the 1970s and 1980s, active Roman Catholic leaders and parishioners in Central America and South America promoted the liberation theology movement, which was politically grounded in Marxist thought and marked a shift in these countries toward a more populist-centered approach.

Elsewhere, in Asia, and specifically in China, the Vatican has had contentious political relationships. The Vatican has grappled with the Chinese government with respect to control of Roman Catholicism in China and the appointing of ecclesiastical leaders. In March 2021, Pope Francis made a historic visit to Iraq in support of the plight of the diminishing Christian population there and elsewhere in the Middle East. During the visit, he was vocal against hostility, extremism, and violence, contending that such things were contrary to true spirituality.

In all of these international affairs, American Catholics have been actively engaged in lobbying the U.S. government with respect to supporting religious freedom, human rights, and democracy abroad. Perhaps most visible in the late 20th century, Senator George Mitchell (D-ME) served as the U.S. special envoy for Northern Ireland under President Bill Clinton. A Roman Catholic, Mitchell's efforts did much to bring an end to many years of conflict in Northern Ireland. Instances such as this, as well as the creation of the position of ambassador of the United States to the Holy See, reflect the recognition of the influence that religious values have on national and international affairs, most notably matters of war and peace.

As previously stated, Roman Catholicism is far from monolithic, and there is a spectrum of organizations and groups within the church focused on the presumption of peace. Pax Christi is one of the most prominent such groups, with a focus on issues of war and peace from a pacifist perspective. Religious demographics and their alignment with political parties in the United States no longer have the solidarity they previously had; the "Roman Catholic vote" is not monolithic.

Notably, Joseph R. Biden, the forty-sixth president of the United States, is only the second Roman Catholic to hold that office, following the thirty-fifth president, John F. Kennedy (1917–1963)—and he does so with none of the controversy caused by questions of allegiance to the Vatican that Kennedy faced when he ran for the presidency in 1960. Though not unified on any social or political subject, Roman Catholicism and individual Roman Catholics in the United States, especially the increasing population of Latino voters, many of whom are staunch Roman Catholics, will likely continue to be an active voice in American politics. American Roman Catholics, whether in military uniform, political office, government service, or as voting citizens, are a vibrant part of the American political system.

*See also:* Afghanistan War; Cold War; Ecclesiastical Statements on War and Peace; Human Rights; Iraq War; Just War Tradition; Pacifism; Peacemaking; Presidential Faith and War; Protestant Denominations; Religious Texts; Weapons of Mass Destruction

## Further Reading

Braun, Christian Nikolaus. "James Turner Johnson and the Roman Catholic Just War Tradition." In *Responsibility and Restraint: James Turner Johnson and the Just War Tradition*, edited by Eric D. Patterson and Marc LiVecche, 125–157. Middletown, RI: Stone Tower Press, 2020.

Hart, D. G. *American Catholic: The Politics of Faith during the Cold War*. Ithaca, NY: Cornell University Press, 2020.

Kengor, Paul, and Robert Orlando. *The Divine Plan: John Paul II, Ronald Reagan, and the Dramatic End of the Cold War*. Wilmington, DE: Intercollegiate Studies Institute, 2019.

National Conference of Catholic Bishops. "The Challenge of Peace: God's Promise and Our Response." May 3, 1983. https://www.usccb.org/upload/challenge-peace-gods-promise-our-response-1983.pdf

National Conference of Catholic Bishops. "The Harvest of Justice Is Sown in Peace." 1993. http://www.usccb.org/beliefs-and-teachings/what-we-believe/catholic-social-teaching/the-harvest-of-justice-is-sown-in-peace.cfm

Olson, Roger E., Frank S. Mead, et al. *Handbook of Denominations in the United States*. 14th ed. Nashville, TN: Abingdon Press, 2018.

Pew Research Center. "The Global Catholic Population." February 13, 2013. https://www.pewforum.org/2013/02/13/the-global-catholic-population/

Powers, Gerard F. "The U.S. Bishops and War since the Peace Pastoral." *U.S. Catholic Historian* 27, no. 2 (2009): 73–96.

Tentler, Leslie Woodcock. *American Catholics: A History*. New Haven, CT: Yale University Press, 2020.

Weigel, George. *Tranquillitas Ordinis: Present Failure and Future Promise of American Catholic Thought on War and Peace*. New York: Oxford University Press, 1987.

Weigel, George. *Witness to Hope: The Biography of John Paul II*. New York: HarperCollins, 1999.

# S

## September 11, 2001, Terrorist Attacks

The September 11, 2001, terrorist attacks (commonly referred to as 9/11) in New York City and Washington, DC, are a defining moment in recent American history. The attacks resulted in the deaths of more than 3,000 individuals in the wake of the hijackings of four airplanes by nineteen hijackers. The planes were flown into the World Trade Center (two planes) and the Pentagon, and another unsuccessful attempt resulted in the crash of the airplane in a field near Shanksville, Pennsylvania. The attacks have been likened to the surprise attack on the United States on December 7, 1941, at Pearl Harbor, Hawaii. More Americans died on 9/11 than on December 7, 1941. The fact that the event was planned and carried out by militant Islamist extremists within the terrorist organization al-Qaeda, led by Osama bin Laden (1957–2011), brought a visibly religious dimension to the acts that were not always present in previous terrorist attacks of the last quarter of the 20th century, though religiously motivated terrorist attacks had been increasing since the early 1990s.

Of the two houses of worship closest to the World Trade Center, St. Nicholas Greek Orthodox Church, next to the World Trade Center, and St. Paul's Chapel (Episcopal), only the former was destroyed; the latter, standing across from the World Trade Center, was undamaged. In the aftermath, St. Paul's became a site for rest and prayer for rescue and recovery workers at the Ground Zero site of the collapse of the Twin Towers of the World Trade Center. The many first responders to the attack and crash sites included military, police, and fire chaplains as well as civilian clergy of many faith traditions. Their presence and ministry extended far beyond September 11. They served for many months in a variety of settings and capacities, including the recovery operations at the World Trade Center site, which came to be known as Ground Zero or "the Pile."

It is not surprising that after a national tragedy in any nation where there is a large religious population, there is often a visible display of prayer, memorial services, and increased attendance in houses of worship. That was evident in the days and weeks after the 9/11 attacks. There was an initial surge of religiosity and increased attendance at worship services, but the increase did not last. Surveys found that within weeks or months, it subsided. There was not a sustained religious renewal. Some observers believe that this phenomenon revealed the limits of organized religion in the 21st century and is an indication of the growing trend away from organized religious participation.

Religious services such as one at the Washington National Cathedral on September 14, 2001, in which Billy Graham's remarks in a nationally televised event that was attended by national political, religious, and military leaders sought to bring hope and healing to Americans were common. In the days and weeks following 9/11, religious groups and organizations made statements condemning the tragedy of 9/11, but they also called for interfaith dialogue and protection of American civil liberties. For example, the United States Conference of Catholic Bishops issued a statement on November 14, 2011, titled "A Pastoral Message: Living with Faith and Hope after September 11."

Also common in the aftermath of trauma, tragedy, and war, many physical memorials were created to provide memory, meaning, consolation, and inspiration for any who saw them. These often had religious connotations or included religious texts. The most prominent of these during the first days and weeks after the attacks was what came to be known as the "Cross at Ground Zero" (now located in the National September 11 Memorial & Museum). The cross was an intact seventeen-foot-high steel crossbeam that was found by workers at the debris site of the World Trade Center a few days after the attack. For many first responders who were Christian, the beam came to represent a Christian cross, symbolic of their faith. The beam became a makeshift shrine at which workers could pause for prayer, hope, healing, and inspiration. Roman Catholic Mass was also celebrated for workers at the site on Sundays.

The beam also became the focal point of a legal battle when the secular organization American Atheists objected to the inclusion of the beam and other religious items when plans for the formation of a national museum at the site were announced. The legal challenge was dismissed by a judge from the U.S. Second Circuit Court of Appeals on grounds that the beam was "historical in nature" and did not discriminate against any other individuals or groups (cited in Mears 2014). The beam, public services, and other items and statements are a dimension of civil religion as well as public and private faith in the United States.

Two political and sociological phenomena that gained greater visibility and vocalization in the aftermath of the attacks were increases in anti-Semitic and anti-Islamic sentiments in the United States. Regarding the former, some conspiracy theorists promoted the attacks on the World Trade Center as an Israeli and Jewish plot to control global events and serve as a catalyst for war. With respect to the latter, and as a derivative of the event, the 9/11 attacks created national attention on the American Muslim population of the United States and brought to the forefront the challenges faced by them with respect to their assimilation and acceptance by non-Muslim Americans as citizens. It also highlighted assumptions of and tensions within American religious pluralism. American Muslims were not part of the attacks in any way (except that some American Muslims died in the attacks, as did American Jews), but the fact that all nineteen hijackers were Muslims and that their attacks had strong Islamist motivations created suspicion among some Americans regarding Islam in the United States.

In many ways, the attacks of 9/11 were a significant event in 21st-century American religion. The attacks affected individual and group self-understanding as well as the understanding and perceptions of other faith traditions in the United States. Religious dimensions of the event also affected American political and military actions in Afghanistan, Iraq, and what was termed the "global war on terrorism." The political and religious consequences of the attacks significantly affected the course of American history in the first two decades of the 21st century and remain a visible and important aspect of contemporary life in the United States.

*See also:* Afghanistan War; Ecclesiastical Statements on War and Peace; Iraq War; Islam and War; Religion, Conflict, and Geopolitics; Rituals and Symbolism; Terrorism

## Further Reading

Beliefnet. "The Real Spiritual Impact of 9/11." September 2003. https://www.beliefnet.com/faiths/2002/09/the-real-spiritual-impact-of-911.aspx

Bush, George W. "Remarks at the National Day of Prayer & Remembrance Service." American Rhetoric: Rhetoric of 9-11, September 14, 2001. https://www.americanrhetoric.com/speeches/gwbush911prayer&memorialaddress.htm

Graham, Billy. "Billy Graham's 9/11 Message from the Washington National Cathedral." Billy Graham Evangelistic Association, September 11, 2019. https://billygraham.org/story/a-day-to-remember-a-day-of-victory/

Jordan, Brian J. *The Cross at Ground Zero*. Bloomington, IN: Xlibris, 2017.

Juergensmeyer, Mark. *Terror in the Mind of God*. 4th ed. Berkeley: University of California Press, 2017.

Kishi, Katayoun. "Assaults against Muslims in U.S. Surpass 2001 Level." Pew Research Center, November 15, 2017. https://www.pewresearch.org/fact-tank/2017/11/15/assaults-against-muslims-in-u-s-surpass-2001-level/

Mayo, Marilyn. "Anti-Semitic 9/11 Conspiracy Theorists Thrive 15 Years after Attacks." Anti-Defamation League, September 9, 2016. https://www.adl.org/blog/anti-semitic-911-conspiracy-theorists-thrive-15-years-after-attacks

Mears, Bill. "Court Says Ground Zero Cross Can Stay." CNN, July 28, 2014. https://www.cnn.com/2014/07/28/us/world-trade-center-cross/index.html

National Commission on Terrorist Attacks. *The 9/11 Commission Report: The Attack from Planning to Aftermath*. Authorized Text, Shorter Edition. New York: W. W. Norton, 2011.

Panagopoulos, Costas. "Trends: Arab and Muslim Americans and Islam in the Aftermath of 9/11." *Public Opinion Quarterly* 70, no. 4 (Winter 2006): 608–624.

Pew Research Center. "Poll: Two Years after 9/11, Growing Number of Americans Link Islam to Violence." September 10, 2003. https://www.pewforum.org/2003/09/10/poll-two-years-after-911-growing-number-of-americans-link-islam-to-violence/

Pew Research Center. "Post September 11 Attitudes." December 6, 2001. https://www.pewresearch.org/politics/2001/12/06/post-september-11-attitudes/

Trinity Church Wall Street. "St. Paul's Chapel and 9/11." https://www.trinitywallstreet.org/about/stpaulschapel/911

Uecker, Jeremy E. "Religious and Spiritual Responses to 9/11: Evidence from the ADD Health Study." *Sociological Spectrum* 28, no. 5 (2008): 477–509. https://doi.org/10.1080/02732170802206047

United States Conference of Catholic Bishops. "A Pastoral Message: Living with Faith and Hope after September 11." November 14, 2001. http://www.usccb.org/issues-and-action/human-life-and-dignity/september-11/a-pastoral-message-living-with-faith-and-hope-after-september-11.cfm

Vecsey, Christopher. *Following 9/11: Religion Coverage in the New York Times*. Syracuse, NY: Syracuse University Press, 2011.

Zuchoff, Mitchell. *Fall and Rise: The Story of 9/11*. New York: HarperCollins, 2019.

# T

## Terrorism

Terrorism is centuries old, but as a result of the September 11, 2001, terrorist attacks, it has shaped much of the 21st-century international religious and political discourse with respect to violence and war. At its core and most basic level, terrorism is the intentional targeting and abuse of innocent civilians and noncombatants for political power.

The term *terrorism* is often emotionally charged and used in a pejorative manner tied to any idea or act that the user of the term opposes—whether it be political, philosophical, economic, cultural, or religious. However, such usage is subjective and lacks definition and specificity. Not all acts of violence or opposition are terrorism.

Widely accepted definitions vary and overlap in their wording, often due to the nature of the work of the agency or organization using the term. In the United States, a commonly accepted definition is that of the U.S. Department of Defense: "The unlawful use of violence or threat of violence to instill fear and coerce governments or societies. Terrorism is often motivated by religious, political, or other ideological beliefs and committed in the pursuit of goals that are usually political" (Joint Chiefs of Staff 2010, vii). Whether terrorism is viewed as a criminal activity or something different and broader, it is a problem of national and international proportions that has been increasing during the last fifty years.

In the United States, since 2001, there have been more than one hundred officially designated terrorist incidents, although many of them were foiled such that no attack occurred. Broadly, these can be categorized as carried out by individuals or groups that are formally or informally tied to right-wing political extremism, Islamist jihadism, and left-wing political extremism. Among the more prominent attacks are the shoe bombing attempt (December 22, 2001); the Beltway sniper attacks (February–October 2002); the United States Holocaust Memorial shooting (June 1, 2009); the Fort Hood shooting (November 5, 2009); the Wisconsin Sikh temple shooting (August 5, 20212); the Boston Marathon bombing (April 15, 2013); the Charleston church shooting (June 17, 2015); the San Bernardino attack (December 2, 2015); the Orlando nightclub shooting (June 12, 2016); the Pittsburgh synagogue shooting (October 27, 2018); and the Naval Air Station Pensacola shooting (December 6, 2019).

Not all terrorism is religiously motivated. However, much of what has been experienced globally and nationally in the 21st century does have strong religious ties and ideology grounded in religion. Sometimes the religious component has been attached to nationalist or ethnic interests. The more factors there are in the terrorist equation for a group or an incident, the more difficult it becomes for it to be combated.

Religiously motivated terrorists perceive their actions as divinely sanctioned and as acts of religious obligation or divine approval. Religious terrorists overlap their cause with what they understand to be divine plans in which the terrorist is a special agent of the divine and on a special mission. They often believe that they have been divinely chosen and that their act will be a turning point in a cosmic spiritual war that is being carried out on a present and physical geopolitical battlefield. Among the common traits of religious terrorists are a belief that the movement or cause in which the terrorist is taking part is pure, a belief that the terrorist act will lead to spiritual victory and a new religious age, a belief that recent and distant history has made the terrorist act necessary, and a belief that the conflict in which the terrorist is engaged is primarily spiritual or cosmic (Demy and Stewart 2001, 69–73).

Although terrorism may occur entirely apart from religion, religiously motivated terrorism is prominent in the 21st century. No religious tradition has a monopoly on religious terrorism, and within the broad spectrum of belief and practice within each tradition, terrorist ideology is not a core attribute. Rather, it is something that is advocated by fringe elements of the faith tradition and is rejected by the faithful majority within that faith tradition. While a minority of any religious tradition may advocate for terrorism, the majority do not, and many religious groups and denominations have issued statements condemning terrorism and promoting peaceful resolution of grievances against the state or others.

Regardless of one's religious or political perspective, terrorism is an abuse of human rights and morally affects all people, whether or not they are personally targeted, injured, or killed. Terrorism expert Christopher Harmon offers much to reflect upon with this statement on terrorism: "One could well argue that if terrorism is not immoral, then nothing is immoral" (Harmon 2000, 190).

*See also:* Afghanistan War; Buddhism and War; Christianity and War; Ecclesiastical Statements on War and Peace; Hinduism and War; Islam and War; Judaism and War; Just War Tradition; Middle East Conflict; Religion, Conflict, and Geopolitics; September 11, 2001, Terrorist Attacks; Weapons of Mass Destruction

## Further Reading

Combs, Cynthia C. *Terrorism in the Twenty-First Century*. 8th ed. New York: Routledge, 2018.
Demy, Timothy, and Gary P. Stewart. *In the Name of God: Understanding the Mindset of Terrorism*. Eugene, OR: Harvest House Publishers, 2001.
Gregg, Heather S. "Defining and Distinguishing Secular and Religious Terrorism." *Perspectives on Terrorism* 8, no. 2 (April 2014): 36–51.
Harmon, Christopher C. *Terrorism Today*. London: Frank Cass, 2000.
Harmon, Christopher C., and Randall G. Bowdish. *The Terrorist Argument: Modern Advocacy and Propaganda*. Washington, DC: Brookings Institution, 2018.
Hoffman, Bruce. *Inside Terrorism*. Rev. ed. New York: Columbia University Press, 2017.
Joint Chiefs of Staff. "Antiterrorism." Joint Publication 3-07.2, November 24, 2010. https://www.bits.de/NRANEU/others/jp-doctrine/JP3_07.2(10).pdf
Juergensmeyer, Mark. *Terror in the Mind of God*. 4th ed. Berkeley: University of California Press, 2017.
Juergensmeyer, Mark, Margo Kitts, and Michael Jerryson. *The Oxford Handbook of Religion and Violence*. Oxford, UK: Oxford University Press, 2012.
National Commission on Terrorist Attacks. *The 9/11 Commission Report: The Attack from Planning to Aftermath*. Authorized Text, Shorter Edition. New York: W. W. Norton, 2011.
Patterson, Eric. "Just War Theory & Terrorism." *Providence: A Journal of Christianity & American Foreign Policy* no. 4 (Summer 2016): 38–44.
Ranstorp, Magnus. "Terrorism in the Name of Religion." *Journal of International Affairs* 50, no. 1. Religion: Politics, Power and Symbolism (Summer 1996): 41–62.
Valeri, Robin Maria, and Kevin Borgeson, eds. *Terrorism in America*. 2nd ed. New York: Routledge, 2019.

## Torture

Torture and the issues surrounding it were not topics that Americans expected to confront at the beginning of the 21st century. However, in the aftermath of the terrorist attacks on September 11, 2001, and the American response to those attacks in Afghanistan and Iraq (Operation Iraqi Freedom), torture as an abuse of human rights became a headline issue in religious and political discourse. Specifically, issues of torture (termed "enhanced interrogation techniques" by various U.S. entities) arose in the context of prisoner abuse at Bagram Airfield-BAF in Afghanistan, in 2003 at Abu Ghraib prison in Iraq, and the Guantánamo Bay detention camp in the Guantánamo Bay Naval Base in Cuba as well as other secret sites around the globe that were run by the CIA. While human rights advocates and religious bodies have long protested torture by dictatorships and regimes around the globe, as well as the ties and support the United States had to some of those regimes, torture in the 21st century by U.S. personnel was unexpected.

Torture has long been contrary to U.S. and international law, but the prohibition in the United States was strengthened in 2015 with passage of the McCain-Feinstein Anti-Torture Amendment by a Senate vote of 78–21 and signed into law in a slightly modified version on November 25, 2015. It prevents torture programs such as those used in the aftermath of the 9/11 attacks from being authorized in the future.

Faith traditions across the religious spectrum issued statements and resolutions against torture and urged politicians and the U.S. government to change its laws and practices. Many religious leaders signed an October 26, 2003, ecumenical statement, "Torture Is a Moral Issue," in addition to issuing individual religious and denominational resolutions and statements. For example, the United States Conference of Catholic Bishops has published a study guide to "Torture Is a Moral Issue" for individual Roman Catholics and congregations to use for further discussion and personal growth.

In many religious traditions, torture is understood to be a violation of human rights and, even more egregious, a denial of human dignity grounded in the belief that humans are created in the image of God (*imago Dei*). In addition to damaging and abusing the one tortured, it is also argued that there are psychological and spiritual ramifications for the torturer as well. One of the major challenges for all who engage in discussion and thought regarding torture is how it is to be defined and at what point an action becomes torture. There are internationally recognized (though not universally agreed upon) definitions, though a lack of clarity with respect to specific acts and terms, such as *brainwashing* or *persuading*, leaves room for argument on what is and is not torture in a particular instance. Distinctions between torture, coercion, manipulation, and brainwashing are problematic. Further, this raises the question, "Is torture ever morally justified?" On this question, even among those who argue against torture, there are some who argue the potential for an exception to the prohibition.

Within the just war tradition, both in its secular and religious manifestations, torture is rejected just as it is in international law (on the latter, see the Convention against Torture and Other Cruel, Inhuman or Degrading Treatment or Punishment, commonly known as the United Nations Convention against Torture (UNCAT)). The rejection of torture within the just war tradition arises for several reasons. These include violation of the principles of just war, violation of the dignity of the individual, an attempt to eliminate atrocities, and the prevention of the escalation of atrocities. At its core, the act of torture disregards and disdains the laws of war and human rights.

The violence of torture differs from other types of extreme violence and miseries that people experience in wartime. Even though a person may intentionally (or accidentally) kill, injure, or maim during war, it is not possible to accidentally or inadvertently torture someone. Torture is always an intentional act.

In part, the just war tradition seeks to provide an ethical framework for thinking about the tragedy of war in an attempt to restrain the violence of war. Proponents of the tradition, seeking to uphold its values, must not succumb to that which they seek to minimize.

The torture debate remains a subject over which there is more religious unanimity than political unanimity in the United States. While there are strong religious and ideological convictions regarding its prohibition, the politics of the debate along with political pragmatism and realism ensure that it will not cease to be a topic that is politically divisive, even though strong laws prohibit it.

*See also:* Ecclesiastical Statements on War and Peace; Human Rights; Iraq War; Just War Tradition; Terrorism

## Further Reading

Central Conference of American Rabbis. "The Use of Torture or Lesser Forms of Coercion to Obtain Information from Prisoners." March 2005. https://www

.ccarnet.org/ccar-resolutions/the-use-of-torture-or-lesser-forms-of-coercion-to-obtain-information-from-prisoners/

Dee, Melinda. "Effect of Torture on the Torturer." University of Utah S. J. Quinney College of Law, November 27, 2017. https://law.utah.edu/effect-of-torture-on-the-torturer/

Evangelicals for Human Rights. "An Evangelical Declaration against Torture: Protecting Human Rights in an Age of Terror." *Review of Faith & International Affairs* 5, no. 2 (2007): 41–58.

*First Things*. "The Truth about Torture?—A Christian Ethics Symposium." January 6, 2010. https://www.firstthings.com/blogs/firstthoughts/2010/01/the-truth-about-torture-e28094-a-christian-ethics-symposium

Gutting, Gary, and Jeff McMahan. "Can Torture Ever Be Moral?" *New York Times* [blog], January 26, 2015. https://opinionator.blogs.nytimes.com/2015/01/26/can-torture-ever-be-moral/

Heimbach, Daniel R. "The Problem with Assessing Torture." *Journal of Faith & War* (December 2010). http://faithandwar.org/index.php/national-security/44-strategic-leadership/98-the-problem-with-assessing-torture

Hunsinger, George, ed. *Torture Is a Moral Issue: Christians, Jews, Muslims, and People of Conscience Speak Out*. Grand Rapids, MI: Eerdmans, 2008.

May, Larry. *War Crimes and Just War*. Cambridge, UK: Cambridge University Press, 2007.

National Council of Churches. "A Statement on the Disavowal of Torture." November 2005. http://nationalcouncilofchurches.us/common-witness/2005/torture.php

National Religious Campaign Against Torture. "Torture Is a Moral Issue: Statements of National Denominations." 2006. http://www.nrcat.org/get-involved/sign-the-statement-of-conscience/endorsements-by-religious-leaders/statements-denouncing-torture

Pew Research Center. "The Religious Dimensions of the Torture Debate." May 7, 2009. https://www.pewforum.org/2009/04/29/the-religious-dimensions-of-the-torture-debate/

United States Conference of Catholic Bishops. "Human Rights/Torture." http://www.usccb.org/issues-and-action/human-life-and-dignity/torture/index.cfm

United States Conference of Catholic Bishops. "Torture Is a Moral Issue." October 23, 2006. http://www.usccb.org/issues-and-action/human-life-and-dignity/torture/national-denominational-and-faith-group-leaders-issue-statement-denouncing-torture-2006-10-23.cfm

# U

## Ukraine War

The Ukraine War is also sometimes known as the Russo-Ukraine War. The February 2022 Russian invasion of Ukraine generated a global response largely, though not exclusively, supporting Ukraine and its military forces fighting in defense of Ukrainian sovereignty and geography. Leading support for Ukraine came from member nations of the North Atlantic Treaty Organization (NATO) and the European Union (EU). Beyond the destruction of Ukrainian cities and infrastructure, the conflict has created one of the greatest political crises in Europe since World War II and the largest humanitarian and refugee crisis since that war, with more than four million refugees and many more internally displaced people.

From religious and political perspectives, Orthodoxy, the prevailing religion in Russia and Ukraine, is closely tied to nationalism, even though the majority of their citizens do not participate in regular church attendance. In January 2019, the global spiritual leader of Orthodox Christians, the ecumenical patriarch in Constantinople (Patriarch Bartholomew), granted autocephaly ("independent" or "self-headed" status) to the newly created Orthodox Church of Ukraine (OCU). This act formally recognized what was then known as the Ukrainian Orthodox Church—and under control of the Russian Orthodox Church—as being self-governing and independent of the Russian Orthodox Church and its spiritual leadership by the patriarch of Moscow. This was the culmination of more than a hundred years of religious struggle within Ukraine and the first time Ukrainian Orthodox Christians had ecclesiastical freedom from Moscow since 1686. However, Russia and the Russian Orthodox Church refused to recognize the OCU. Further complicating the political dimensions of global Orthodoxy, following the creation of the OCU, the Russian Orthodox Church broke all ties with the Holy Synod of the patriarch of Constantinople. This created a political division within Orthodoxy, splitting Christians in a move not experienced since the Great Schism of 1054, in which Eastern Christianity (Orthodoxy) separated from Western Christianity (Catholicism).

The patriarch of Moscow's (Patriarch Kirill) support for the 2022 Russian invasion of and war against Ukraine is tied to Russian Orthodoxy's political alliance with Russian president Vladimir Putin and the tangled history of church-state relations in Russia, especially in the 20th century. Even so, the Orthodox Church in Russia is not unified in support from its members of Patriarch Kirill or the war, and such divisions have weakened the support of Patriarch Kirill among Orthodox Christians globally. In March 2022, the Russian-controlled region of Crimea ordered the drafting of a law banning the Ukrainian Orthodox Church in the Black Sea peninsula.

A 2019 survey of Ukrainians found that almost 65 percent identified as Orthodox, 9.5 percent as Greek Catholic, 1.8 percent as Roman Catholic, 1.6 percent as Protestant, 0.1 percent as Jewish, and 0.1 percent as Muslim. Other groups had smaller demographics, and almost 13 percent did not identify with any group (U.S. Department of State 2019).

In February and March 2014, Russia invaded and annexed the Crimean Peninsula of Ukraine and continues to hold it. In April 2014, pro-Russian separatists declared independence from Ukraine, and Russia supported the declaration. Since then, Ukraine has been fighting in the region. In the spring of 2021, Russia began amassing military forces on the Ukrainian border and in neighboring pro-Russian Belarus.

The threat by Russian president Vladimir Putin to use nuclear weapons if deemed necessary by Russia generated condemnation from the EU and NATO, who did not want the war to move beyond Ukraine's borders but who supported Ukraine with weapons and humanitarian assistance. Most observers in the West across the political and religious spectra viewed the conflict within the ethical, moral, and legal framework of the just war tradition. Consequences and implications of the war reach far beyond the borders of Ukraine, and it is understood in the West as being a major turning point in European politics with political and humanitarian costs not experienced since World War II.

*See also:* Just War Tradition; Presidential Faith and War; Weapons of Mass Destruction

## Further Reading

Denysenko, Nicholas E. *The Orthodox Church in Ukraine: A Century of Separation.* DeKalb: University of Northern Illinois Press, 2018.

Smith, Christopher M. *Ukraine's Revolt, Russia's Revenge.* Washington, DC: Brookings Institution, 2022.

U.S. Department of State. "2019 Report on International Religious Freedom: Ukraine." 2019. https://www.state.gov/reports/2019-report-on-international-religious-freedom/ukraine/

Walzer, Michael. "The Just War of the Ukrainians." *Wall Street Journal*, March 26–27, 2022, C1.

# United Nations

An intergovernmental organization focused on international peace and security, the United Nations (UN) was founded in 1945 in the aftermath of World War II as an entity to support and propagate postwar peace, cooperation, and stability. An outgrowth of an agreement between five great power states as permanent members (the United States, Great Britain, France, the former Soviet Union, and China), the UN aimed to establish peace after World War II and to continue the work of the League of Nations, which had been formed after World War I to maintain international peace and security. The two World Wars of the 20th century were devastating to nations around the globe. With millions of people dead, European colonialism collapsing, and the memory and effects of the Holocaust fresh, the UN arose to monitor and protect international and human rights.

The UN System consists of six principal organs, including the General Assembly, the Security Council, and the International Court of Justice (ICJ). The fifteen-member UN Security Council is led by the five permanent members. To date, the UN has grown to 193 member states comprising its General Assembly.

The UN routinely interacts with more than 3,000 nongovernmental organizations (NGOs) that are given "official" UN status; the majority of them work through the UN's Economic and Social Council (ECOSOC). Of these 3,000, about 10 percent are deemed faith-based organizations (FBOs) that seek to influence debate and policy decisions of the UN. As a secular international body, the UN shares ideals and values with many religious groups and organizations, especially with respect to human rights and a desire for a peaceful and stable world in which humans may flourish.

While faith-based and secular humanitarian NGOs such as Catholic Relief Services have observer status in UN activities, they are entities external to the UN General Assembly and do not have the same voting status as nations. Faith-based communities have provided humanitarian services to assist the poor, the marginalized, and victims of natural disaster, war, and persecution. Such organizations also focus on human needs, including education, health, and religious freedom.

In 2016, the Committee of Religious Non-Governmental Organizations (NGOs) at the United Nations was created with the dual purpose of offering a forum for exchanging ideas regarding the spiritual, ethical, and moral aspects of the UN's work and to serve as a religious forum for promoting the three pillars of the UN: human rights, peace and security, and development.

One area of concern for many with respect to human rights is freedom of religion and persecution because of one's faith commitments. The 1948 Universal Declaration of Human Rights (UDHR) directly addressed religious freedom and the right to change one's religious affiliation (Article 18). However, it was not until 1981 that the UN issued its Declaration on the Elimination of All Forms of Intolerance and of Discrimination Based on Religion or Belief. Five years later, in 1986, the UN created the position of Special Rapporteur on freedom of religion or belief. These efforts, along with the requirement that nations provide reports to the UN every four and a half years regarding human rights development, are important actions in and of themselves but also because of the strong linkage one often sees between conflict and human rights violations, including religious persecution.

In contemporary conflicts, faith-based NGOs continue to address issues of war and peace, including human rights, genocide, the marginalized, and refugees displaced by war and conflict. In the 21st century, such issues include but are not limited to treatment of the Rohingya, Uyghur, and Kurd populations; conflict in regions such as Sudan and Yemen; and civil wars and conflict creating refugee issues worldwide.

Although there are many religious groups and faith traditions represented with observer status at the UN Headquarters in New York City, the work of these groups on the ground in battle zones and regions shattered by conflict provides some of the greatest humanitarian assistance and relief available to victims of conflict.

Anywhere there are UN peacekeepers, there are likely to be NGOs and FBOs working as well. In many instances, NGOs and FBOs rely on the services of the UN forces for safety and protection as they carry out their humanitarian missions. There are quite a few instances in Afghanistan where religious NGO and FBO workers have been targeted and killed. This demonstrates the need for NGOs to have an awareness of what the UN is doing and to work closely with the UN regarding local security concerns.

From a national perspective in the context of great power competition, the UN is often viewed as an ineffective organization that is incapable of exerting ultimate authority over veto-holder states (the United States, Great Britain, France, Russia, and China). It does not wield any significant military force capable of intervening in conflict or providing blanket security. However, the UN provides a critical role in laying a basis for multinational agreement through the formulation of treaties. Treaties, even when not ratified, can serve as a basis for agreement, testing for common ground, forwarding discussion, and establishing regional and international consensus.

The UN arose in the aftermath of World War II out of international concern and consensus that the world should not experience a third world war. Although the hopes and aspirations of the League of Nations of World War I were not realized, after World War II, there remained the strong desire to again attempt an international organization of similar scope as the earlier League of Nations. With varying degrees of success and failure, the UN continues to function as an international balancing force to state interests. Part of its commitments are the desire for the reduction of war and the promotion of peace on a global level. To that end, there is much overlap with the humanitarian and religious values of secular and religious entities working on the ground in conflict zones around the world.

*See also:* Christianity and War; Genocide; Human Rights; Religious Freedom and Religious Persecution; Responsibility to Protect

## Further Reading

Carrette, Jeremy, and Hugh Miall. *Religion, NGOs, and the United Nations: Visible and Invisible Actors in Power*. London: Bloomsbury Academic, 2018.

Caspar, Jayson. "'Water on a Stone': UN Expert on the Hard Work of Religious Freedom." *Christianity Today* online edition, November 16, 2020. https://www.christianitytoday.com/news/2020/november/un-religious-freedom-ahmed-shaheed-irf-forb-ministerial.html

The Committee of Religious NGOs at the United Nations. "About." Accessed March 11, 2020. https://rngos.wordpress.com/

Ferris, Elizabeth. "Faith-Based and Secular Humanitarian Organizations." *International Review of the Red Cross* 87, no. 858 (2005): 311–325. https://www.icrc.org/en/doc/assets/files/other/irrc_858_ferris.pdf

Haynes, Jeffrey. "Faith-Based Organizations at the United Nations." European University Institute, Robert Schuman Centre for Advanced Studies, EUI Working Papers, RSCAS 2013/70, September 2013. https://cadmus.eui.eu/bitstream/handle/1814/28119/RSCAS_2013_70.pdf

United States Institute for Peace. "Faith-Based NGOs and International Attempts at Peacebuilding." October 22, 2001.

# V

## Vietnam War

The Vietnam War (1955–1975) (with major U.S. participation in 1965–1973) is the most debated military conflict in recent American history. It was very divisive in American society, and American religious groups and denominations were as religiously and politically divided about the war as the population as a whole. The memory and effects of the war have shaped the military and religious responses to every conflict since it ended. American war dead during the war exceeded 58,000, and beyond the military and political consequences, the war affected all areas of American culture.

In the 21st century, political and military leaders have frequently voiced concern that U.S. actions in Iraq and Afghanistan would lead to a "quagmire." Use of the term *quagmire* is an intentional choice that links contemporary conflicts with the Vietnam War and journalist David Halberstam's (1934–2007) book *The Making of a Quagmire: America and Vietnam during the Kennedy Era* (1965). The term subsequently became associated with what is known as "quagmire theory" in international relations.

Viewed as a Cold War proxy war at the time, the conflict had significant internal religious dynamics early in the war. Until his assassination in 1965, South Vietnam's controversial Roman Catholic president Ngo Dinh Diem (1901–1963) initially had strong U.S. support. Diem was the first president of South Vietnam, and his government established Catholicism as a national religion, even though 85 percent of the population was Buddhist. His government favored Roman Catholics and limited some of the rights of non-Catholics. This led to Buddhist-Catholic struggles within the country, and on June 11, 1963, a Buddhist monk named Thich Quang Duc (1897–1963) set himself on fire at a busy Saigon intersection in protest of government policies. The self-immolation was photographed and became an internationally known protest to the Diem government.

Although the majority of South Vietnam was Buddhist, many Americans, in and out of the U.S. government, saw in Diem's Christianity the potential of a strong ally against the spread of communism in Asia. The fact that the war was understood by Americans as having a strong religious dimension made the politics of the war and responses to it extremely fragmented and volatile in the United States.

During the mid-1960s, some clergy in the mainline Protestant denominations began to publicly oppose the American war effort. Such protests increased in the aftermath of the early 1968 North Vietnamese Tet Offensive during which many cities in South Vietnam, including Saigon and the American embassy there, came under attack. Militarily, the offensive was unsuccessful, but it raised doubts in the minds of many Americans regarding President Lyndon Johnson's assurances that the end of the war was near. The Tet Offensive became a turning point for many Americans and their previous support of the war effort.

Although many theologically liberal pastors and religious leaders turned against the war, their congregations often did not share the same political views such that in mainline Protestant denominations and in some Roman Catholic congregations, there was a political divide between the pulpit and the pew. Likewise, in the prominent U.S. religious periodicals, there was a political split. In 1968, the liberal magazine *The Christian Century* turned against the war, whereas its conservative rival *Christianity Today* continued to support the war effort. The highly publicized anti-war protests and trials of religious leaders such as William Sloane Coffin, Jr. (1924–2006), Daniel Berrigan (1921–2016), and Philip Berrigan (1923–2002) accentuated the religious polarity of the war in American religion. This split was the beginning of a religiopolitical trend that continues to the present. As the war continued longer than expected by Americans, even evangelicals and other religious conservatives privately began to voice concerns regarding the course of the war. For example, in April 1969, evangelist Billy Graham (1918–2018) wrote a lengthy letter to his friend President Richard M. Nixon (1913–1994) expressing reservations regarding the Nixon administration's execution of the war. By the end of the 1960s, Americans across the religious and political spectrum were anxious for the war to end.

When coupled with declining membership in many denominations from the 1960s onward, the Protestant religious landscape in the United

States began a decades-long shift from mainline denominations to more theologically and politically conservative evangelical denominations, such as Assemblies of God, the Church of the Nazarene, the Southern Baptist Convention, and the Pentecostal Holiness Church, and groups such as the National Association of Evangelicals. The political divide also affected the number of military chaplains that various denominations endorsed for service in the military. Denominations with strong anti-war doctrinal positions or factions either refused to permit their clergy to serve as chaplains or reluctantly permitted participation, with the result being that military members from those faith traditions did not have adequate numbers of chaplains serving from their denominations.

Congregants in liberal churches who disagreed with the political stances of their denominations migrated to more politically and theologically conservative denominations and churches and formed the core of what in the late 1970s through 1990s became known as the Religious Right in American politics. Similarly, by 1971, American Catholic bishops had reversed their collective stance regarding the war and declared that it no longer could be considered a just war that followed the tenets of the centuries-old just war tradition. Within the African American religious community, there arose challenges in 1967 after Martin Luther King, Jr. (1929–1968) publicly denounced the war. King and other African Americans strongly supported President Johnson's civil rights and social policies. Thus, when King publicly denounced the president's military strategy, it created a loss of support from many within that community for the war, further weakening Johnson's political base. At the time Johnson left office, to be followed by Richard Nixon, African American churches were continuing to turn against the war.

Within American Judaism, there was also strong opposition to the war. Rabbi, philosopher, and theologian Abraham Joshua Heschel (1907–1972), one of the most prominent Jewish theologians and philosophers of the 20th century, strongly and vocally opposed the war (although Jewish chaplains and other military personnel also served in Vietnam). This again illustrates the political spectrum within individual American religious communities during the war.

Religious values of individual Americans have consequences with respect to the war. During the war, there was a significant shift in conscientious objection status based on religion with respect to military service and the draft (Selective Service System). Although conscientious objection to war has always been a part of American history, until 1940, most conscientious objectors had come from American peace churches (e.g., Mennonites, Society of Friends (Quakers), Church of the Brethren). During the Vietnam War, there was a broadening of legal, political, and religious views on conscientious objection such that there was a significant increase in the number of men granted conscientious objector status who came from Protestant mainstream denominations (e.g., Methodist, Lutheran, Episcopal, Presbyterian) or secular backgrounds. Many such denominations and religious groups actively promoted conscientious objection and opposition to the war. This brought religious opposition to the war into mainstream American society with political and religious consequences that remain to the present.

When the war came to an end in 1975, following the collapse of Saigon in April 1975 and capitulation of the government and military in South Vietnam, thousands of people fled South Vietnam. It was the largest ever exodus of Vietnamese to the United States. American religious organizations and denominations across the political spectrum provided humanitarian assistance to refugees, known at the time as "Vietnamese boat people," and helped thousands of them immigrate to the United States. The arrival of the Vietnamese in the United States also exponentially increased the Buddhist population of the nation, helping to create religious diversity that continues in the 21st century. The enormous religious and humanitarian endeavor became a foundational event in late 20th- and 21st-century humanitarian and disaster relief work by religious groups.

Earlier in the war, and especially after 1967 and 1968, across the religious spectrum, as religious leaders became activists in the anti-war movement, the religious base fractured, and political conservatives migrated to more like-minded denominations and religious organizations. The result was the beginning of a significant shift in the religious demographics in the United States. The social and political consequences of that shift continue to the present and affect how Americans view religion, politics, and war in the 21st century. Just as there was no unified religious response to the Vietnam War, neither was there one to subsequent American wars fought in the late 20th and 21st centuries, whether in the Middle East, Afghanistan, Africa, or elsewhere. Much of the contemporary religiopolitical divisions regarding war are deeply rooted in the American experience of the Vietnam War.

*See also:* American Exceptionalism; American Peace Churches; Conscientious Objection; Ecclesiastical Statements on War and Peace;

Evangelicalism; Graham, William Franklin, Jr. ("Billy"); King, Martin Luther, Jr.; Korean War; Music; Pacifism; Protestant Denominations; Roman Catholicism

## Further Reading

Bogaski, George. *American Protestants and the Debate over the Vietnam War: Evil Was Loose in the World.* Lanham, MD: Lexington Books, 2014.

Fairclough, Adam. "Martin Luther King, Jr. and the War in Vietnam." *Phylon* 45, no 1 (1st qtr. 1984): 19–39.

Fiske, Edward B. "Religion; The Clergy on Vietnam." *New York Times*, January 7, 1968, Sec. E, 9.

Griggs, Walter S., Jr. "The Selective Conscientious Objector: A Vietnam Legacy." *Journal of Church and State* 21, no. 1 (Winter 1979): 91–107.

Halberstram, David. *The Making of a Quagmire: America and Vietnam during the Kennedy Era.* New York: Random House, 1965.

Kaplan, Edward K. "Heschel & the Vietnam War." *Tikkun* 22, no. 4 (2007): 14–68. https://www.muse.jhu.edu/article/592924

King, Martin Luther, Jr. "Martin Luther King, Jr. on the Vietnam War." *The Atlantic*, February 2018. https://www.theatlantic.com/magazine/archive/2018/02/martin-luther-king-jr-vietnam/552521/

Lattin, Don. "'The Vietnam Years': How the Conflict Ripped the Nation's Religious Fabric." Religion News Service, September 8, 2017. https://religionnews.com/2017/09/08/the-vietnam-years-how-the-conflict-ripped-the-nations-religious-fabric/

Mislin, David. "How Vietnam War Protests Accelerated the Rise of the Christian Right." *Smithsonian Magazine*, May 3, 2018. https://www.smithsonianmag.com/history/how-vietnam-war-protests-spurred-rise-christian-right-180968942/

Moskos, Charles C., and John Whiteclay Chambers II. *The New Conscientious Objection: From Sacred to Secular Resistance.* New York: Oxford University Press, 1993.

Owens, Mackubin Thomas. "Vietnam and the Just War Tradition." In *America and the Just War Tradition*, edited by Mark David Hall and J. Daryl Charles, 226–250. Notre Dame, IN: University of Notre Dame Press, 2019.

Padgett, Timothy D. *Swords & Plowshares: American Evangelicals on War, 1937–1973.* Bellingham, WA: Lexham Press, 2018.

Patterson, Eric. "Just War & National Honor: The Case of Vietnam." *Providence* 10 (Winter 2018): 4–14.

Preston, Andrew. *Sword of the Spirit, Shield of Faith: Religion in American War and Diplomacy.* New York: Alfred A. Knopf, 2012.

Quinley, Harold E. "The Protestant Clergy and the War in Vietnam." *Public Opinion Quarterly* 34 (Spring 1970): 43–54.

Settje, David E. *Faith and War: How Christians Debated the Cold and Vietnam Wars*. New York: New York University Press, 2011.

Smylie, James H. "American Religious Bodies, Just War, and Vietnam." *Journal of Church and State* 11, no. 3 (Autumn 1969): 383–408.

## Wars of Israel

Beginning with the Israeli War of Independence (November 1947–July 1949), which started as a civil war, Israel has been in more than a dozen significant conflicts and wars since the nation was founded in 1948. In the 1960s and 1970s, the Six-Day War (June 1967) and the Yom Kippur War (October 1973) gained international headlines and significant U.S. interest, not the least of which was the June 1967 Israeli attack on the USS *Liberty* that was part of the preemptive operations of the Six-Day War.

In the 1970s and 1980s, instability, civil war, and multidimensional war in Lebanon resulted in Israeli operations against Palestinian insurgency as well as the 1982 Lebanon War and fifteen years of conflict between the Israeli Defense Forces and Muslim guerilla forces led by Iranian-backed Hezbollah. From 1987 to 1993, there was what is called the First Intifada (literally from Arabic meaning "tremor" or "shuddering" and more commonly understood as "rebellion"), a large-scale Palestinian uprising in the West Bank and Gaza Strip. During the Gulf War (1991), Iraqi forces fired missiles into Israel in an attempt to draw them into the war in hopes of generating support from other nations of the Middle East against Israel and the U.S.-led coalition. Israel was persuaded by the coalition not to respond, but the incident illustrates the volatility of politics and conflict in the region.

Post-2000, the First Intifada was followed by the Second Intifada (2000–2005). In 2006, there was a Second Lebanon War, and from January 2008 to January 2009, the Gaza War. This last conflict was followed by major military operations in 2012 and 2014 in the Gaza Strip. Against the backdrop of all of these conflicts, there have been larger wars in the Middle East, such as the Gulf War and Iraq War, and continuous instability.

Israel and the conflicts involving Israel are always a factor in the politics of the Middle East and a significant part of U.S. strategy and policies in the region. Apart from secular support for Israel by Americans, much of the significance of Israel for the United States is undergirded by religious support from within American Judaism and American Protestantism, specifically American evangelicals.

With respect to politics and religion in the United States, the wars of Israel, especially in the 21st century, have been contentious and as divided as any religious or political subject. In 2107, President Donald Trump announced that the United States recognized Jerusalem as the capital of Israel, and in 2018, the United States officially opened its embassy in Jerusalem. For American evangelicals, this was welcomed, but organizations such as the National Council of Churches (NCC), which represents more than three dozen "mainline" denominations, this was opposed and condemned. The NCC believes that the United States should be neutral in the Israeli-Palestinian conflict. Other religious and political organizations, such as major lobbying groups that include Christians United for Israel and the American Israel Public Affairs Committee (AIPAC), supported the move.

There has been significant international support for economic and diplomatic actions against Israel in support of the Palestinian cause. Part of the Palestinian political cause is the promotion of an international economic campaign known as BDS (boycott, divestment, and sanctions). Palestinians believe that these efforts should continue until Israel withdraws from what are called the "occupied territories" and agrees to demands. In the United States, there has been a mixed political reaction to the movement, and as of January 2019, twenty-seven states had passed various anti-BDS measures. BDS is a means by which Iran and other foes of Israel can isolate and harm Israel economically—something that thus far has been unachievable militarily.

The recent wars and conflicts of Israel, especially in Lebanon and Gaza, have demonstrated numerous challenges of the law of armed conflict, international humanitarian law, and military operations in an environment with many civilians. In an evolving world of nonstate actors such as Hezbollah, terrorism, and the ever-present and multifaceted concerns of the Palestinian-Israeli peace process, issues of war and peace in Israel will continue to receive divided and international religious and political attention. As the strongest ally of the United States in the Middle East, actions by Israel will also remain controversial in American religious and political life.

*See also:* Contemporary Non-U.S. Conflicts; Evangelicalism; Gulf War; Human Rights; Judaism and War; Middle East Conflict; Religion, Conflict, and Geopolitics; United Nations

**Further Reading**

Amstutz, Mark R. *Evangelicals and American Foreign Policy.* New York: Oxford University Press, 2014.

Borg, David. "The End of Evangelical Support for Israel? The Jewish State's International Standing." *Middle East Quarterly* 21, no. 2 (Spring 2014). http://www.meforum.org/3769/israel-evangelical-support

Bunton, Martin. *The Palestinian-Israeli Conflict: A Very Short Introduction.* New York: Oxford University Press, 2013.

Dershowitz, Alan. *The Case against BDS: Why Singling Out Israel for Boycott Is Anti-Semitic and Anti-Peace.* New York: Post Hill Press, 2018.

Israel Ministry of Foreign Affairs. "Israel's Wars." Accessed February 1, 2020. https://mfa.gov.il/MFA/AboutIsrael/History/Pages/Israel-Wars.aspx

Katz, Yakov, and Amir Bohbot. *How Israel Became a High-Tech Military Superpower.* New York: St. Martin's Press, 2017.

Marcus, Ralph D. *Israel's Long War with Hezbollah.* Washington, DC: Georgetown University Press, 2017.

Mearsheimer, John J., and Stephen M. Walt. *The Israel Lobby and U.S. Foreign Policy.* New York: Farrar, Straus and Giroux, 2007.

Muravchik, Joshua. "The Seventh Day & Counting: The Elusive Peace of the Six-Day War." *Providence* (Spring 2017). https://providencemag.com/2017/08/the-seventh-day-and-counting-the-elusive-peace-of-the-six-day-war/

Olson, Jason M. *America's Road to Jerusalem: The Impact of the Six-Day War on Protestant Politics.* Lanham, MD: Lexington Books, 2018.

Oren, Michael B. "The Coming Middle East Conflagration." *The Atlantic,* November 4, 2019. https://www.theatlantic.com/ideas/archive/2019/11/israel-preparing-open-war/601285/

Oren, Michael B. *Six Days of War: June 1967 and the Making of the Modern Middle East.* New York: Random House, 2002.

# Weapons of Mass Destruction (Nuclear, Biological, Chemical)

The acquisition, proliferation, and use of weapons of mass destruction (WMDs) remains a topic of significant national and international political importance. As such, WMDs have in the past and continue to receive attention from many religious groups and denominations. A weapon of mass destruction is a weapon that has the capacity for injury, death, and destruction on a scale unachievable by other weapons. Because of this lethality, WMDs inevitably and indiscriminately injure and kill noncombatants as well as combatants. Because of their destructive power, the possession of such weapons, even if not used, raises major ethical, legal, political, and religious concerns in domestic politics and international relations.

Debates regarding the development, possession, and use of WMDs has drawn attention from religious communities and leaders since such weapons were first used (gas) in World War I. WMDs are commonly listed under three types—nuclear, biological, and chemical weapons, commonly referred to as "NBC" weapons. Radiological weapons are sometimes also included, although this type is implied as an adjunct to nuclear weapons use because radiological effects occur both during and after a nuclear explosion.

The classification of a WMD includes not only the scale of destructive capacity and the three most commonly listed modern types but also the potential of use by enemies as a serious threat to a nation and potentially its survival. WMDs are a form of killing power that shapes domestic and international relations, affects U.S. security and defense strategies, determines arsenal planning and budgeting, and fundamentally reshapes warfighting and homeland defense. This is evidenced by the Cold War nuclear arms race between the United States and the Union of Soviet Socialist Republics (USSR or Soviet Union), the impetus for the U.S. invasion of Iraq (2003), and concerns about nonstate actors using WMDs in terrorist attacks, such as the 9/11 attacks of 2001. Further concerns regarding WMDs in the 21st century have arisen in the aftermath of their use in 2017 in the civil war in Syria by forces under the control of President Bashar al-Assad, as well as ongoing international resistance to the development of nuclear weapons by Iran and North Korea.

Regarding religion and contemporary politics, many faith traditions have addressed concerns regarding WMDs, especially from the 1970s onward. Within Christianity, some religious groups and denominations, such as those known as American peace churches, condemned all weapons, including WMDs, favoring pacifism instead. Others addressed WMDs in the context of the just war tradition and in religiopolitical debates, including the 1983 U.S. Catholic Bishops' pastoral letter, "The Challenge of Peace" (discussed below) and statements regarding the use of WMDs as chemical weapons in Syria and the potential use of nuclear WMDs by Saddam Hussein as a justification for the U.S. and coalition invasion of Iraq during the George W. Bush administration.

The term *weapons of mass destruction* was coined for modern use to describe bomber formations of planes in the 1930s before World War II. The most well-known case of WMD use is that of the Allied dropping of the atomic bombs on the Japanese cities of Hiroshima and Nagasaki on August 6 and 9, respectively, in 1945. Allied bombing missions had previously destroyed the cities of Dresden and Tokyo over the course of days and weeks, as well as many other cities, but the crews of the U.S. B-29 bombers *Enola Gay* (dropping the bomb on Hiroshima) and *Bockscar* (dropping the bomb on Nagasaki) each deployed WMDs that killed tens of thousands in a single explosion.

A 1946 U.S. Strategic Bombing Survey (USSBS) following the Pacific War compared the effects of the single atomic bombs at Hiroshima and Nagasaki with the conventional bombing of Tokyo. Estimates of the number of people killed and wounded differ in range, but the USSBS analysis compares the effort in Tokyo of 279 bomber planes during the course of a total of 93 urban attacks with 1,129 tons of conventional bombs to the single atomic bomb attacks at Hiroshima and Nagasaki. In sum, the Tokyo attacks destroyed 15.8 square miles and killed an estimated 83,000 people and injured 102,000 over a number of days. In comparison, the single WMD at Hiroshima destroyed 4.7 square miles in seconds, killing more than 70,000 people and injuring as many, and the bomb at Nagasaki killed more than 40,000 and injured as many. Thus, a single atomic bomb killed at least half as many people as the conventional bombs from almost 300 planes—maximum destruction at a mass scale with very little effort.

During the Korean War (1950–1953), there was some military and political discussion about using nuclear weapons against communist Chinese targets, but the weapons were not deployed. Throughout the era of the Cold War (1945–1990), WMDs increasingly became a concern as U.S. and Soviet stockpiles of the weapons increased. Although many people in the West argued for the development and acquisition of the weapons, there were always religious and political voices of concern or opposition that sought de-escalation of the nuclear arms race and structured disarmament. In the United States, one of the strongest religious voices (though not the only one) to specifically address WMDs was the United States Conference of Catholic Bishops (USCCB).

Given the unprecedented potential for mass destruction, the gruesome yet successful use of force of the atomic bomb accelerated the worldwide race for nations of means to acquire this WMD for asymmetric power to threaten and defend. This touched off the Cold War starting in 1945 and the religious response debating the morality of nuclear weapons use. One of the most influential among these responses, "The Challenge of Peace," was issued in 1983 by the USCCB as a pastoral letter calling for peace and the abolition and nonproliferation of nuclear weapons. The letter applies strict traditional just war *jus in bello* (law in waging war) criteria of proportionality and discrimination of noncombatants to nuclear weapons, providing a moral critique of the U.S. bombing of Hiroshima and Nagasaki and setting a standard for nuclear ethics marking WMDs as indiscriminate and immoral. Further, the USCCB specifically denounced the destruction of cities wholesale, or "city-busting," as indiscriminate and illegitimate (Powers 209, 73–75).

Religious responses to WMDs predated nuclear ethics and the 1983 pastoral letter; chemical weapons have been used in war and conflict as far back as April 1915 near Ypres, Belgium, when Germany placed over 5,000 chlorine gas cylinders near Allied trenches during World War I. For more than one hundred years, there have been religious voices calling for nations to abandon the creation, stockpiling, and use of WMDs.

Though the 1983 USCCB letter and its follow-up pastoral letter, "The Harvest of Justice Is Sown in Peace" (1993), were widely received and promoted, the letters were not without criticism within the Roman Catholic community and externally as well. Critics argued that the document was grounded in a presumption against war rather than a presumption against injustice, the latter being the classical position of the religious and secular constructs of the just war tradition of which Roman Catholicism has been a major advocate.

The World Council of Churches, National Council of Churches, National Association of Evangelicals, and other groups have issued statements regarding nuclear weapons. Many denominations have expressed support or nonsupport for the use of force of WMDs, although virtually all express concern over proliferation.

The nuclear issue did not cease with the end of the Cold War. Regarding Saddam Hussein's gassing of the Kurds in the aftermath of the Gulf War

(1991), critiques feared and believed that he continued to retain WMD capabilities. It was this belief that led, in part, to the Iraq War. Additionally, in the 1990s, there was concern about "loose," untracked nuclear weapons that were mismanaged by the former Soviet Union during decommissioning procedures. It was uncertain what nations or nonstate actors might acquire these untracked weapons.

One example of the use of WMD technologies acquired from the former Soviet Union involved sarin gas attacks—one in the city of Matsumoto, Japan, in June 1994 and one at multiple locations in the Tokyo subway in March 1995. Shoko Asahara, the leader of the Aum Shinrikyo domestic terrorist group responsible for the attacks, planned the attack with the assistance of a former Soviet Union scientist.

In the 21st century, chemical WMD usage in Syria by various forces, including the Islamic State in Iraq and the Levant (ISIL or ISIS), Syrian Ba'athists, and the Syrian government of Bashar al-Assad, starting in 2012, remains an ongoing international global security concern. Various religious NGOs continue working to alleviate humanitarian crises related to the use of chemical WMDs in the Middle East.

In both Christian and Islamic theology, there are some strands that believe that the end of the present age as we know it will be brought about by cataclysmic events and warfare. These beliefs are grounded in interpretations of what are deemed to be prophetic passages of the sacred texts of each religious tradition. For some adherents, this end of human history is linked to destructive forces with kinetic power commensurate to WMDs. Though not always identified as WMDs, the prophetic ideologies do not negate their use.

Perhaps the religious significance of the use of force of WMDs is best demonstrated by a statement made by Robert Oppenheimer (1904–1967), the lead scientist of the Manhattan Project, the secret weapons laboratory that developed the atomic bombs used at Nagasaki and Hiroshima, Japan. Upon seeing the successful testing of the bomb, known as the Trinity Test (July 16, 1945), Oppenheimer made a statement about the bomb that included a referral to a sacred Hindu text: "We knew the world would not be the same. A few people laughed. A few people cried. Most people were silent. I remembered the line from the Hindu scripture, the Bhagavad Gita: Vishnu is trying to persuade the Prince that he should do his duty and, to impress him, takes on his multi-armed form and says, 'Now I am become death, the destroyer of worlds'" (cited in Freed and Giovannitti 1965).

As long as there are WMDs, there will be continued voices within many religious traditions calling for abandoning them in all circumstances. The presence of such weapons heightens the relevance and voices of those within all religious traditions who seek a peaceful political resolution of national differences and the promotion of peace rather than war.

*See also:* American Peace Churches; Apocalypticism; Christianity and War; Cold War; Genocide; Human Rights; Iraq War; Islam and War; Just War Tradition; Korean War; Middle East Conflict; Protestant Denominations; Responsibility to Protect; Roman Catholicism; Terrorism; United Nations; World War I; World War II

## Further Reading

Braun, Christian Nikolaus. "James Turner Johnson and the Roman Catholic Just War Tradition." In *Responsibility and Restraint: James Turner Johnson and the Just War Tradition*, edited by Eric D. Patterson and Marc LiVecche, 125–157. Middletown, RI: Stone Tower Press, 2020.

Christianson, Drew, and Carole Sargent, eds. *A World Free of Nuclear Weapons: The Vatican Conference on Nuclear Disarmament*. Washington, DC: Georgetown University Press, 2020.

Cook, David. *Contemporary Muslim Apocalyptic Literature*. Syracuse, NY: Syracuse University Press, 2005.

Everts, Sarah. "When Chemicals Became Weapons of War." 2015. https://chemicalweapons.cenmag.org/when-chemicals-became-weapons-of-war/

Freed, Fred, and Len Giovannitti, dirs. "The Decision to Drop the Bomb." In *The Decision to Drop the Bomb*. NBC News, January 5, 1965. Interview of Robert Oppenheimer on the Trinity Test explosion.

National Association of Evangelicals. "Nuclear Weapons." January 1, 2011. https://www.nae.net/nuclear-weapons/

National Conference of Catholic Bishops. "The Harvest of Justice Is Sown in Peace." November 17, 1993. http://www.usccb.org/beliefs-and-teachings/what-we-believe/catholic-social-teaching/the-harvest-of-justice-is-sown-in-peace.cfm

National Council of Catholic Bishops. "The Challenge of Peace: God's Promise and Our Response." May 3, 1983. https://www.usccb.org/upload/challenge-peace-gods-promise-our-response-1983.pdf

National Council of Churches. "Nuclear Disarmament: The Time Is Now." November 12, 2009. http://nationalcouncilofchurches.us/common-witness/2009/nuclear-disarm.php

Powers, Gerard F. "The U.S. Bishops and War since the Peace Pastoral." *U.S. Catholic Historian* 27, no. 2 (2009): 73–96. http://www.jstor.org/stable/40468576

Wellerstein, Alex. "Counting the Dead at Hiroshima and Nagasaki." Bulletin of the Atomic Scientists. https://thebulletin.org/2020/08/counting-thedead-at-hiroshima-and-nagasaki/

# World War I

From 2014 to 2018, nations around the world commemorated the centennial of World War I. In part, this was done to acknowledge the service and sacrifice of more than nine million combatants from many nations who died in the war. It is also important to recognize that the war shaped and reshaped the 20th century and that its effects continue in the 21st century. In the 20th century, the League of Nations, World War II, aspects of international humanitarian law and the law of armed conflict, and pacifism and peace movements all had linkages with the war. For each of these, there were religious dimensions that were very strong and presently continue. Further, contemporary conflict in the Middle East has some of its roots in the geopolitical decisions of the Allies (also known as the Entente Powers) during and after the war.

Many Americans, President Woodrow Wilson included, were reluctant to enter the war. It was seen as something that Europeans had brought upon themselves and a conflict that did not and should not involve the United States. The war had been raging for more than two and a half years before the United States entered conflict on April 6, 1917. After U.S. entry, the war continued for another one and a half years, until November 11, 1918, when the guns fell silent.

Pastors such as the influential Henry Sloane Coffin (1877–1954) of Madison Avenue Presbyterian Church in New York City, one of the most prominent pulpits in the country, vocally opposed the war in Europe. For many, the opposition was not due to pacifism but to the belief that the war was not necessary. However, once war was declared by the United States, they supported the effort, not because war was good but because they believed in President Wilson's idea that a new world order could be established after the war and that it might lead to perpetual world peace.

In the idea of long-standing peace after the war was the remnant of the Christian theological idea known as postmillennialism—that the world, through intentional human endeavor, will get better and better and bring in the biblically prophetic Kingdom of God on earth. Although the war had shattered this theological idea in Europe, vestiges of it remained in some parts of Protestantism in the United States.

Prior to the war, based on the ideas of social Darwinism, some European intellectuals (religious and otherwise) promoted the idea that war was necessary and inevitable to purge the continent of weak nations so that others could flourish. From the 1870s until the end of the war in 1918, aspects of political and philosophical social Darwinism easily blended with European theological postmillennialism and created an idea of redemption by war. In the United States, the liberal theology known as the Social Gospel was prominent and easily merged with Wilson's internationalism. For many religious liberals, the Social Gospel was bringing about the Kingdom of God in the United States, and Wilson was helping bring it about in the world. In so doing, religious liberals and religious conservatives aligned with patriotic and religious motivations (though different) in a common desire to see the defeat of the Central powers.

President Wilson was reluctant to enter the war and had hopes that he would be able to broker peace among the belligerents. From the beginning of the war, he sought neutrality and noninvolvement for the United States. But when this no longer was viable, he drew heavily upon his Presbyterian Christian faith to lead the American war effort and seek lasting postwar peace.

In 1917, neither pacifists nor proponents of war, whether their ideas were religiously motivated or politically motivated, commanded a majority in American society. As the war progressed and circumstances changed such that there was little realistic alternative for the United States to enter the war, various groups coalesced to create a religious and patriotic front. Although some pacifists remained opposed to the war and did not participate, by 1917, the U.S. peace movement had reached its zenith.

In the same way that leading Protestant figures and organizations such as the Federal Council of Churches made the transition from not favoring U.S. participation in the war to favoring it, Roman Catholic and Jewish leaders also followed suit. History scholar Andrew Preston writes, "Religious leaders, and through them their congregations, invested America's role in the war with transcendent meaning and millennial yearning. They provided the moral platform from which the United States would launch a new world order" (Preston 2012, 337).

There was a spectrum of opinion about the war among religious conservatives as well as religious liberals. Religious liberals tended to promote a theology of postmillennialism, whereas religious conservatives tended to adhere to a theology of premillennialism in which there was a distrust of internationalism. However, premillennialists saw prophetic significance in the British capture of Jerusalem (December 1917) from the Turks, who were allied with Germany. This, coupled with the Balfour Declaration (1917) promising a homeland to Jews in the Middle East, became part of the religious and political dynamics of the 20th- and 21st-century Middle East. In the 21st century, American evangelical support for Israel, politically and religiously, is directly tied to events in the Middle East during World War I.

After the United States declared war, most religious groups strongly supported the war and embraced both just war and crusade rhetoric and perspectives. For example, the nationally known Protestant evangelist Billy Sunday (1862–1935) initially saw the war as not an American concern. However, after the sinking of the *Lusitania* and the execution of Edith Cavell by Germany, Sunday came to support the British efforts against the Central Powers. He gave strong vocal support to President Wilson, and after war was declared by the United States, he fervently blended patriotism and preaching and declared that neutrality was impossible. Patriotic posters and propaganda easily mixed religious images and ideas with American military and political goals. One example is the government-sponsored film, poster, and music of *Pershing's Crusaders* that vividly portrayed the head of the American Expeditionary Forces (AEF), General John J. Pershing (1860–1948), as a 20th-century Christian crusader. Religious and political rhetoric were often intertwined to gain support, sell war bonds, and enlist volunteers.

Many religious organizations, such as the YMCA, provided aid and assistance in the war zones as well as on the home front. In the aftermath of the war, religious denominations and groups were extremely active and influential in the commemorations of the war, war monuments, and perpetuating the legacy and lessons of the war. While the war was not a religious war, religion was a strong motivating force for war and for peace. In the interwar period, many national and international religious organizations contributed to the peace movement and efforts to create a lasting legacy of peace through the League of Nations and other international groups. Though unsuccessful in their efforts, religious organizations became steadfast in their advocacy in the realm of international politics and humanitarian efforts. Such a presence continued throughout the 20th century and into the 21st century.

In the 21st century, one finds strong support for the state of Israel among American evangelicals, and as noted above, much of this can be traced historically to World War I—as can much of the continued turmoil and conflict in the region. Religious support for the United Nations by organizations such as the National Council of Churches can be traced to the failed League of Nations and rising postwar internationalism. One can also find religious and political activism seeking to ban the use of chemical weapons during and after World War I. This would be expanded later in the 20th century to calls for the banning of weapons of mass destruction (WMDs) by some religious groups. Although the Wilsonian dream of lasting world peace was not achieved, many contemporary religious leaders, denominations, and organizations find in the tragedy and aftermath of World War I historical examples and justification for active and vocal political action in the 21st century.

*See also:* American Exceptionalism; American Peace Churches; Just War Tradition; Literature; Music; Pacifism; Presidential Faith and War; Protestant Denominations; Rhetoric, Sermons, and Prayers; Roman Catholicism; Weapons of Mass Destruction; World War II

## Further Reading

Bolt, Robert. "World War I." In *The Wars of America: Christian Views*, edited by Ronald A. Wells, 163–188. Macon, GA: Mercer University Press, 1991.

Burleigh, Michael. *Sacred Causes: The Clash of Religion and Politics, from the Great War to the War on Terror*. New York: HarperCollins, 2007.

Burnidge, Cara Lee. *A Peaceful Conquest: Woodrow Wilson, Religion, and the New World Order*. Chicago: University of Chicago Press, 2016.

Ebel, Jonathan H. *Faith in the Fight: Religion and the American Soldier in the Great War*. Princeton, NJ: Princeton University Press, 2010.

Hall, Mark David, and J. Daryl Charles, eds. *America and the Just War Tradition: A History of U.S. Conflicts*. Notre Dame, IN: University of Notre Dame Press, 2019.

Hankins, Barry. *Woodrow Wilson: Ruling Elder, Spiritual President*. New York: Oxford University Press, 2016.

Jenkins, Philip. *The Great and Holy War: How World War I Became a Religious Crusade*. New York: HarperOne, 2014.

Miller, Richard B., ed. *War in the Twentieth Century: Sources in Theological Ethics*. Louisville, KY: Westminster/John Knox Press, 1992.

Morgan, David T. "The Revivalist as Patriot: Billy Sunday and World War I." *Journal of Presbyterian History (1962–1985)* 51, no. 2 (1973): 199–215.

Preston, Andrew. *Sword of the Spirit, Shield of Faith: Religion in American War and Diplomacy*. New York: Alfred A. Knopf, 2012.

Stromberg, Roland N. *Redemption by War: The Intellectuals and 1914*. Lawrence: Regents Press of Kansas. 1982.

# World War II

Unlike wars of the last half of the 20th century and opening decades of the 21st century, World War II (1939–1945) was a war that Americans rallied behind and enthusiastically supported. They did so with war bond sales, scrap metal drives, victory gardens, patriotic slogans, and significant religious support across the American religious spectrum. In the Pacific and European theaters of operations as well as on the home front, religion was a major force in sustaining the morale and motivation necessary to endure the deprivations and duration of the global war.

Even before the United States entered the war, religious rhetoric and imagery was strongly tied to the conflict. For example, it was on the eve of World War II that British prime minister Neville Chamberlain (1869–1940) sought to avoid war with Germany and Adolf Hitler (1889–1945) with the Munich Agreement between Germany and Britain. He returned to England on September 30, 1938, and declared in a speech that his diplomatic efforts had gained "peace for our time." The phrase was recognizable to Britons based on the petitionary prayer phrase "The Order for Morning Prayer" in the *Book of Common Prayer* (1662): "Give us peace in our time." A nation steeped in the faith and liturgy of the Church of England, the King James Version of the Bible, and the *Book of Common Prayer* knew those words well.

By the time the United States formally entered the war on December 8, 1941, the day after the surprise Japanese attack on U.S. forces at Pearl Harbor, Hawaii (and other sites on the Hawaiian island of Oahu), much of the world had already been at war for two years. Religious leaders in Europe and the United Kingdom had wrestled with ethical and religious issues pertaining to military operations and the course of the war.

Political pacifism was strong in many denominations in the years between the World Wars. During the interwar years, the United States retreated from the stage of international relations (although it did participate in various treaties and arms negotiations), withdrawing to hemispheric isolation. This was supported and encouraged by many religious groups in the United States. Religious leaders were often part of the peace movements and called for disarmament during the interwar years (though American evangelicals generally rejected pacifism). So strong were the political and religious sentiments that President Franklin D. Roosevelt was unable to have legislation passed by Congress that would commit the United States to minimal collective security. Traditional peace churches such as the Quakers and Mennonites continued their long history or promoting Christian pacifism. Other groups, such as the Catholic Association for International Peace and the theologically liberal Federal Council of Churches, also emerged to give strong voice to the interwar peace movement. Yet, there were also strong religious (Roman Catholic and Protestant) voices with a national audience that rejected pacifism and isolationism. Among these were Reinhold Niebuhr (1892–1971), Archbishop (Detroit) Edward Mooney (1882–1958), and John R. Mott (1865–1955). Most conservative churches provided a more moderate voice on issues of war, peace, and international affairs (though many of them had been marginalized as far as a national voice due to the Fundamentalist-Modernist controversies that occurred in American Protestantism in the 1920s and 1930s).

Although there was some diminishment of pacifism in 1939–1940, especially after the fall of France to Nazi Germany, there remained a strong pacifist strand in the United States As a result, when Pearl Harbor was attacked on December 7, 1941, many ecumenically minded religious groups and their members faced an unexpected spiritual/moral as well as political crisis. Even so, in his December 8, 1941, "Day of Infamy" speech to Congress and the American people, U.S. president Franklin D. Roosevelt set a tone of moral and religious assuredness, declaring, "No matter how long it may take us to overcome this premeditated invasion, the American people in their righteous might will win through to absolute victory" (Roosevelt 1941).

Religious reluctance to support the war effort dissipated in the first few months of the U.S. war, even though the opening months of 1942 were especially difficult and filled with military setbacks, especially in the Pacific theater. To the extent that they looked for theological and ethical justification, most religious groups supported the war effort on the grounds of the just war tradition. After the war, during the Nuremberg trials (1945–1946) and Tokyo trials (1946–1948), the Allies prosecuted Axis leaders for such things as "crimes against humanity," "war crimes," and "crimes against peace." These prosecutions furthered the principles of the just war tradition and set the stage for the principles and activities of the United

Nations, international law, and ideas of humanitarian law that remain to the present.

From the beginning of the American war effort, political and religious rhetoric were easily blended. As noted above, President Roosevelt used religious terminology in his first address to the nation and to the U.S. Congress after the bombing of Pearl Harbor. He would do so throughout the war. On the evening of the Allied invasion of Europe on D-Day, June 6, 1944, he prayed on national radio for the safety and victory of Allied forces. Earlier, on January1, 1942, shortly after the United States entered the war, he called for a national day of prayer. Similarly, after Roosevelt's death in office, his successor, President Harry S. Truman, called for a similar day of prayer on May 13, 1945, in the aftermath of victory in Europe. Three months later, he called for Sunday, August 19, 1945, to be a national day of prayer giving thanks for victory. Truman also stated in diaries and speeches that prayer was a part of the decision-making process in the use of the atomic bombs.

The war raised several moral issues for denominations, the military, and the nation as a whole that strongly influenced future efforts, policies, and practices. After Pearl Harbor, fearing the possibility that American citizens of Japanese lineage on the nation's West Coast might be subversive and act against national security, 120,000 Japanese Americans were placed in relocation camps for the duration of the war (after being forced to sell their property at large losses). This was accomplished through an executive order signed by President Roosevelt on February 19, 1942. The policy was terminated in early 1945. This displacement along with the nation's refusal to accept large numbers of Jewish refugees became topics of religious concern after the war. By the summer of 1942, the United States had become aware of German plans to exterminate the Jewish population, and reports of these activities continued to grow in the following months and years. Jewish leaders in the United States called for intervention, but the nation did not respond with significant action. As early as 1943, American publications were stating that the nation was guilty of moral failure and complicity in what would become known as the Holocaust.

After the war, when the scope and devastation of the Holocaust came into full light, the spiritual, moral, ethical, political, and religious ramifications reshaped postwar understanding of human rights, genocide, international law, and interreligious dialogue. It directly affected the creation of the United Nations (1945), the establishment of the state of Israel (1948), and the adoption of the Universal Declaration of Human Rights (UDHR; 1948). Each of these had significant religious effects in the last half of the 20th century and the first decades of the 21st century.

Area bombing and the intentional bombing of civilian populations was another issue that was debated by religious leaders in the United States and United Kingdom at the time, and debates regarding the ethical and theological dimensions of it continue to the present. The United States joined the British bombing effort in Europe in 1943, and in the fall of 1944, the United States began heavy bombing raids on the Japanese mainland. The latter culminated in the dropping of the atomic bombs on Hiroshima (August 6, 1945) and Nagasaki (August 9, 1945). With the dropping of these two bombs, the era of nuclear warfare began, and it would spark continuous political and religious debate into the 21st century.

Part of the political dimension of any nation at war in any conflict is the will of the citizens to engage in and sustain the war effort. What happens on the home front directly affects the battlefront. Religion almost always plays a part in sustaining or opposing the war effort. This was certainly true during World War II. Beyond worship services, prayers, sermons, and the exhortation of religious leaders, there was a vast amount of religion used in U.S. propaganda efforts and in daily culture that linked religion and war. In propaganda, one sees the blending of religion and war in government-sponsored posters that used religious imagery. One example of this is a 1943 Office of War Information (OWI) poster with the words "This Is the Enemy"; it shows a hand and arm wearing a Nazi uniform stabbing a Bible with a bayonet. Another example is a 1942 OWI poster showing three arms and hands, two with tools and one with a rifle, reaching upward with the words "Strong in the strength of the Lord we who fight in the people's cause will never stop until that cause is won." Posters, placards, and art depicting religious items and actions were widely accepted and not uncommon on the home front.

In popular culture, music and movies frequently utilized religious themes. Based on two events—one from the attack on Pearl Harbor and the other from a U.S. bombing mission in the European theater—songs such as "Praise the Lord and Pass the Ammunition" (1942) and "Comin' in on a Wing and a Prayer" (1943) quickly rose to the top of the music charts and were frequently heard on the radio. Sheet music with powerful graphics also sold hundreds of thousands of copies. Another example is

*God Is My Co-Pilot*, a book (1943) and movie (1945) about aviator Robert Scott's wartime service in the Pacific theater.

Religion among those in military service was very prominent and had an enormous effect on troop morale and spiritual well-being. When service members entered the military, they brought their religion with them, and there was a large growth in religious lay leaders and military chaplains. After the war, there was a significant rise in religious and humanitarian organizations that arose based on the experiences of service members. Many of those continue to the present and are a prominent voice in contemporary humanitarian efforts and policy making.

Events such as the famous Patton "weather prayer" and the sinking of the USS *Dorchester* on February 3, 1943, in which four chaplains (two Protestant, one Roman Catholic, and one Jewish) sacrificed their lives by giving their lifejackets to others, became well-known stories encouraging patriotism and religion. In 1948, the U.S. Postal Service issued a stamp commemorating the sacrifice of the four chaplains.

After the war, religion, politics, and the war remained intermingled in American society, especially with the rise of the Cold War and portrayals of it as Christianity versus communism and atheism. In postwar popular culture, the mixture of religion and war was seen in a variety of books, memoirs, and movies. General (later president) Dwight D. Eisenhower titled his wartime memoir *Crusade in Europe* (1948). An example of religion and war from books and film in the 1950s is *Heaven Knows Mr. Allison* (book in 1952, movie in 1957). The war became an integral aspect of the concept of civil religion, providing illustrations and examples of it for the growing religiopolitical construct. Further linking religion and war, in the aftermath of World War II, Congress authorized the World War II Victory Medal for those who had served in the military during December 7, 1941 to December 31, 1946. The reverse side of the medal bears the words "Freedom of Speech and Religion." This again illustrates the prevalence of religion during the era.

The memory and commemoration of the events of the World War II remain prominent in American life in the 21st century. Within religious communities, there is strong commitment to veterans of the war, but there are also continued debates about the use of nuclear weapons, the wide-range bombing of civilians in area bombing raids, and, among some religious groups, the viability of religious pacifism. The tragedy of the Holocaust remains a central component of religious pronouncements and discussions of the war. In some instances, the Holocaust has served as a topic of common concern in the fostering of Jewish-Christian dialogue.

***See also:*** American Exceptionalism; American Peace Churches; Cold War; Holocaust; Human Rights; Just War Tradition; Literature; Military Chaplains; Music; Pacifism; Presidential Faith and War; Protestant Denominations; Rhetoric, Sermons, and Prayers; Roman Catholicism; Weapons of Mass Destruction; World War I

## Further Reading

Bullert, Gary B. "Reinhold Niebuhr and *The Christian Century:* World War II and the Eclipse of the Social Gospel." *Journal of Church and State* 44, no. 2 (Spring 2002): 271–290.

Hall, Mark David, and J. Daryl Charles, eds. *America and the Just War Tradition: A History of U.S. Conflicts*. Notre Dame, IN: University of Notre Dame Press, 2019.

Inboden, William C. "The Prophetic Conflict: Reinhold Niebuhr, Christian Realism, and World War II." *Diplomatic History* 38, no. 1 (January 2013): 49–82.

Marshall, Peter J., ed. *The Wartime Sermons of Peter Marshall*. Geneseo, NY: Clarion Call Publishing, 2005.

Miller, Richard B., ed. *War in the Twentieth Century: Sources in Theological Ethics*. Louisville, KY: Westminster/John Knox Press, 1992.

Padgett, Timothy D. *Swords & Plowshares: American Evangelicals on War, 1937–1973*. Bellingham, WA: Lexham Press, 2018.

Pierard, Richard V. "World War II." In *The Wars of America: Christian Views*, edited by Ronald A. Wells, 189–226. Macon, GA: Mercer University Press, 1991.

Preston, Andrew. *Sword of the Spirit, Shield of Faith: Religion in American War and Diplomacy*. New York: Alfred A. Knopf, 2012.

Roosevelt, Franklin D. "Speech by Franklin D. Roosevelt, New York (Transcript)." December 8, 1941. https://www.loc.gov/resource/afc1986022.afc1986022 _ms2201/?st=text&r=-0.033,-0.216,1.111,1.14,0

Sittser, Gerald L. *A Cautious Patriotism: The American Churches and the Second World War*. Chapel Hill: University of North Carolina Press, 1997.

Snape, Michael. *God and Uncle Sam: Religion and America's Armed Forces in World War II*. Rochester, NY: Boydell Press, 2105.

Stahl, Ronit Y. *Enlisting Faith: How Military Chaplaincy Shaped Religion and State in Modern America*. Cambridge, MA: Belknap Press, 2017.

"*Strong in the Strength of the Lord*. Ca. 1939–1945. Poster. 102 × 71 cm. Designed by David Stone Martin for the Office of War Information." University of Washing Libraries, Digital Collection. https://digitalcollections.lib.washington .edu/digital/collection/posters/id/72/

Sutton, Matthew Avery. *Double Crossed: The Missionaries Who Spied for the United States during the Second World War*. New York: Basic Books, 2019.

*This Is the Enemy*. 1943. Poster. Lithograph on paper. 71.3 × 51 cm (28 1/16 × 20 1/16 in.). Designed by Barbara J. Marks for the Office of War Information. Cooper Hewitt Museum. https://collection.cooperhewitt.org/objects/18622269/

Walters, Kevin L. "Beyond the Battle: Religion and American Troops in World War II." Unpublished PhD diss., University of Kentucky, 2013. https://uknowledge.uky.edu/cgi/viewcontent.cgi?article=1011&context=history_etds

# Annotated Bibliography

Not every item listed in the further reading sections of the entries is listed below. Rather, what is presented are the standard and most significant works pertaining to the overall subject of this book.

**Atchison, Liam, Keith Bates, and Darin D. Lenz, eds. *Civil Religion and American Christianity.* Rev. ed. Middletown, RI: Stone Tower Press, 2020.**
The blending of presidential faith, politics, and the wars of the United States have done much to bolster the presence of civil religion in the country. Contributors in this volume study particular presidencies and events to show how civil religion permeates American culture and politics.

**Atwood, Craig D., and Roger E. Olson. *Handbook of the Denominations of the United States.* 14th ed. Nashville, TN: Abingdon Press, 2018.**
This is a standard volume on demographics and summary histories of religious groups in America.

**Bailyn, Bernard. *The Ideological Origins of the American Revolution.* Enl. ed. Cambridge, MA: Belknap Press, 1992.**
This volume is a standard work for anyone interested in the American Revolution and the intellectual underpinnings of it. It is a short volume, easily understood, and highly informative.

**Beschloss, Michael. *Presidents of War: The Epic Story, from 1807 to Modern Times.* New York: Crown Publishing, 2018.**
Beschloss provides an engaging study of American presidents who have led the nation during times of war. It is well written, enjoyable, and educational.

**Bhatt, Chetan.** *Hindu Nationalism: Origins, Ideologies and Modern Myths.* **Oxford, UK: Berg, 2001.**

This book shows the linkage between Hinduism, nationalism, and the convergence of the two in politics and attitudes toward war. Although the focus is not the United States, the work presents the strong views of Hindu nationalism that show how religion, politics, and violence can merge.

**Biggar, Nigel.** *In Defence of War.* **New York: Oxford University Press, 2013.**

Biggar presents a contemporary view and defense of the just war tradition and its heritage within Christianity. The volume is a standard work in just war tradition studies.

**Bogaski, George.** *American Protestants and the Debate over the Vietnam War: Evil Was Loose in the World.* **Lanham, MD: Lexington Books, 2014.**

This book recounts the intersection of religion, war, and politics during the Vietnam War and provides insights into contemporary attitudes toward war by American Protestants.

**Bolt, Robert. "World War I." In** *The Wars of America: Christian Views,* **edited by Ronald A. Wells, 163–188. Macon, GA: Mercer University Press, 1991.**

This chapter provides a succinct overview of the attitudes of American Christians during World War I and how those attitudes were manifested in political influence and action.

**Boyer, Paul.** *When Time Shall Be No More: Prophecy Belief in Modern American Culture.* **Cambridge, MA: Harvard University Press, 1992.**

This is a standard work on one aspect of American religious culture and belief and how it affected social, political, and religious thought. Its emphasis on apocalypticism is valuable for understanding the attitudes of some American Christians with respect to war, weapons of mass destruction, and support of Israel.

**Bremer, Francis, J.** *John Winthrop: America's Forgotten Founding Father.* **Oxford, UK: Oxford University Press, 2005.**

This study shows the importance of religion and its effects on politics and the founding of the American nation based on the life of one of the country's most influential leaders during the era.

**Brodrecht, Grant.** *Our Country: Northern Evangelicals and the Union during the Civil War Era.* **New York: Fordham University Press, 2018.**
Religious attitudes and fervor during the American Civil War were deeply rooted. This history shows how those commitments were manifested during the war. It provides an excellent study of the interplay of religion, politics, and war in American history.

**Brunstetter, Daniel, and Cian O'Driscoll, eds.** *Just War Thinkers: From Cicero to the 21st Century.* **London and New York: Routledge, 2018.**
This volume provides an excellent overview of the thoughts and writings of major proponents of the just war tradition.

**Bullert, Gary, B.** "Reinhold Niebuhr and *The Christian Century*: World War II and the Eclipse of the Social Gospel." *Journal of Church and State* **44, no. 2 (Spring 2002): 271–290.**
Niebuhr was an influential American theologian and public figure in mid-20th-century America. His work influenced much of American Protestantism and politics.

**Burkhardt, Todd.** *Just War and Human Rights: Fighting with Right Intention.* **Albany: State University of New York Press, 2017.**
This is an important work that shows the linkage between the just war tradition and the upholding of human rights.

**Burleigh, Michael.** *Sacred Causes: The Clash of Religion and Politics, from the Great War to the War on Terror.* **New York: HarperCollins, 2007.**
This volume is important in that it addresses many of the misconceptions about religion and war over the last century and how they linger in the present.

**Burnidge, Cara Lee.** *A Peaceful Conquest: Woodrow Wilson, Religion, and the New World Order.* **Chicago: University of Chicago Press, 2016.**

This book studies President Wilson's deep religious commitments and how they influenced his presidency and legacy.

Byrd, James P. *A Holy Baptism of Fire: The Bible and the American Civil War.* New York: Oxford University Press, 2021.
This is an excellent work on the role of the Bible in the Civil War and the role of religion in the military history of the early American nation.

Byrd, James P. *Sacred Scripture, Sacred War: The Bible and the American Revolution.* New York: Oxford University Press, 2013.
This is an essential work for anyone wanting to understand how religion, politics, and war overlapped during the founding years of the United States.

Carlson, John D., and Jonathan H. Ebel, eds. *From Jeremiad to Jihad: Religion, Violence, & America.* Berkeley: University of California Press, 2012.
The book argues that the convergence of religion and violence in American history has often been misunderstood and misrepresented, and it seeks to correct such mistakes.

Carter, Jimmy. "Just War—or a Just War?" *New York Times*, March 9, 2003. https://www.nytimes.com/2003/03/09/opinion/just-war-or-a-just-war.html
This is an important article by a former president that references the just war tradition and the Iraq War.

Chapple, Christopher Key. "Peace, War, and Violence in Hinduism." *Oxford Bibliographies Online*, January 27, 2011. https://doi.org/10.1093/obo/9780195399318-0038
Writings and resources regarding perspectives on peace and war in one of the world's oldest religions are provided in this excellent bibliography.

Charles, J. Daryl, and Timothy J. Demy. *War, Peace, and Christianity: Questions and Answers from a Just-War Perspective.* Wheaton, IL: Crossway Publications, 2010.
This book addresses more than 100 common questions about the just war tradition.

Cherry, Conrad, ed. *God's New Israel: Religious Interpretations of American Destiny.* Englewood Cliffs, NJ: Prentice-Hall, 1972.

This is a standard work on the religious background of the idea of American exceptionalism.

**Clouse, Robert G., ed. *War: Four Christian Views*. Downers Grove, IL: InterVarsity Press, 1981.**
Proponents of four views of Christianity and war present their views and interact with the others. The views presented include nonresistance, pacifism, just war, and preventive war.

**Cole, Darrell. *When God Says War Is Right: The Christian Perspective on When and How to Fight*. Colorado Springs, CO: Waterbrook, 2002.**
The author provides a brief and engaging work on Christianity, war, and contemporary religious commitments.

**Cook, David. *Contemporary Muslim Apocalyptic Literature.* Syracuse, NY: Syracuse University Press, 2008.**
The belief in a violent and cataclysmic end to human history is shared in several religions. The author shows its prominence in Islam and how some adherents link it to terrorism, weapons of mass destruction, and contemporary events.

**Cowles, C. S., et al. *Show Them No Mercy: Four Views on God and Canaanite Genocide*. Grand Rapids, MI: Zondervan Publications, 2003.**
Presenters evaluate and interact with varying views on violence in the Bible and reconciling war in the Old Testament with the teachings of Jesus in the New Testament. The views presented include radical discontinuity, moderate discontinuity, eschatological continuity, and spiritual continuity.

**Craigie, Peter C. *The Problem of War in the Old Testament*. Grand Rapids, MI: William B. Eerdmans, 1978.**
This major study of war and peace in the Hebrew Bible addresses issues of God as warrior, the prohibition of murder, holy war, and defeat in the biblical text.

**Dalai Lama. "The Reality of War." Accessed June 14, 2022. https://www.dalailama.com/messages/world-peace/the-reality-of-war**
In this primary source document, the most prominent global Buddhist leader speaks to the realities of contemporary warfare and argues that absolute pacifism is not always the best solution.

Dallaire, Roméo. *Shake Hands with the Devil: The Failure of Humanity in Rwanda.* Toronto: Random House Canada, 2003.
The story of the failure of the United Nations and others to prevent genocide in Rwanda in the 1990s is recounted by the senior officer of the UN peacekeeping forces present throughout the event.

Demy, Timothy J. "Arming for Armageddon: Myths and Motivations of Violence in American Christian Apocalypticism." In *Armed Groups: Studies in National Security, Counterterrorism, and Counterinsurgency*, edited by Jeffrey Norwitz, 225–235. Newport, RI: Naval War College Press, 2008.
This chapter argues that not all apocalyptic Christian theology is violent or extremist.

Demy, Timothy J. "War." In *The Oxford Encyclopedia of the Bible and Ethics*, edited by Robert L. Brawley, vol. 2, 395–403. New York: Oxford University Press, 2014.
This entry provides an overview of war as presented in biblical texts.

Dorsett, Lyle W. *Serving God and Country: U.S. Military Chaplains in World War II.* New York: Dutton Caliber, 2013.
This is a brief and engaging story of military chaplains.

Dunham, Michael. *Buddha's Warriors: The Story of the CIA-Backed Tibetan Freedom Fighters, the Chinese Communist Invasion, and the Ultimate Fall of Tibet.* New York: Penguin Group, 2004.
The brother of the present Dalai Lama and others were enlisted and trained by the United States to fight Chinese communists. This the story of that endeavor and the role religion played in political and military decisions for two decades.

Ebel, Jonathan H. *Faith in the Fight: Religion and the American Soldier in the Great War.* Princeton, NJ: Princeton University Press, 2010.
This volume stresses the importance of religion in American society as well its importance to the common soldier during World War I.

Fairclough, Adam. "Martin Luther King, Jr. and the War in Vietnam." *Phylon* 45, no. 1 (1st qtr. 1984): 19–39.

This article studies the complex and shifting history of Martin Luther King, Jr., the civil rights movement, and the Vietnam War.

**Faust, Drew Gilpin.** *The Republic of Suffering: Death and the American Civil War.* **New York: Random House, 2008.**
Faust's book shows the rise and power of words and ideas in the development of public discourse and civil religion.

**Fiske, Edward B. "Religion; The Clergy on Vietnam."** *New York Times,* **January 7, 1968: Sec. E, 9.**
This is one the first reports of clergy opposition to the war in Vietnam.

**Franklin D. Roosevelt Presidential Library and Museum. "A 'Mighty Endeavor': D-Day." Accessed June 13, 2022. https://www.fdrlibrary. org/d-day**
This is a primary source document of religion, politics, and war on one of the most important days in American military history.

**Frazer, Gregg L.** *God against the Revolution: The Loyalist Clergy's Case against the American Revolution.* **Lawrence: University Press of Kansas, 2010.**
Not all Americans were in favor of seeking independence from Britain, and loyalist clergy had a strong voice in such opposition.

**Frost, J. William.** *A History of Christian, Jewish, Hindu, Buddhist, and Muslim Perspectives on War and Peace.* **Lewiston, NY: Edwin Mellen Press, 2004.**
This is a straightforward and readable comparison of war and peace in five faith traditions.

**Gaddis, John Lewis.** *The Cold War: A New History.* **New York: Penguin Books, 2006.**
Gaddis explains how the history and politics of the Cold War shaped much of American political discourse and its diverse ideologies in the 21st century.

**Gibbs, Nancy, and Michael Duffy.** *The Preacher and the Presidents: Billy Graham in the White House.* **New York: Center Street, 2007.**

American presidents looked to Billy Graham for friendship, counsel, and pastoral care, especially during wartime.

**Graham, Billy. "Billy Graham's 9/11 Message from the Washington National Cathedral." Billy Graham Evangelistic Association, September 9, 2018. https://billygraham.org/story/a-day-to-remember-a-day-of-victory/**
By 2001, Graham was in his final years, and national respect for him was enormous, as many U.S. Christians viewed him as "America's pastor." A week after the 9/11 attacks, Graham delivered a nationally televised sermon of hope and comfort in the presence of presidents and political leaders across the ideological spectrum.

**Graham, Billy.** *I Saw Your Sons at War: The Korean Diary of Billy Graham.* **Minneapolis, MN: Billy Graham Evangelistic Association, 1953.**
This is one of Graham's earliest writings as he was emerging as a national figure. He recounts visiting U.S. troops in South Korea during the Korean War.

**Graham, Billy.** *Just as I Am.* **New York: HarperOne Publishers, 1997.**
Graham's autobiography tells of the life and ministry of the 20th-century global influencer as a voice of Christianity. His interactions with U.S. presidents during the Cold War, the Vietnam War, and beyond are well known, and his book is extremely engaging.

**Griggs, Walter S., Jr. "The Selective Conscientious Objector: A Vietnam Legacy."** *Journal of Church and State* **21, no. 1 (Winter 1979): 91–107.**
This article speaks to one aspect of conscientious objection to war during the Vietnam War and the role of religion in such cases.

**Guelzo, Allen C.** *Abraham Lincoln: Redeemer President.* **Grand Rapids, MI: Eerdmans, 2002.**
This is a very readable study of Lincoln and civil religion and the image of Lincoln in the minds of many Americans.

**Gupta, Vidya Bhushan.** *Hinduism in America.* **Demarest, NJ: Vid Publications, 2004.**

This book provides a good overview of the growing presence of Hinduism in the United States.

**Haberski, Raymond J.** *God and War: American Civil Religion since 1945.* **New Brunswick, NJ: Rutgers University Press, 2012.**
This book shows that civil religion has not decreased in the decades since the end of World War II.

**Halberstram, David.** *The Making of a Quagmire: America and Vietnam during the Kennedy Era.* **New York: Random House, 1965.**
This is one of the earliest books to argue that the Vietnam War was not in American interests long term and would be politically divisive.

**Hall, David D.** *The Puritans: A Transatlantic History.* **Princeton, NJ: Princeton University Press, 2019.**
This book shows the close exchange of political and religious ideas among Puritans in the Old and New Worlds.

**Hall, Mark David, and J. Daryl Charles, eds.** *America and the Just War Tradition: A History of U.S. Conflicts.* **Notre Dame, IN: University of Notre Dame Press, 2019.**
The work provides a strong study of religion, politics, and ethical thought in U.S. wars.

**Hankins, Barry.** *Woodrow Wilson: Ruling Elder, Spiritual President.* **New York: Oxford University Press, 2016.**
The volume addresses Wilson's deeply held religious commitments and how they influenced his politics and presidency.

**Harris, Christopher.** "Mason Locke Weems's *Life of Washington:* The Making of a Bestseller." *Southern Literary Journal* 19, no. 2 (Spring 1987): 92–101.
The article shows how George Washington became a legend in American thought and civil religion.

**Hatch, Nathan O.** *The Sacred Cause of Liberty: Republican Thought and the Millennium in Revolutionary New England.* **New Haven, CT: Yale University Press, 1977.**

This is an important study of religion, politics, and ideology during the era of the American Revolution.

**Hedin, Benjamin. "Martin Luther King, Jr.'s Searing Antiwar Speech, Fifty Years Later."** *New Yorker*, **April 3, 2017. https://www.newyorker.com/culture/culture-desk/martin-luther-king-jr-s-searing-antiwar-speech-fifty-years-later**
The article recounts the shift in Martin Luther King, Jr.'s thoughts, from pro-war to anti-war, and the impact of that shift on religious and political support for the Vietnam War.

**Heimbach, Daniel R. "The Bush Just War Doctrine: Genesis and Application of the President's Moral Leadership in the Persian Gulf War." In** *From Cold War to New World Order: The Foreign Policy of George H. W. Bush*, **edited by Meena Bose and Rosanna Perotti, 441–464. Westport, CT: Greenwood Press, 2002.**
This significant article discusses President George H. W. Bush's use of the just war tradition in his decision for war against Iraq.

**Helgeland, John. "Christians and the Roman Army, A.D. 173–337."** *Church History* **43, no. 2 (1974): 149–63, 200.**
The author argues that the primary concern of Christians and the military in the early church was not pacifism but the nature of the Roman army's religion.

**Helgeland, John, Robert J. Daly, and J. Patout Burns.** *Christians and the Military: The Early Experience.* **Philadelphia: Fortress Press, 1985.**
This volume sets a new course for the study of early Christians and the Roman military, showing that there was not an absolute rejection of military service and embracing of pacifism. It largely consists of primary sources.

**History on the Net. "When Patton Enlisted the Entire Third Army to Pray for Fair Weather." May 8, 2020. https://www.historyonthenet.com/when-patton-enlisted-the-entire-third-army-to-pray-for-fair-weather**
This is a short presentation of the story of the famous "Patton Prayer" during the Battle of the Bulge in World War II.

**Holmes, Arthur F., ed.** *War and Christian Ethics: Classic and Contemporary Readings on the Morality of War.* 2nd ed. Grand Rapids, MI: Baker Books, 2005.
This volume consists of primary source readings on war and peace, from Plato to the present.

**Hutcheson, Richard G., Jr., and Mark A. Jumper.** *The Churches and the Chaplaincy.* Rev. ed. Middletown, RI: Stone Tower Press, 2021.
Hutcheson's work is a landmark study in military chaplaincy and American society. This revised edition shows the relevance of military chaplaincy in the 21st-century United States.

**Inboden, William.** *Religion and American Foreign Policy, 1945–1960.* Cambridge, UK: Cambridge University Press, 2010.
American Protestantism, especially liberal Protestantism, and Roman Catholicism were enormously influential in the post–World War II years of U.S. foreign policy.

**Inboden, William C.** "The Prophetic Conflict: Reinhold Niebuhr, Christian Realism, and World War II." *Diplomatic History* 38, no. 1 (January 2013): 49–82.
This article addresses the influence of American theologian and public intellectual Reinhold Niebuhr during World War II.

**Jenkins, Philip.** "Billy Graham and the Hell Bombs." Patheos, February 23, 2018. https://www.patheos.com/blogs/anxiousbench/2018/02/billy-graham-hell-bombs/
This is a short article on Billy Graham and war during the Cold War.

**Jenkins, Philip.** *The Great and Holy War: How World War I Became a Religious Crusade.* New York: HarperOne, 2014.
This is an engaging study of religion, politics, and war in World War I.

**Jerryson, Michael K.** "Buddhist Traditions and Violence.". In *The Oxford Handbook of Religion and Violence*, edited by Mark Juergensmeyer, Margo Kitts, and Michael K. Jerryson, 41–66. New York: Oxford University Press, 2016.

This chapter shows that pacifism is an ideal in Buddhism but not a universal mandate.

**Jerryson, Michael K., and Mark Juergensmeyer.** *Buddhist Warfare.* **New York: Oxford University Press, 2010.**
This volume presents cases of Buddhist warfare and argues that such cases are not an anomaly in Buddhist thought.

**Johnson, James Turner.** *Morality and Contemporary Warfare.* **New Haven, CT: Yale University Press, 1999.**
Johnson presents a moral analysis of war and contemporary trends in warfare from a just war perspective. He has been a major voice for the just war tradition for more than three decades.

**Kaplan, Edward K. "Heschel & the Vietnam War."** *Tikkun* 22, no. 4 (2007): 14–68. https://www.muse.jhu.edu/article/592924
This article presents the political thought of one of the great 20th-century American rabbis and Jewish theologians with respect to the Vietnam War.

**Kengor, Paul, and Robert Orlando.** *The Divine Plan: John Paul II, Ronald Reagan, and the Dramatic End of the Cold War.* **Wilmington, DE: Intercollegiate Studies Institute, 2019.**
Pope John Paul II and President Ronald Reagan formed a unique alliance to undermine communism and bring the Cold War to an end.

**Kidd, Thomas S.** *America's Religious History: Faith, Politics, and the Shaping of a Nation.* **Grand Rapids, MI: Zondervan, 2019.**
This is a very readable and enjoyable work on the interplay of religion and politics throughout the nation's history.

**Kidd, Thomas S.** *God of Liberty: A Religious History of the American Revolution.* **New York: Basic Books, 2010.**
Kidd presents the powerful role of religion in the American Revolution and its centrality in the culture of the era.

**King, Martin Luther, Jr. "'I've Been to the Mountaintop.'" April 3, 1988. https://kinginstitute.stanford.edu/encyclopedia/ive-been-mountaintop**
This is a primary source document of one of Martin Luther King, Jr.'s most powerful and best-known speeches. It was given the night before his assassination.

King, Martin Luther, Jr. "Martin Luther King, Jr. on the Vietnam War." *The Atlantic*, February 2018. https://www.theatlantic.com/magazine/archive/2018/02/martin-luther-king-jr-vietnam/552521/
Martin Luther King, Jr.'s turn against support for the Vietnam War was a pivotal moment with respect to religion and the war. This presents his opposition in his own words.

King, Martin Luther, Jr. *A Testament of Hope: The Essential Writings of Martin Luther King, Jr.* Edited by James Melvin Washington. San Francisco: Harper & Row, 1986.
This book brings together Martin Luther King, Jr.'s major writings that show how religion, civil rights, and politics were intertwined for him.

Kirby, Dianne, ed. *Religion and the Cold War.* New York: Palgrave Macmillan, 2002.
This is an edited volume that shows the powerful influence American religion had on politics and U.S. foreign policy during the Cold War.

Lambert, Frank. *The Founding Fathers and the Place of Religion in America.* Princeton, NJ: Princeton University Press, 2003.
Many of the nation's founders had deep religious commitments. Others had significant philosophical values that informed their actions. Lambert presents those spiritual and intellectual currents.

Larson, Mark J. *Calvin's Doctrine of the State: A Reformed Doctrine and Its American Trajectory, the Revolutionary War, and the Founding of the Republic.* Eugene, OR: Wipf & Stock, 2009.
This study shows the importance of political thought on the American Revolution to the Protestant reformer.

Lincoln, Abraham. "Second Inaugural Address." *The Atlantic Monthly* 284, no. 3 (September 1999): 60. https://www.theatlantic.com/past/docs/issues/99sep/9909lincaddress.htm
This is one of Lincoln's most famous speeches.

MacAskill, Ewen. "George Bush: 'God Told Me to End the Tyranny in Iraq.'" *The Guardian* (U.S. edition), October 7, 2005. https://www.theguardian.com/world/2005/oct/07/iraq.usa
This newspaper article recounts religious aspects of President Bush's decision to go to war against Iraq in 2003.

**Mailer, Gideon.** *John Witherspoon's American Revolution.* **Chapel Hill: University of North Carolina Press, 2017.**
Often overlooked among the nation's founders, this excellent biography of John Witherspoon shows the importance of religion during the American Revolution and the founding years of the nation.

**Marsden, George M.** *Religion and American Culture: A Brief History.* **Grand Rapids, MI: Eerdmans Publishing, 2018.**
Marsden's writings are superb, and his scholarship is exceptional. This volume provides a very readable overview of the role of religion in the United States and how it has shaped social, cultural, and political life.

**Marshall, Peter J., ed.** *The Wartime Sermons of Peter Marshall.* **Geneseo, NY: Clarion Call Publishing, 2005.**
Peter Marshall was a nationally known Protestant pastor and writer and the chaplain of the U.S. Senate. These sermons from World War II provide a clear view of the public face of much of Protestantism in the United States during the war.

**Martin, William.** *A Prophet with Honor: The Billy Graham Story.* **Grand Rapids, MI: Zondervan, 2007.**
This is a well-written biography of a national figure in 20th-century American life.

**Masefield, Stephen.** *The Faith of George W. Bush.* **New York: Penguin, 2003.**
This is a short, well-written account of the religious values and commitments of President Bush and how they influenced his presidency and decisions regarding politics and war.

**McGready, Blake.** "Revisiting the Prayer at Valley Forge." *Journal of the American Revolution*, **October 15, 2018. https://allthingsliberty.com/2018/10/revisiting-the-prayer-at-valley-forge/**
This is an excellent article on the popular concept of General George Washington and religion during the harsh winter of 1777–1778.

**McKenna, George.** *The Puritan Origins of American Patriotism.* **New Haven, CT: Yale University Press, 2007.**

This is an excellent book and an easy read. It demonstrates the importance of religion in American public and political discourse and shows the vibrant presence of civil religion in the nation throughout its history.

Miller, Randall M., Harry S. Stout, Charles Reagan Wilson, eds. *Religion and the American Civil War*. New York: Oxford University Press, 1998.
This is a valuable and well-written study of the significance and effects of religion during the war.

Miller, Richard B., ed. *War in the Twentieth Century: Sources in Theological Ethics*. Louisville, KY: Westminster/John Knox Press, 1992.
This is a resource book of primary source documents for studying 20th-century religion and war.

Miller, Robert J. *Both Prayed to the Same God: Religion and Faith in the American Civil War*. Lanham, MD: Lexington Books, 2007.
The American Civil War divided the nation, yet soldiers and citizens on both sides shared common religious values.

Mislin, David. "How Vietnam War Protests Accelerated the Rise of the Christian Right." *Smithsonian Magazine*, May 3, 2018. https://www.smithsonianmag.com/history/how-vietnam-war-protests-spurred-rise-christian-right-180968942/
War and the responses to it generate political and religious dynamics that far outlast the period of conflict.

Mohammad-Arif, Aminah. "The Paradox of Religion: The (Re)Construction of Hindu and Muslim Identities amongst South Asian Diasporas in the United States." *South Asia Multidisciplinary Academic Journal*, no. 1 (2007). https://doi.org/10.4000/samaj.55
This article looks at the integration of religion, politics, and identity among South Asian immigrants in the United States.

Mojzes, Paul. *North American Churches and the Cold War*. Grand Rapids, MI: Eerdmans, 2018.
This is an excellent work that shows the interplay of politics and religion during the decades of the Cold War.

**Morgan, David T.** "The Revivalist as Patriot: Billy Sunday and World War I." *Journal of Presbyterian History (1962–1985)* 51, no. 2 (1973): 199–215.

This is an excellent article on a nationally known evangelist of the early 20th century and how his views and messages influenced the thought of some American Protestants.

**Moskos, Charles C., and John Whiteclay Chambers II.** *The New Conscientious Objection: From Sacred to Secular Resistance.* **New York: Oxford University Press, 1993.**

This book links religion and conscientious objection and shows the spectrum of contemporary religious and political thought on the issue.

**Muehlenbeck, Philip.** *Religion and the Cold War: A Global Perspective.* **Nashville, TN: Vanderbilt University Press, 2012.**

This volume explores how religion informed the ideological and military clashes across the globe in the second half of the 20th century.

**Neusner, Jacob, Bruce Chilton, and Robert E. Tully.** *Just War in Religion and Politics.* **Lanham, MD: University Press of America, 2013.**

The just war tradition has secular and religious strands in the 21st century. This study evaluates the interaction of tradition with contemporary politics and religion.

**Newport, Kenneth G. C., and Crawford Gribben, eds.** *Expecting the End: Millennialism in Social and Historical Context.* **Waco, TX: Baylor University Press, 2006.**

This volume studies apocalypticism and its influence on politics and perspectives on conflict and war.

**Noll, Mark A.** *Christians in the American Revolution.* **2nd ed. Vancouver, Canada: Regent College Publishing, 2006.**

This is a short but standard work on the intersection of religion and war during the American Revolution.

**Noll, Mark A.** *The Civil War as a Theological Crisis.* **Chapel Hill: University of North Carolina Press, 2006.**

Noll studies the American Civil War through the lens of religion and notes the deep fissures it created in American theology of the era.

**O'Connell, David.** *God Wills It: Presidents and the Political Use of Religion.* **New York: Routledge, 2015.**
The volume shows how American presidents have used religion and religious rhetoric in the furtherance of political goals.

**O'Donovan, Oliver.** *The Just War Revisited.* **Cambridge, UK: Cambridge University Press, 2003.**
This is a good overview of the renewed interest in the just war tradition.

**Olson, Roger E., Frank S. Mead, Samuel S. Hill, and Craig D. Atwood.** *Handbook of Denominations of the United States.* **14th ed. Nashville, TN: Abingdon Press, 2018.**
Updated every few years, this book provides a brief history and the current demographics of most Christian traditions in the United States.

**Omer, Atalia, R. Scott Appleby, and David Little, eds.** *The Oxford Handbook of Religion, Conflict, and Peacebuilding.* **New York: Oxford University Press, 2019.**
This is a standard work for viewing religion, war, and peace efforts in the 21st century.

**Oren, Michael B.** *Power, Faith, and Fantasy: America in the Middle East, 1776 to the Present.* **New York: W. W. Norton & Co., 2007.**
Written by the former Israeli ambassador to the United States, this very readable history surveys the long history of American interest in a national homeland for the Jewish people in the Middle East.

**Ostransky, Bronislav.** *The Jihadist Preachers of the End Times: ISIS Apocalyptic Propaganda.* **Edinburgh, UK: Edinburgh University Press, 2019.**
Religion, weapons of mass destruction, and apocalyptic belief and rhetoric are central to the propaganda of the so-called Islamic State.

**Padgett, Timothy D.** *Swords & Plowshares: American Evangelicals on War, 1937–1973.* **Bellingham, WA: Lexham Press, 2018.**
This is a detailed study of the religious and political values of a large segment of American society with respect to World War II, the Korean War, and Vietnam War. It is an essential work for studying evangelicals and war.

**Patterson, Eric.** *Ending Wars Well: Order, Justice, Conciliation in Contemporary Post-Conflict.* **New Haven, CT: Yale University Press, 2012.**
Patterson's work is a major study that extends the just war tradition to postwar considerations that support justice and human rights.

**Patterson, Eric.** *Just American Wars: Ethical Dilemmas in U.S. Military History.* **New York: Routledge, 2019.**
This volume looks at the major wars of the nation through the lens of ethics and analyzes the military and political decisions of the wars.

**Patterson, Eric. "Just War Theory & Terrorism."** *Providence: A Journal of Christianity & American Foreign Policy* **(Summer 2016): 38–44.**
This is a succinct presentation on the just war tradition's understanding of terrorism.

**Pew Research Center. "The Changing Global Religious Landscape." Religion & Public Life Project, April 5, 2017. https://www.pewforum.org/2017/04/05/the-changing-global-religious-landscape/**
This is an important study that shows the changes in American religious life in recent decades and how those changes affect American politics.

**Pew Research Center. "Religious Landscape Study." 2014. https://www.pewforum.org/religious-landscape-study/**
This is an excellent study and site for understanding the current and shifting religious demographics in the nation.

**Pierard, Richard V. "Billy Graham and Vietnam: From Cold Warrior to Peacemaker."** *Christian Scholar's Review* **10, no. 1 (1980): 37–51.**
As with many religious leaders during the Cold War and Vietnam War, Graham's views became more nuanced and cautious as the years passed.

**Preston, Andrew.** *Sword of the Spirit, Shield of Faith: Religion in American War and Diplomacy.* **New York: Alfred A. Knopf, 2012.**
Preston offers the best work to date that traces the interactions of religion, war, and politics in American history.

**Reichberg, Gregory M.** *Religion, War, and Ethics: A Sourcebook of Textual Traditions.* **New York: Cambridge University Press, 2014.**
For anyone studying religion and war, this is a standard work.

Reid, Daniel G., and Tremper Longman III. *God Is a Warrior.* Grand Rapids, MI: Zondervan, 1995.
This is a biblical study of the divine warrior motif in the Old and New Testaments against the broader background of ancient Near Eastern warrior mythology.

Republican National Committee. "America Resurgent, Republican Platform." Accessed March 1, 2020. https://www.gop.com/platform/american-exceptionalism/
This is a primary source document on 21st-century American exceptionalism.

Roosevelt, Franklin D. *Speech by Franklin D. Roosevelt, New York Transcript.* December 8, 1941. Library of Congress. https://www.loc.gov/resource/afc1986022.afc1986022_ms2201/?st=text&r=-0.033,-0.216,1.111,1.14,0
This is President Roosevelt's most famous speech.

Ruotsila, Markku. *Fighting Fundamentalist: Carl McIntire and the Politicization of American Fundamentalism.* New York: Oxford University Press, 2016.
Carl McIntire was a flamboyant and outspoken religious leader who believed that conservative religious values were the core aspect of political values and should be vocally and visibly present in American politics, especially when opposing 20th-century communism and its global spread.

Settje, David E. *Faith and War: How Christians Debated the Cold and Vietnam Wars.* New York: New York University Press, 2011.
Settje explores the diverse responses of American Christians to the Cold War and Vietnam War.

Shattuck, Gardiner H., Jr. *A Shield and Hiding Place: The Religious Life of the Civil War Armies.* Macon, GA: Mercer University Press, 1987.
This is a brief study on religion during the Civil War and its wide-ranging effects on the armies and the population.

Shelby, Tommie, and Brandon M. Terry, eds. *To Shape a New World: Essays on the Political Philosophy of Martin Luther King, Jr.* Cambridge, MA: Belknap Press, 2018.

## 238 | Annotated Bibliography

The life and thoughts of Martin Luther King, Jr. reverberate strongly in 21st-century America, and his views on war and peace continue to be influential.

**Sittser, Gerald L.** *A Cautious Patriotism: The American Churches and the Second World War.* **Chapel Hill: University of North Carolina Press, 1997.**
Religious fervor during the war was not automatic, and there was a diversity of views regarding American participation in the war. This volume studies the apathy and fervor of various denominations with respect to the war.

**Smith, Gary Scott.** *Religion in the Oval Office: The Religious Lives of American Presidents.* **New York: Oxford University Press, 2015.**
This work studies the private and public religious lives of American presidents and how faith shaped their politics and policies.

**Smylie, James H.** "American Religious Bodies, Just War, and Vietnam." *Journal of Church and Staten* **11, no. 3 (Autumn 1969): 383–408.**
This article shows the contentious nature of the war in American religion, especially with respect to the just war tradition.

**Snape, Michael.** *God and Uncle Sam: Religion and America's Armed Forces in World War II.* **Rochester, NY: Boydell Press, 2015.**
Snape presents the best study to date of religion in the U.S. military during World War II. It is an indispensable volume.

**Sorabji, Richard, and David Rodin.** *The Ethics of War: Shared Problems in Different Traditions.* **Aldershot, Hants, England: Ashgate, 2006.**
The work provides a good comparative study of war and peace in the world's major faith traditions.

**Stahl, Ronit Y.** *Enlisting Faith: How Military Chaplaincy Shaped Religion and State in Modern America.* **Cambridge, MA: Belknap Press, 2017.**
Stahl demonstrates the role of the ministries of chaplains in the military and how their influence shaped postwar American religious attitudes.

# Annotated Bibliography | 239

**Stellato, Jesse, ed.** *Not in Our Name: American Antiwar Speeches, 1846 to the Present.* **University Park: Pennsylvania State University Press, 2012.**
This is a good source for anti-war sermons and rhetoric from the American Civil War to the present.

**Stout, Harry S.** *Upon the Altar of the Nation: A Moral History of the Civil War.* **New York: Viking, 2005.**
Stout shows the religious and ideological underpinnings of the American Civil War in this short, well-written work.

**Stout, Harry S. "War." In** *The New England Soul: Preaching and Religious Culture in Colonial New England,* **233–255. 2nd ed. New York: Oxford University Press, 2011.**
This is an exceptional and widely recognized study of the role of sermons. The pages cited focus on sermons before and during the American Revolution.

**Stromberg, Roland N.** *Redemption by War: The Intellectuals and 1914.* **Lawrence: Regents Press of Kansas, 1982.**
This is a key work in understanding the mindset of those who pushed the world to war in 1914, especially with respect to acceptance of social Darwinism and the belief that there was a need to purge weaker powers from global prominence.

**Tierney, Dominic.** *How We Fight: Crusades, Quagmires, and the American Way of War.* **New York: Little Brown, 2010.**
This is an excellent study on the relationship between ideology and politics as it pertains to U.S. wars.

**Tocqueville, Alexis de.** *Democracy in America.* **New York: G. Dearborn & Co., 1838.**
This is a classic work written in 1835 by a French visitor to the United States. In the book, he gives vignettes of his travels and impressions of the new American nation.

**Turek, Lauren Francis.** *To Bring the Good News to All Nations: Evangelical Influence on Human Rights and U.S. Foreign Policy.* **Ithaca, NY: Cornell University Press, 2020.**

This volume traces the complexities and trends of religion, especially evangelicalism, on American foreign policy and advocacy of global human rights.

**Wacker, Grant.** *America's Pastor: Billy Graham and the Shaping of a Nation.* **Cambridge, MA: Harvard University Press, 2014.**
This is the most in-depth study of Billy Graham currently available. It offers important information on Graham's attitudes toward U.S. wars and his interactions with numerous American presidents.

**Walters, Kevin L. "Beyond the Battle: Religion and American Troops in World War II." Unpublished PhD diss., University of Kentucky, 2013. https://uknowledge.uky.edu/cgi/viewcontent.cgi?article=1011&context=history_etds**
This is an extensive study on personal faith and the American soldier during World War II.

**Walzer, Michael.** *Just and Unjust Wars: A Moral Argument with Historical Illustrations.* **5th ed. New York: Basic Books, 2015.**
This is one of the standard works on the just war tradition. Written in the aftermath of the Vietnam War, it presents the tradition from a historical and nonreligious perspective.

**Wells, Ronald A., ed.** *The Wars of America: Christian Views.* **Macon, GA: Mercer University Press, 1991.**
The study offers chapter on the major wars of the United States and the role of Christianity in those conflicts. See also the more recent work of Hall and Charles, eds., *America and the Just War Tradition.*

**Wilsey, John D.** *American Exceptionalism and Civil Religion: Reassessing the History of an Idea.* **Downers Grove, IL: InterVarsity Press, 2015.**
This is an excellent and very readable presentation on the intersection of civil religion and American exceptionalism throughout the nation's history.

**Witte, John, and M. Christian Green.** *Religion and Human Rights: An Introduction.* **New York: Oxford University Press, 2011.**
The shared values and foundations of religion and human rights are presented in a very readable work.

**Woodworth, Steven E.** *While God Is Marching On: The Religious World of Civil War Soldiers.* **Lawrence: University of Kansas Press, 2001.**
This is a very interesting and readable account of the religious lives of soldiers during the war, and it demonstrates the role and importance of religion in the lives of warriors who embrace it.

**Yoder, John Howard.** *Christian Attitudes to War, Peace, and Revolution.* **Edited by Theodore J. Koontz and Andy Alexis-Baker. Grand Rapids, MI: Brazos Press, 2009.**
This volume contains a series of essays by John Howard Yoder, a prominent pacifist and Mennonite ethicist.

# Index

Page numbers in **bold** indicate the location of main entries.

Afghanistan War, **1–4**
    Al-Qaeda, 1, 2
    Biden, Joe, 3
    Bin Laden, Osama, 1
    Bush, George W., 2
    conscientious objection, 42
    "global war on terrorism," 2
    Hussein, Saddam, 2
    military withdrawal, 3
    Taliban, 1, 3
Al-Qaeda, 1, 2, 84, 114, 147, 177
American Civil War, **4–8**
    aftermath, 6–7
    "Battle Hymn of the Republic," 6
    "city on a hill," 8, 9
    denominational divisions, 5
    Gettysburg Address, 6
    millennialism, 5–6
    presidential faith and war, 139
    as reform movement, 5
    religious revivals, 6
    slavery, 6, 7
    "The Star-Spangled Banner," 10
American exceptionalism, **8–12**
    American Revolution, 18
    associated words and phrases, 8–9
    ideological roots, 10
    Manifest Destiny, 8–9
    *Pax Americana*, 10
    20th century, 10
    21st century, 10
    American Friends Service Committee, 13, 44, 56, 126, 128, 130
American peace churches, **12–14**
    American Friends Service Committee, 13
    Church of the Brethren, 12, 13
    conscientious objection, 12, 42
    major emphases, 13
    Mennonites, 12, 13
    "Responsibility to Protect" (R2P), 13
    September 11, 2001, 13
    Society of Friends, 12
    Vietnam War, 12
    weapons of mass destruction, 202
American Revolution, **14–19**
    American exceptionalism, 15, 18
    beginnings of civil religion, 18
    clergy, 16, 17
    colonial warfare before, 15
    intellectual roots, 14–15
    loyalists, 17
    millennialism, 16

American Revolution (*Continued*)
  pacifists, 17
  political ideology and resistance, 15–16
  political justifications for, 15–16
  presidential faith and war, 138
  Quebec Act of 1774, 17
  religious groups, 17–18
  rhetoric, sermons, and prayers, 163
  sermons, 16
Apocalypticism, **19–22**
  Armageddon, Battle of, 19
  Christianity and, 19–21
  Islam and, 21–22
  Judaism and, 21–22
  millennialism, 5–6, 20–21
  recent wars and, 19
  violence, 21–22
  weapons of mass destruction, 205
Art, **22–25**
  Islamist responses, 24
  Lincoln, Abraham, 23–24
  religion, politics, and war, 22–23, 24
  Rockwell, Norman, 24
  September 11, 2001, 24–25
  21st century, 24
  Washington, George, 23–24
  World War II, 24

"Battle Hymn of the Republic," 6, 36, 119, 164
Benedict XVI, Pope, 146, 161
Biden, Joe, 3, 140, 175
Bin Laden, Osama, 1, 62, 177
*Book of Common Prayer*, 110, 211
Buddhism and war, **27–31**
  Cold War, 29
  compassion and nonviolence, 28–29, 30
  Dalai Lama, 29
  demographics in U.S., 28
  forms and branches of Buddhism, 27–28
  just war tradition, 29
  Tibet, 28, 29
  Vietnam War protest, 29
  violence, 29–30
Bush, George H. W., 62, 119, 138, 139
Bush, George W., 2, 70, 81, 82, 119, 140, 203

Carter, Jimmy, 53, 119, 138
"The Challenge of Peace: God's Promise and Our Response," 48, 159, 172, 173, 203, 204
Christianity and war, **33–37**
  American Civil War, 36
  demographics in U.S., 33
  early Christianity, 35
  Gulf War, 36
  just war tradition, 33, 34
  music, 36
  pacifism, 34, 36
  Patton, George, 36
  religious texts, 156–157
  Roosevelt, Franklin D., 36
  20th–21st century thinkers, 35
  World War II, 36
Church of the Brethren, 12, 13, 17, 42, 130, 134, 196
Churchill, Winston, 37–38, 120, 139
Clinton, Bill, 8, 119, 150, 174
Cold War, **37–40**
  American exceptionalism and civil religion, 38

Churchill, Winston, 37–38
collapse of Communism, 39
Eisenhower, Dwight D., 38, 39
"In God We Trust," 38–39
John Paul II, Pope, 39
NATO, 37, 38
Pledge of Allegiance, 39
Protestant denominations, 38, 39
Reagan, Ronald, 38
Soviet Union, 37, 38
Truman, Harry S., 38
Vietnam War, 193
Conscientious objection, **40–43**
Afghanistan War, 42
American Civil War, 41
American peace churches, 42
classifications, 41
Department of Defense definition, 41
Gulf War, 42
Iraq War, 42
*United States v. Seeger*, 42
Universal Declaration of Human Rights (UDHR), 41
Vietnam War, 41–42
*Welsh v. United States*, 42
World War I, 41
World War II, 41
Contemporary non-U.S. conflicts, **43–45**
deadliest conflicts, 43–44
religious humanitarian assistance, 44
"Responsibility to Protect" (R2P), 45
Syrian Civil War, 43, 44

Dalai Lama, 29, 30, 147

Ecclesiastical statements on war and peace, **47–49**
"The Challenge of Peace: God's Promise and Our Response," 48
"The Harvest of Justice Is Sown in Peace," 48
National Conference of Catholic Bishops, 48
Eisenhower, Dwight D., 38, 39, 138, 140, 165, 215
Evangelicalism, **49–54**
demographics in U.S., 50
"Evangelical Quadrilateral," 50
foreign policy, 53
key personalities, 52, 53
National Association of Evangelicals, 52
political diversity, 51
social diversity, 51
Vietnam War, 52

Ford, Gerald R., 119, 138
Fosdick, Harry Emerson, 47, 164
Francis, Pope, 55, 115, 147, 174

Genocide, **55–58**
criticism, 56
definition, 55
Francis, Pope, 55
Holocaust, 73
monitoring, 56
Nongovernmental Organizations (NGOs), 56
"Responsibility to Protect" (R2P), 57, 158
21st century, 56–57
United Nations, 55, 56
Gettysburg Address, 6, 162

Graham, William Franklin, Jr. ("Billy"), **58–62**
  critic of communism, 59
  education, 58–59
  Korean War, 59, 105
  September 11, 2001, 59
  U.S. presidents, 59–60
  Vietnam War, 59–60
  weapons of mass destruction, 60
Gulf War, **62–65**
  Bush, George H. W., 62
  Christianity, 36
  conscientious objection, 42
  Hussein, Saddam, 63
  Iraq War, 81
  Islam, 63
  Israel, 199
  just war tradition, 64
  Operation Desert Shield, 62
  Operation Desert Storm, 62
  Operation Provide Comfort, 63–64
  religious leaders, 62–63
  religious overtones, 63
  religious rhetoric, 63

"The Harvest of Justice Is Sown in Peace," 48, 159, 172, 204
Hinduism and war, **67–71**
  *ahimsa* (nonviolence), 69
  Bharatiya Janata Party (BJP), 69
  demographics in U.S., 67
  Modi, Narendra, 69
  nationalism, 68–70
  origins, 67–68
  violence, 68–69
  Vishwa Hindu Parishad (VHP), 69

Holocaust, **71–75**
  anti-Semitism, 71–73
  definition, 71–72
  Frank, Anne, 73
  genocide, 73
  human rights, 73
  Judaism and War, 92
  Remembrance, 73
  U.S. response and, 72–73
  Wiesel, Elie, 73
  World War II, 71–75
Human rights, **75–79**
  characteristics, 76–77
  defining rights, 76
  generations of rights, 77–78
  Holocaust, 73
  pacifism, 132
  religious freedom, 75
  religious freedom and religious persecution, 148–149
  religious traditions and, 75–76
  torture, 76
  Universal Declaration of Human Rights (UDHR), 77–78
Hussein, Saddam, 2, 63, 81, 203, 204

Iraq War, **81–84**
  Bush, George W., 81, 82
  conscientious objection, 42
  Gulf War, 81
  Hussein, Saddam, 81
  religious leaders and groups, 81–82
  torture, 82
  weapons of mass destruction, 81, 82

Islam and war, **84–89**
   Afghan wars, 87
   *dar-al-Islam*, 87
   *dar-al-Kufr*, 87
   demographics in U.S., 85
   *jihad*, 86–87
   major traditions, 85
   Qur'an, 86
   religious texts, 157
   September 11, 2001, 87
   U.S. political organizations, 88
Islamic State in Iraq and the Levant (ISIL or ISIS), 21, 44, 83, 84, 87, 114, 147, 205

John Paul II, Pope, 39, 146
Johnson, James Turner, 35, 159, 173
Johnson, Lyndon B., 60, 138, 194
Judaism and war, **91–95**
   anti-Semitism, 92
   demographics in U.S., 91
   Hebrew scriptures, 93
   Holocaust, 92
   *milhemet hova*, 93
   *milhemet reshut*, 93
   military chaplains, 91
   religious texts, 154, 156
   Talmud, 93
   *tikkun olam*, 93–94
   wars of Israel, 92
Just war tradition, **95–99**
   American wars, 98
   Aquinas, Thomas, 35, 95, 97, 159, 172
   Augustine, 35, 51, 96, 97
   Christianity and, 33, 96, 97
   Dalai Lama, 29
   early proponents of, 96
   Gulf War, 64
   history, 95–97
   *jus ad bellum*, 97
   *jus in bello*, 97
   *jus post bellum*, 97
   just peace, 96
   presuppositions of, 97–98
   principles of, 97
   Responsibility to Protect (R2P), 159–160
   secularization of, 96–97

Kennedy, John F., 8, 138, 140, 175, 193
King, Martin Luther, Jr., 47, 51, **101–104**
   assassination, 101
   "Beyond Vietnam: A Time to Break Silence" speech, 102
   civil disobedience, 102–103
   civil rights movement, 101–102
   "I Have a Dream" speech, 101
   law, 102–103
   peace movements, 133
   peacemaking, 136
   sermons and speeches, 101–102
   Vietnam War, 101–102, 195
   "Why I Am Opposed to the War in Vietnam" speech, 102
Korean War, **104–107**
   Cold War, 104–105
   Federal Council of Churches, 105
   Graham, Billy, 59, 105
   MacArthur, Douglas, 105
   Pious VII, Pope, 105
   weapons of mass destruction, 105
   World War II, 110

# 248 | Index

League of Nations, 133, 189, 191, 207, 209, 210
Lincoln, Abraham, 8, 23–24, 138, 139
   Gettysburg Address, 6, 162
Literature, **109–111**
   *Beowulf*, 110
   *Book of Common Prayer*, 110
   Greek and Roman, 110
   religious influence, 109
   veterans and, 109

Mennonites, 12, 13, 17, 42, 82, 98, 130, 212
Middle East conflict, **113–116**
   Al-Qaeda, 114
   Hamas, 114
   Hezbollah, 114
   Holocaust, 114
   Iraq War, 114
   Islamic State in Iraq and the Levant (ISIL or ISIS), 114
   religious geography, 114
   religious persecution, 115
   Sunni/Shia division, 115
   Syrian Civil War, 114
   21st century conflicts, 113
   U.S. religious groups, 115
Military chaplains, **116–119**
   First Amendment, 117
   noncombatant status, 117–118
   religious diversity, 117
   World War II, 117
Millennialism, 5–6, 16, 20, 21, 207, 208, 209
Music, **119–123**
   "Battle Hymn of the Republic," 119
   Christian hymns, 120

Christianity, 36
"Christmas in the Trenches," 120
"Comin' in on a Wing and a Prayer," 119, 215
country and western songs, 121
"Down by the Riverside," 120
"God Bless America," 121
Holocaust, 120
"Praise the Lord and Pass the Ammunition," 119, 215
protest songs, 120
rhetoric, sermons, and prayers, 165
September 11, 2001, 121
"Sky Pilot," 120
*Symphony of Sorrowful Songs*, 120
"The Star-Spangled Banner," 119
War of 1812, 119
*War Requiem*, 121
World War II, 119, 121, 215

National Association of Evangelicals (NAE), 44, 47, 52, 195, 204
National Conference of Catholic Bishops, 44, 48, 159, 173, 178, 184, 195
   weapons of mass destruction, 203–204
Nixon, Richard M., 60, 138, 194, 195
Nongovernmental organizations (NGOs), **125–128**
   American Friends Service Committee (Quaker), 127–128
   contemporary work, 127–128

definition, 126–127
Doctors without Borders
  (Médecins Sans Frontières),
  125
faith-based organizations
  (FBOs), 125–126, 127
genocide, 56
humanitarian assistance, 127–128
International Committee of the
  Red Cross (ICRC), 125
origins, 125
United Nations, 126, 127
YMCA, 125

Obama, Barack, 8, 24, 140, 161
Orthodox churches, 35, 39, 50, 81,
  115, 130, 142, 147, 171, 177,
  187–188

Pacifism, **129–132**
  critique, 131–132
  human rights, 132
  peace churches, 130
  peace movements, 134
  principles, 129, 131
  religious foundations, 130–131
  as a term, 129
  weapons of mass destruction, 130
  World War I, 130
  World War II, 130
Peace movements, **132–135**
  Afghanistan War, 132
  Catholic Worker Movement, 134
  Cold War, 133, 134
  Iraq War, 132–133
  King, Martin Luther, Jr., 133
  pacifism, 134
  Peace of God, 133–134
  peacemaking, 134

Protestantism, 134
Roman Catholicism, 134
Truce of God, 133–134
Vietnam War, 133
weapons of mass destruction, 133
World War II, 133
Peace of God, 133–134
Peacemaking, **135–137**
  just war tradition, 135
  King, Martin Luther, Jr., 136
  organizations, 136
  pacifism, 129–132
  peace movements, 134
  21st century, 136
  United Nations, 135
Presidential faith and war, **137–142**
  American Revolution, 138
  Biden, Joe, 140
  Bush, George H.W., 139
  Bush, George W., 139, 140
  civil religion, 138
  Cold War, 140
  Eisenhower, Dwight D., 140
  Graham, Billy, 140
  Lincoln, Abraham, 139
  military service, 138
  Obama, Barack, 140
  Roosevelt, Franklin D., 139
  September 11, 2001, 140
  Truman, Harry S., 139, 140
  Trump, Donald, 140
  Washington, George, 138
  World War II, 139
Protestant denominations, **142–144**
  Cold War, 38, 39
  demographics in U.S., 142
  political diversity, 143
  religious diversity, 143
  21st century, 142

Quakers. *See* Society of Friends

Reagan, Ronald, 8, 38, 39, 138, 173
Religion, conflict, and geopolitics, **145–148**
  Benedict XVI, Pope, 146
  Francis, Pope, 147
  John Paul II, Pope, 146
  Orthodox Churches, 147
  peace and security, 147
  terrorism, 147
  20th century, 146
  21st century, 145, 146, 147
Religious freedom and religious persecution, **148–151**
  consequences, 149–150
  human rights, 148–149
  International Religious Freedom Act (IRFA), 150
  21st century, 150
  Universal Declaration of Human Rights (UDHR), 148
Religious identity in the armed forces, **151–153**
  First Amendment of U.S. Constitution, 152
  interpretation of, 154–155
  military chaplains, 151, 152
  persistent challenges, 152–153
  religious accommodation, 152
  religious demographics, 152
  religious faith groups and faith traditions, 152
Religious texts, **153–158**
  Asian religions, 154
  *Book of Common Prayer*, 110, 211
  Christianity, 156–157
  in guidance and decision-making, 154, 155, 157
  Islam, 157
  Judaism, 154, 156
  Qur'an, 86
  weapons of mass destruction, 205
Responsibility to Protect (R2P), 13, 45, 57, 64, **158–162**, 173
  Benedict XVI, Pope, 161
  contemporary application, 160
  contemporary non-U.S. conflicts, 13, 45, 57
  critique, 159–160
  humanitarian intervention, 160–161
  International Criminal Court (ICC), 159
  Johnson, James Turner, 159, 173
  just war tradition, 159–160
  origins, 158–159
  religious responses, 160–161
  "The Challenge of Peace," 159
  "The Harvest of Justice Is Sown in Peace," 159
  three pillars, 158
  United Nations (UN), 13, 158, 159, 160
  Universal Declaration of Human Rights (UDHR), 158
Rhetoric, sermons, and prayers, **162–167**
  American Revolution, 16, 163
  Bush, George W., 82
  Cold War, 165
  Eisenhower, Dwight D., 165–166
  Fosdick, Harry Emerson, 47, 164

Gettysburg Address, 162
Graham, Billy, 166
Iraq War, 82
King, Martin Luther, Jr., 101–102
Lincoln, Abraham, 162
Marshall, Peter, 165
music, 165
pacifism, 164
pocket scriptures, 165
political leaders, 163
presidential, 139
radio, 165
religious dissent, 164
Roosevelt, Franklin D., 164
September 11, 2001, 163
Sheen, Fulton J., 165
Truman, Harry S. 164
World War II, 164
Rituals and symbolism, **167–170**
abuse of, 168–169
civil religion, 170
debate, 168
effects of, 167–168
Gulf War, 169
military chaplains, 169
military honors, 169
politics, 168
September 11, 2001, 168, 170
trench art, 169
World War I, 169
World War II, 169
Roman Catholicism, **171–176**
Catholic Relief Services, 173
Catholic social teaching, 173
"The Challenge of Peace," 172, 173
Cold War, 173

demographics in U.S., 172
"The Harvest of Justice Is Sown in Peace," 172
John Paul II, Pope, 173–174
just war tradition, 172
Northern Ireland, 174
Pax Christi, 174
political action, 171
Responsibility to Protect (R2P), 173
21st century, 172, 174
U.S. presidents, 174–175
weapons of mass destruction, 172
Roosevelt, Franklin D., 36, 120, 138, 139, 212, 213
rhetoric, sermons, and prayers, 164

September 11, 2001, terrorist attacks, 1, 2, 8, 10, 13, 23, 24–25, 36, 48, 51, 53, 59, 62, 63, 81, 85, 88, 121, 168, **177–180**, 202
aftermath, 178–179
Al-Qaeda, 177
Bin Laden, Osama, 177
churches destroyed, 177
Graham, Billy, 178
Ground Zero, 177
political and sociological phenomena, 178
religious responses, 178
symbols, 178
Society of Friends (Quakers), 12, 42, 82, 98, 120, 130, 134, 196, 212
American Friends Service Committee, 127–128

Taliban, 1, 3
Terrorism, **181–183**
   definition, 181
   human rights, 183
   prominent incidents, 181–182
   religion, conflict, and geopolitics, 147
   religious and political distinctions, 182
   religiously motivated, 182
   September 11, 2001, 181
"The Star-Spangled Banner," 10, 119
Torture, **184–186**
   Abu Ghraib, 184
   Afghanistan War, 184
   debate, 184–185
   ethics of, 184–185
   Guantanamo Bay Naval Base, 184
   human rights, 76, 184, 185
   international law, 185
   Iraq War, 82, 184
   just war tradition, 185
   religious responses, 184
   "Torture Is a Moral Issue," 184
   United Nations Convention Against Torture, 185
   U.S. law, 184
Truce of God, 133–134
Truman, Harry S., 38, 39, 105, 138, 139, 140, 164, 213
   rhetoric, sermons, and prayers, 164
Trump, Donald, 69, 140, 200

Ukraine War, **187–189**
   European Union, 187, 188
   just war tradition, 188
   NATO, 187, 188
   Orthodox Christianity, 187–188
   Putin, Vladimir, 188
   religious demographics, 188
United Nations (UN), **189–192**
   conscientious objection, 41
   establishment of, 189
   faith-based organizations (FBOs), 126, 189–190
   genocide, 55, 56, 57
   Holocaust, 73
   human rights, 76, 78, 189–190
   International Court of Justice (ICJ), 189
   Iraq War, 81
   Middle East conflict, 114
   nongovernmental organizations (NGOs), 126, 127, 189–191
   peace movements, 133
   peacemaking, 135
   religious freedom and persecution, 148, 190
   "Responsibility to Protect" (R2P), 13, 45, 57, 158–161
   three pillars, 190
   torture, 189
   21st century, 190
   UN General Assembly, 58, 159, 189, 190
   UN Security Council, 150, 160, 161, 189
   UN System, 189
   Universal Declaration of Human Rights (UDHR), 41, 76, 158, 190
   World War I, 189, 191
   World War II, 189, 191
United States Conference of Catholic Bishops. *See*

# Index | 253

National Conference of Catholic Bishops
Universal Declaration of Human Rights (UDHR), 41, 77–78, 127, 148, 158, 190, 214

Vietnam War, **193–198**
  Berrigan, Daniel, 194
  Berrigan, Philip, 194
  Buddhist protest, 29, 193–194
  Coffin, William Sloane, Jr., 194
  Cold War proxy, 193
  collapse of Saigon, 196
  conscientious objection, 41–42, 195–196
  Duc, Thich Quang, 193–194
  Evangelicalism, 52
  Graham, Billy, 59–60, 194
  Halberstam, David, 193
  Heschel, Abraham Joshua, 195
  Johnson, Lyndon B., 195
  Judaism, 195
  King, Martin Luther, Jr., 101–102, 195
  Nixon, Richard, 194, 195
  peace movements, 133
  Protestant denominations, 194–195
  "quagmire," 193
  refugees, 196
  religious opposition, 194–195
  Roman Catholic-Buddhist dynamics, 193
  social and political consequences, 196

War on terror, 2, 118, 179
Wars of Israel, **199–201**
  First Intifada, 199
  Gaza War, 199
  Gulf War, 199
  Hezbollah, 199
  Judaism and war, 92
  Palestinian cause, 200
  Second Intifada, 199
  Second Lebanon War, 199
  Six-Day War, 199
  U.S. religion, 200
  women and war, 199
  Yom Kippur War, 199
Washington, George, 15, 23–24, 36, 119, 138
Weapons of mass destruction (nuclear, biological, chemical), **201–207**
  American peace churches, 202
  apocalypticism, 205
  atomic bomb, 203–204, 205
  Aum Shinrikyo, 205
  *Bhagavad Gita*, 205
  Bush, George W., 81, 203
  "city-busting," 204
  Cold War, 202, 203
  debate and classification, 202
  definition, 201–202
  Graham, Billy, 60
  Hiroshima, 203, 204, 205
  Hussein, Saddam, 203, 204
  Iran, 202
  Iraq War, 81, 82
  Islamic State in Iraq and the Levant (ISIL or ISIS), 205
  just war tradition, 202, 204
  Korean War, 105, 203
  Manhattan Project, 205
  Nagasaki, 203–204, 205
  NBC (Nuclear, Biological, and Chemical) weapons, 202

Weapons of mass destruction (*Continued*)
  North Korea, 202
  Oppenheimer, Robert, 205
  Pacific theater, 203–204, 205
  pacifism, 130
  peace movements, 133
  religious significance, 205–206
  September 11, 2001, 202
  Syria, 202, 205
  "The Challenge of Peace," 203–204
  "The Harvest of Justice Is Sown in Peace," 204
  United Nations, 81
  U.S. Conference of Catholic Bishops, 203–204
  U.S. Strategic Bombing Survey (USSBS), 203
  World War I, 202, 204
  World War II, 203
Wilson, Woodrow, 139, 207, 208, 209, 210
World War I, **207–211**
  Balfour Declaration, 209
  Cavell, Edith, 209
  conscientious objection, 41
  League of Nations, 210
  millennialism, 208
  pacifism, 130, 207
  Pershing, John J., 209
  religious organizations, 209
  rituals and symbolism, 169
  Sunday, Billy, 209
  U.S. religious leaders, 208
  weapons of mass destruction, 210
Wilson, Woodrow, 207, 208, 209
World War II, **211–217**
  art, 24
  bombing, 214
  *Book of Common Prayer*, 110, 211
  Christianity, 36
  Cold War, 215
  conscientious objection, 41
  D-Day, 36, 213
  "Day of Infamy" speech, 212
  Eisenhower, Dwight D., 215
  ethical concerns, 211, 213
  Hiroshima and Nagasaki, 214
  Holocaust, 71–75, 213, 215
  literature, 110, 215
  memory and commemoration, 215
  military chaplains, 117
  Moody, Edward, 212
  Mott, John R., 212
  music, 119, 214
  Niebuhr, Reinhold, 212
  peace movements, 133
  pacifism, 130, 211–212
  Patton, George, 36, 215
  postwar tribunals, 212
  presidential faith and war, 139
  religious rhetoric, 213, 214
  religious support, 212–213
  rituals and symbolism, 169
  Roosevelt, Franklin D., 212, 213
  weapons of mass destruction, 203, 205

# About the Authors

**Timothy J. Demy, ThD, PhD,** is a professor of military ethics at the U.S. Naval War College, in Newport, Rhode Island. He is the author and editor of numerous articles, encyclopedias, and books on the subjects of war, peace, politics, religion, ethics, and security. His writings include *Religion and Contemporary Politics: A Global Encyclopedia*, 2 vols. (ABC-CLIO); *Evangelical America: An Encyclopedia of Contemporary American Religious Culture (*ABC-CLIO); *The Reformers on War, Peace, and Justice*; and *War, Peace, and Christianity: Questions and Answers from a Just-War Perspective.*

Demy earned a ThM and ThD from Dallas Theological Seminary, a PhD from Salve Regina University, and master's degrees from the University of Texas at Arlington, the University of Cambridge and the U.S. Naval War College. He previously served as a U.S. Navy chaplain for twenty-seven years.

**Gina Granados Palmer, PhD,** is an assistant professor of leadership and ethics at the U.S. Naval War College, in Newport, Rhode Island, and an entrepreneur with a background in mechanical engineering and production technology. Focusing on leadership, ethics, technology, war, and the balance between diplomacy and defense, her doctoral dissertation considers literary and visual representations of the war in the Pacific theater at the end of World War II. She has published articles on artificial intelligence and future warfare as well as the just war tradition. She is the editor of two forthcoming books on warfare, politics, and global security.

Palmer received her PhD at Salve Regina University and a BS in mechanical engineering from California Polytechnic State University, San Luis Obispo. Her master's thesis at Harvard University's Division of Continuing Education was awarded the Dean's Prize for Outstanding Thesis in International Relations.